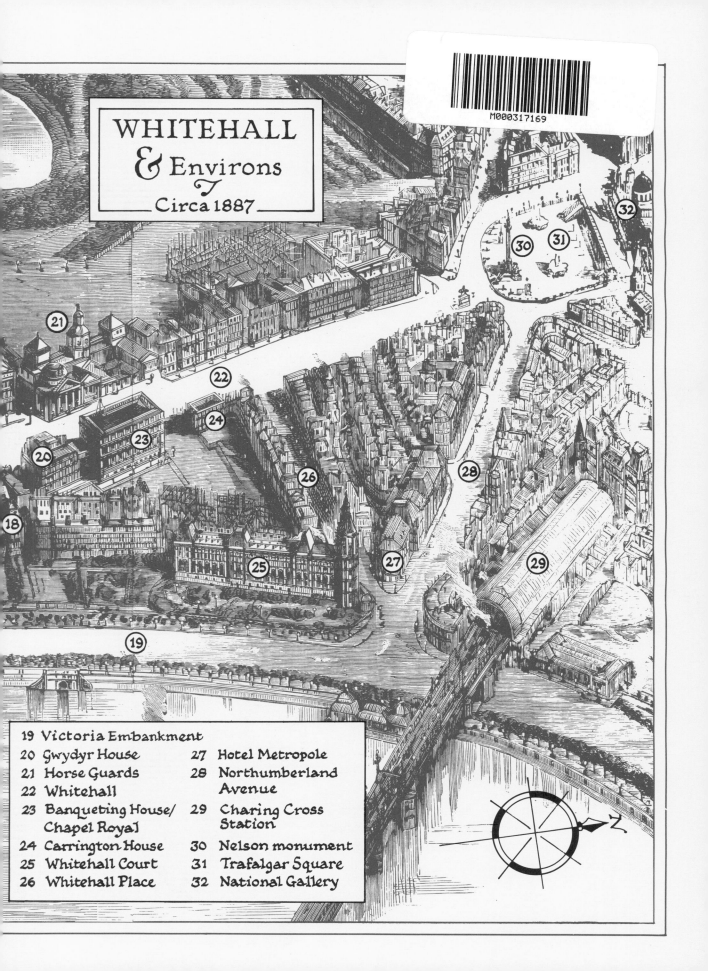

WHITEHALL & Environs Circa 1887

19 Victoria Embankment
20 Gwydyr House
21 Horse Guards
22 Whitehall
23 Banqueting House/ Chapel Royal
24 Carrington House
25 Whitehall Court
26 Whitehall Place
27 Hotel Metropole
28 Northumberland Avenue
29 Charing Cross Station
30 Nelson monument
31 Trafalgar Square
32 National Gallery

FROM PALACE TO POWER

An Illustrated History of Whitehall

FROM PALACE TO POWER

An Illustrated History of Whitehall

SUSAN FOREMAN

Foreword by Simon Jenkins

THE **A**lpha *PRESS*

in association with

sussex
ACADEMIC
PRESS

Text and choice of illustrations in this edition © Susan Foreman 1995

The right of Susan Foreman to be identified as author of this work
has been asserted in accordance with the Copyright, Designs and
Patents Act 1988.

First published in the United Kingdom in 1995 by

The Alpha Press, in association with Sussex Academic Press
18 Chichester Place,
Brighton BN2 1FF

British Library Cataloguing in Publication Data

Foreman, Susan
From Palace to Power: An Illustrated History
of Whitehall
I. Title
942.132

ISBN (hardback) 1 898595 10 0

Typeset in 11/15 pt Bembo
Jacket and text design by Ian Wileman
Endpaper maps prepared by Peter McClure

Printed and bound in Great Britain by Butler and Tanner, Frome, Somerset

2 4 6 8 10 9 7 5 3 1

Jacket front
Board of Trade and Whitehall as seen from the corner of Downing Street. (Lithograph
by Thomas Shotter Boys, published in *London as it is*, 1842.) The Board of Trade,
designed by Sir John Soane, is in the left foreground, the projecting porch beyond is that
of Dover House. On the right are the two buildings that survive today: the Banqueting
House and, partially hidden by trees, Gwydyr House. Beyond the Banqueting House are
houses later demolished to clear the War Office site. In the middle distance can be seen
the spire of St Martin-in-the-Fields.

Jacket back and frontispiece
Whitehall, about 1880, from Cassell's *Old and New London*. Shows Soane and Barry's
New Treasury Buildings and Scott's Old Public Offices on the right-hand side of
Whitehall.

Page vi
The Admiralty and Horse Guards, engraved by J. Storer from a drawing by F. Nash,
1805.

Note: This book deals with the district of Whitehall. In terms of modern
boundaries, this is the area bounded by Bridge Street, Great George Street,
Horse Guards Road, the southern side of Trafalgar Square, Northumberland
Avenue and Victoria Embankment.

CONTENTS

FOREWORD

No street in the world can have bred more triumph and more blood than Whitehall. Its brief half mile embodies the power of empire. The power may have declined, but the architecture that was its physical expression survives. The buildings stand today as they did at the height of empire. If ever a landscape was a mirror of history, it is here in the heart of Westminster.

Whitehall has none of the pompous uniformity of most boulevards of empire. Vienna ruled from the terraces of the Hofburg, the emperors of Russia from behind the gigantic walls of the Kremlin. Washington is a carpet of classical temples. Whitehall began life as a thoroughfare servicing the riverside palaces of Westminster, safe from the squalor and disease of the City. It was never a planned avenue, more a neighbourhood high street. The great palace of Whitehall never achieved its expected scale. Apart from the Banqueting House, it did not challenge Versailles or the Louvre. Round its walls, courtiers built themselves townhouses and speculators built terraces where these houses sold their gardens.

From Old Scotland Yard to Richmond Terrace and Downing Street, the character of Whitehall was and still is derived not from the old palace but from its suburb. The rambling royal quarters have long disappeared, fragments emerging from the basements of later structures. But many courtiers' houses remain, their story charted in this book. Whitehall is a monument not to monarchy but to the acolytes of monarchy, the aspiring middle class.

Only with the growth of the British Empire did grandiosity get the better of domesticity. The Foreign Office, War Office, Home Office and Treasury all moved into buildings of imperial dignity. Their façades were clothed in the pilasters and cornices of power. Walls were laden with symbolic statuary. When Sir George Gilbert Scott offered Palmerston a Gothic Foreign Office, the Prime Minister would have none of it. Great powers spoke through the classical orders not the pagan fantasies of northern Europe. Whitehall briefly took leave of its former personality.

But only briefly. Less than half Whitehall was demolished in the past century. The premises of the Prime Minister and Cabinet, of the Admiralty and Lord Chancellor, of the Welsh and Scottish offices, all remain domestic in character. Faceless bureaucracy touched Whitehall only in the new defence ministry. The egress into Parliament Square narrowly escaped demolition, while the only modern insert is the stylish and unobtrusive health department. The street still pours out of Trafalgar Square in a stream of red buses, past a curious theatre and a nest of cosy pubs. It ends beneath the world's greatest clock and a theatre of more substantial pretension. Whitehall's architecture is now uncontroversial and safe for all time. The same is less true of its inhabitants.

Simon Jenkins
The Times

INTRODUCTION

From Palace to Power: an illustrated history of Whitehall is the 450-year story – in contemporary pictures, maps and photographs, as well as letters and diaries of the time – of the historical transformation of 'The Street' recognised throughout the world as a symbol of Government.

From its early beginnings as a muddy track, later a site occupied by York Place, opulent London home of the archbishops of York, to the 23-acre conglomeration of offices and bedchambers, tennis courts and bowling greens that made up a royal palace, and the magnificent dream of Inigo Jones's designs for a new Whitehall Palace that was never realised; from the Great Fire of 1698 that destroyed most of the earlier Whitehall to the rise of imposing government offices, and the architectural competitions that produced grandiose and ornate departments – the historical development and transformation of Whitehall is juxtaposed with the political fortunes of Whitehall's inhabitants.

The first 'player' at Whitehall was Henry VIII, who wanted a finer palace than his own. He seized his opportunity when Cardinal Wolsey overplayed his hand and fell from favour. Later, Queen Elizabeth built a succession of more and more elaborate banqueting halls. During the reign of James I, masques and plays by Shakespeare and Ben Jonson were staged in the Cockpit and at Inigo Jones's Banqueting House.

'The Street' was the scene of one of the most dramatic moments of English history, when James's I's son, King Charles I, paid with his life for his political misjudgments. The austere regime of Oliver Cromwell, who destroyed much of the beauty of old Whitehall, was immediately followed by the roistering rule of King Charles II and his numerous mistresses, who adorned so many of the Palace bedchambers. Whitehall was returned to a more prosaic way of life with the reign of William and Mary.

Under the Stuarts, Whitehall became the heart of English life and culture. The Court was in permanent residence at the Palace and the seat of government was at Whitehall. Only with King William III, who found that the closeness of the Palace to the river did not agree with his constitution and spent little time there, did Whitehall lose its influence. After the Great Fire in 1698, which largely destroyed the Palace, the nobility moved into the area, building lavish homes overlooking the River Thames (that other hub of English life). Simultaneously, government officials also took up residence and work along 'The Street'.

During the late 18th and 19th centuries, the face of Whitehall gradually changed to show a façade resembling that which we know today. This was the age of the architectural competition when more and more elaborate designs in the Gothic or classical tradition were produced, as were schemes for tearing down and rebuilding Whitehall and its surrounding streets. The personalities of the architects – characters such as Sir John Soane and Sir George Gilbert Scott – come through vividly in quotations from their journals and letters. Contemporary opinion of their buildings – not always seen in positive terms – is reflected in comments from journalists, MPs and the general public.

The tragedy and sacrifice of the Great War is embodied in the history of the building of the Cenotaph, originally only intended to be a temporary structure for a one-off occasion. The depth of feeling of the crowds at the first commemoration of the Armistice is contrasted with happier events such as Coronations. The triumphal firework celebrations, and elaborate coronation arches built for special occasions, are depicted on contemporary postcards.

Many celebrated writers also worked as civil servants in Whitehall; among the best-known were Chaucer, Vanbrugh, Pepys and Trollope. Perhaps one of the least well-remembered is the poet Humbert Wolfe. The 1920s' admiration for his poetry is only now recalled because of the settings of his poems by Gustav Holst, composer of the suite 'The Planets'. Wolfe is perhaps not seen at his best in the following apposite lines, written in 1936 for the prologue to the Ministry of Labour Sports and Social Club Pageant of Whitehall:

'And here beside the barge-enchanted Thames
Kings lost their heads or found their diadems,
Statesmen their schemes contrived, the Church her mystery,
'Till Whitehall from a street became our history.'

Whitehall did not escape unscathed from the Second World War. Photographs, taken at the time, show the bomb damage in Downing Street and outside the Treasury. Pictures of wartime roof spotters above Whitehall offices and of the policeman wearing his tin hat on guard duty outside No 10 Downing Street, testify to Whitehall's perceived importance as a national rallying point for a nation at a time of peril. A network of tunnels ran through the area, one of which was utilised as the Cabinet War Rooms underneath the building now occupied by the Treasury. It was from these rooms that Prime Minister Winston Churchill, the War Cabinet and Chiefs of Staff directed the war effort.

Throughout the early 1990s, the swaddling of buildings in plastic sheeting or criss-crossed with scaffolding became a familiar sight. What has emerged, in typically British style, presents, more by luck than judgement, a harmonious and varied façade assembled over the centuries. 'Whitehall' is a name and a street redolent of the history of England.

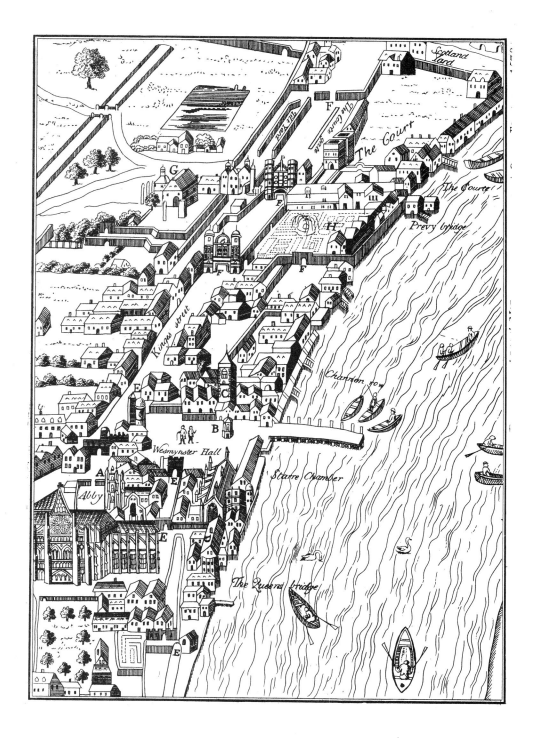

1 *A copy of Ralph Agas's* Civitas Londinium *map showing Westminster as it was in the time of Queen Elizabeth I. This section covers an area stretching from Westminster to Scotland Yard, and includes views of Whitehall Palace, the King Street and Holbein Gates, the Cockpit, Tilt Yard and the Queen's Garden, and stairs giving access to the River Thames.*

1
YORK PLACE

'Sir, You must no more call it York-Place, that's past;
For, since the Cardinal fell, that title's lost:
'Tis now the King's and call'd Whitehall.'

William Shakespeare, *Henry VIII*, iv, i

WHITEHALL grew from small beginnings, a few great houses along the thoroughfare
between Westminster and London. In 1230, Hubert de Burgh, justiciar of England and
Westminster resident, transferred his property to trustees who, ten years later, sold it to the then
Archbishop of York. It was thereafter known as York Place, the London home of successive
archbishops. During Wolsey's tenure (1514–29) it was transformed into a magnificent residence.
The Archbishop, later Cardinal Wolsey, built a Great Hall and Chamber, a wine cellar and orchard,
and entertained lavishly. A frequent guest was King Henry VIII, who coveted York Place – far
superior to his own palace. When the disgraced Wolsey was dismissed in 1529, the King took over
the building and soon after renamed it the Palace of Whitehall.

Whitehall, now the home of central government, has passed through many transformations. The site was once meadowland, with no houses to be seen except a few around Westminster Abbey and, some distance away, those in the village of Charing. The River Thames was the main highway and the area was marshy, although some embankment work had been carried out by the 13th century.

Whitehall was the palace of the Tudors and the Stuarts. It was, said the 19th-century historian, Macaulay, 'the most celebrated palace in which the sovereigns of England have ever dwelt'. At its zenith in the late 16th and early 17th centuries, Whitehall was a sprawling mass of buildings linked by galleries and extending over 23 acres. By the mid-17th century it was 'an anarchy of buildings of every date and type, crowded between the river and the park'.

Whitehall grew from small beginnings. In the Middle Ages the area consisted of a few great houses along King Street, which was then the main thoroughfare – together with the River Thames, of course – between Westminster and London. Many members of the Court built large houses with gardens backing on to the river, thereby taking advantage of both river and road transport. In those days the river was a more convenient thoroughfare than the narrow, ill-kept streets. 'Stairs' or landing-places at the end of almost every lane led down to the river, and every mansion in the Strand had its own private way. When Henry VII came to the throne in 1485, Westminster Palace was still the King's principal residence and the administrative heart of his kingdom.

York Place was named after the See of York and its history can be traced back to the last years of the 12th century when some houses in Westminster were owned by the Bishop of London, and later by his cousin William of Ely, the King's Treasurer. In 1223 they were granted by the Abbey to Hubert de Burgh, justiciar of England and second only in power to the King. In 1230 Hubert de Burgh transferred his property to trustees who, about ten years later, sold it to the Archbishop of York, Walter de Grey. This became the London base of the See of York until Archbishop Wolsey's time.

Wolsey, appointed Archbishop in 1514 and Cardinal in the following year, carried out extensive repairs and new building. York Place was bounded by the Thames, by tenements belonging to Westminster Abbey, by King Street and by the area known as 'Scotland', where the Scottish kings lodged when in London. Wolsey enlarged the grounds by buying all the land in the 'Scotland' area, and acquiring the interest in a number of tenements and gardens in King Street adjoining York Place.

Cardinal Wolsey lived in grand style, parading his wealth by giving sumptuous banquets and holding elaborate masques at York Place, some of which King Henry VIII attended. While in office he was responsible for building the Great Hall, the Great Chamber (and its wine cellar below), the Chapel and Long Gallery, and he established an orchard. The King was a frequent visitor and it is hardly surprising that Henry coveted the house and its grounds which were so much more luxurious than his own palaces.

Wolsey was forced to leave York Place in October 1529 when he was disgraced and deprived of the Great Seal which he had held as Chancellor. He asked the King in recompense to take all his worldly possessions, and a deed made in Spring 1530 describes the 'messuage, gardens and land . . . commonly called York Place, to hold to the use and behoof of the Lord the King, his heirs and assignees for ever'. The King did not wait for the legal formalities to be completed and, only a few days after Wolsey left for exile in Esher, came from Greenwich by water to take over the 'handsome and well-furnished apartments, provided with everything that could be wished'.

The title of York Place seemed no longer fitting, and it was decreed that the whole of the Palace and the Park should be called the 'Kyng's Paleys at Westminster'. The name 'Whitehall' as an alternative to York Place is first recorded in 1530, but was not in general use until about 1542. Why it was chosen is not entirely clear, nor was it at the time. (Philip II of Spain, husband of Mary Tudor, in a marginal note on despatches is said to have mentioned 'the palace which is called Huytal, but why it is called Huytal I am sure I don't know'.) The name may have referred to the colour of the new stone buildings of the Palace, but there was also a contemporary custom of naming any ceremonial or festive hall 'the White-hall'. A great fire destroyed the Palace in 1698 and today all that remains of 'Whitehall' is the elegant Banqueting House designed by Inigo Jones, built between 1619 and 1622, and now sandwiched between grey government buildings.

2 *King Henry VIII (1491–1547), who reigned from 1509 until his death at Whitehall Palace. From:* The Life and Reign of King Henry the Eighth, *by Edward, Lord Herbert for Cherbury,* MDCLXXII.

Pit Ticket

3   *The Cockpit was built during 1530–1 and formed part of that range of sporting facilities erected by King Henry VIII on the west side of Whitehall. Cockfighting was a popular sport in Tudor times and continued into the reign of James I. In 1624 the Cockpit was converted into a theatre designed by Inigo Jones. Further improvements were made, but eventually it fell into disuse and was demolished, probably at the end of 1675, and replaced by Lord Treasurer Danby's house in the following year. William Hogarth's engraving of 1759 shows a cockfight in progress and a pickpocket at work. The shadow falling across the arena was thought to be either a spectator who had failed to honour his bet and had been suspended from the roof – or possibly the shadow of the King himself.*

2
WHITEHALL PALACE:
SIXTEENTH AND SEVENTEENTH
CENTURIES

'It is a dismal sight to behold such a glorious, famous and much-renowned palace reduced
to a heap of rubbish and ashes, which the day before might justly contend with any palace in the
world for riches, nobility, honour and grandeur.'

Report in the *Wren Society*, vol. vii, 1930, recounting details of the
Great Fire that almost entirely destroyed Whitehall Palace in 1698.

KING Henry continued the improvement of Whitehall Palace, building a park, galleries
and a sports area on the west or park side, which included a Tilt Yard, Cockpit, tennis courts and
bowling alley. Elizabeth I built three banqueting houses, none of which lasted; one of them was
used for performing masques and Shakespeare plays such as *Love's Labour's Lost*. The Banqueting
House that survives today was designed by Inigo Jones and built during James I's reign. It was the
backdrop to the execution of Charles I. Oliver Cromwell then moved into the Palace, and after the
Restoration in 1660, King Charles II, 'a merry monarch, scandalous and poor', took up residence.
He was succeeded by his brother, the Catholic James II, who reigned only four years before
abdicating in favour of the Protestant William and Mary of Orange. Under them, the influence
of Whitehall Palace waned and the devastating fire of 1698 only accelerated its demise.

The Tudors

Henry VIII continued the process of enlargement of York Place by taking over more properties and land with a view to building a new royal palace on the site and embellishing it with a large park. To achieve this he purchased land from Westminster Abbey and Eton College. From Eton he acquired the hospital of St James, which he rebuilt as St James's Palace, and about 850 acres of land known as St James's Fields (named after the hospital). From the Abbey he obtained on the west side properties between the Axe Brewhouse (on the site of Downing Street) and Charing Cross. Together with the Eton land, this area formed St James's Park, from which Henry used a portion to build the recreation and sporting side of Whitehall Palace.

Parts of the old York Place and neighbouring houses were demolished but the heart of Wolsey's home – the courtyard, hall, wine cellar and chapel – was kept. Henry even took building materials from Wolsey's new college at Ipswich and dismantled a timber-framed gallery just built at Esher by the Archbishop, re-erecting it as the Privy Gallery at Whitehall.

An Act of Parliament passed in 1536 'declaryng the lymytts of the kyngs Palays of Wetsm.' states that the old Palace was in ruins and the King had lately obtained one great mansion place and house, and

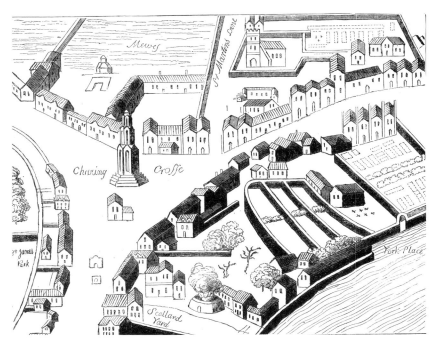

4   *A section of Ralph Agas's* Civitas Londinium *map, showing 'the village of Charing Cross', and 'Scotland' and St James's Park.*

'moste sumptuously and curiously hath buylded and edified many and distincte beautifull costely and pleasaunt lodgynges buyldynges and mansions for his gracis singuler pleasure comforte and cōmodite' [and had] 'made a Parke, walled and envyroned with brick and stone'.

The precinct of Henry's Palace of Westminster was then redefined to be from Charing Cross to Westminster Hall, including all the territory now occupied by present-day Whitehall, and incorporating the whole length of King Street.

A new flight of steps to the river was laid down and three galleries – the Privy Gallery, Stone Gallery and Long Gallery (the last with a ceiling painted by Holbein) – were created in order to facilitate communication between the different parts of the palace. To commemorate the achievements of the Tudor dynasty, the King commissioned a fresco from Holbein, completed in 1537, on the walls of the Privy Chamber. This depicted King Henry VII and his wife, Elizabeth of York, and Henry VIII and Jane Seymour, but the fresco was destroyed by the Great Fire of 1698 which ruined Whitehall Palace. Part of Holbein's original cartoon for the work may be seen in the National Portrait Gallery.

The new Palace, awkwardly bisected by the street which it

5 *Plan of Westminster from* Norden's Survey, *taken in 1593. (Reproduced from J. T. Smith's* Antiquities of Westminster, *1807.) 'Herein are comprehended all the buildings from Temple Bar to Mill Bank Street.' The plan shows the Tilt Yard, the Holbein and King Street Gates, the stairs running down to the river and the Privy Garden.*

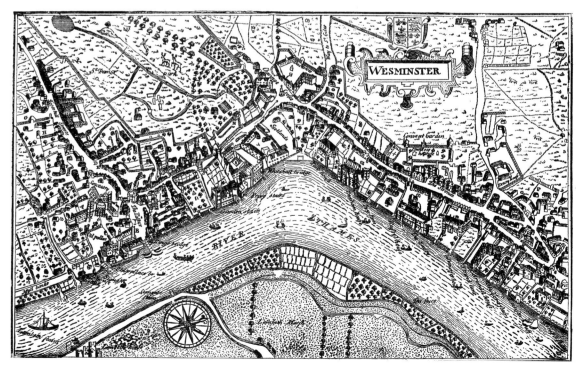

Garden staars   White Hall   White Hall staars   Iork howse   Durham howse   Ivy lane   Bedford howse

6 *Whitehall Palace from the river, from C. J. Visscher's* View of London, *1616.*

straddled and which separated the main living quarters along the river from the park and recreation area, was linked to the Privy Gallery over the road by the Holbein Gate. Further south, the King Street Gate was also used as a bridge. The road was divided into three sections: the first part was from the present-day Trafalgar Square to what is now Dover House and was about as wide as it is today. The second part, from Dover House to Richmond Terrace, known as 'The Street', like the first part, was a public right of way through the Palace precincts. The 'Street' was very narrow, with the Holbein and King Street gates erected in the early 1530s. The third part of the road extended to Parliament Street and was known as King Street, being slightly wider, with houses on each side. There was also a public right of way running west to east, down to Whitehall Palace Stairs.

The Holbein and King Street gates differed markedly in architectural style. The writer and traveller, Thomas Pennant, thought the Holbein Gate 'the most beautiful gate at Whitehall'. Built in 1531–2, it had chequered flint and stone, battlemented octagonal turrets at each corner, Tudor rose and portcullis badges, and was in the English Gothic tradition. It is not known why it was called the Holbein Gate – the artist

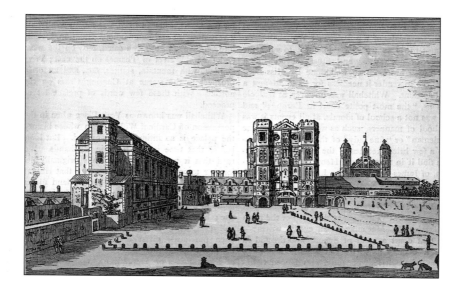

7 *Whitehall, about 1650, from a copy of a print by Israel Silvestre, taken from the collection of Alexander Sutherland.*

did not design it, as was once thought, but he may have used one of the rooms over the gateway as a workshop or lodging. The gate had a main arch to allow coaches and other traffic through, and a small archway on the east side for pedestrians. The west side was occupied by a room and a staircase. The upper storey of the Holbein Gate was used as the Paper Office as early as 1672 and there is evidence that King Henry previously used the apartment as a study.

On the west side King Henry built a sumptuous gallery from which the court could watch joustings and military exercises in the adjoining Tilt Yard. The Tilt Yard Gallery derived its name from the wooden barrier that extended along the centre of the lists. A century later, Charles I was to walk through this gallery, from the park to Whitehall, to his execution. It was one of the regular thoroughfares to and from the Palace.

The King Street Gate was to the south, and is called by the authors of *The King's Works* (the official history of public building from the Middle Ages to the mid-19th century) a 'gauche essay in classical design'. It is clearly shown on Agas's map (facing p. 1), but the exact date of its erection is not known. The gate was a rectangular stone building of two storeys with circular corner turrets and openings for vehicles and pedestrians. Busts made in glazed biscuitware adorned the façade. The gate was used from the early 17th century as lodgings rather than as a means of access to the Cockpit side. A third, more modest, gateway – the Court or Whitehall Gate – was on the east side. This probably dated from

the 15th century and gave access to the Great Court, the royal apartments, the Great Hall and the chapel.

The King also built a river wall of hardstone ashlar in advance of the medieval river wall of York Place. The view of the Palace from the Thames was dominated by the two-storeyed landing-place or Privy Bridge. On the upper floor was the Shield Gallery, decorated by the shields of all those taking part in tournaments, and from a balcony above, members of the Court could watch pageants taking place on the water. Access to the Palace from the river was gained by two sets of stairs. Whitehall Stairs gave a public right of way directly through the palace buildings and out to the street through the Court Gate. For privacy, Henry built a new set of stairs further south, the Privy Stairs, for the sole use of the royal family and their friends.

The Preaching Place was built in 1548 in the centre of the then Privy Garden. The presence of this elaborate pulpit caused the garden to be renamed the Sermon Court. 'In the same garden which was before applied to lascivious and courtly pastimes', said Foxe, Dr Latimer and others preached probably to four times as many as could have heard them in the Chapel, including the young King Edward VI.

John Stow, the 16th-century historian, in his *Survey of London* says: 'On the right hand [ie the west side] be divers fair tennis courts, bowling alleys, and a cok-pit, all built by King Henry VIII, and then one other arched gate with a way over it thwarting the street from the King's garden to the said park.' The sporting complex on the west or park side of the street was composed of the Tilt Yard and Gallery above, the Cockpit, a pheasant yard, tennis courts and bowling alley, with the park on their west. The Tilt Yard occupied the site later to become the Horse Guards.

To the south lay the Cockpit and tennis courts. Both cock-fighting and bear-baiting were popular pastimes of the day. The Cockpit, built during 1530–1, was laid out as an octagon within a square, with battlements and an octagonal tower. Inside was a ring of seats round the table, pens for the cocks and seats for the King and Queen. It was on ground later occupied by the Board Room of the old Treasury and next to Palace apartments known as the Cockpit Lodgings. Courtiers could walk along Cockpit Passage and look down into the Brake or Great Open Tennis Court, and a small open court and the Small Close Tennis Court. To the right towered the Great Close Tennis Court building, at right angles to the entrance to Cockpit Passage, which seems to have been used for banquets as well as for tennis.

King Henry's Whitehall Palace was the largest in Europe but had been built to no coherent design and was not, at first sight from the outside, impressive. However, the interior was praised by many. Von Wedel, a German visitor to England in 1584, considered the interior 'very beautiful and royal indeed'. A Venetian Count who visited while Henry's rebuilding work was in progress

'saw a palace, built by the late Cardinal, which now belongs to the King . . . the building is now being enlarged; and I saw three so-called "galleries" which are long porticoes and halls, without chambers, with windows on each side, looking on gardens and rivers, the ceiling being marvellously wrought in stone with gold, and the wainscot of carved wood representing a thousand beautiful figures and round about there are chambers, and very large halls, all hung with tapestries.'

King Henry VIII died at Whitehall on 28 January 1547. 'Then was the corpse in the chest had into the midst of his privy chamber and set upon trestles with a rich pall of cloth of gold and a cross thereon.' The body was embalmed and wrapped in lead; the chapel, cloister, hall and the king's apartment were all hung with black.

Edward, the King's son, was brought to Whitehall three weeks after Henry's death to prepare for his Coronation. During his short reign the boy spent most of his time either at Whitehall or at Greenwich, where he died in July 1553. A month later, his embalmed body was brought to Whitehall for burial at Westminster Abbey.

After her accession, Henry's elder daughter Queen Mary I spent some time at Whitehall Palace, receiving there special emissaries from the Emperor concerning her proposed marriage with Philip of Spain. In November 1554, Parliament was summoned to the Presence Chamber to receive a special ambassador from the Pope. When Philip visited England in 1557, he and the Queen stayed at the Palace. Later that year Mary returned to Whitehall for the opening of Parliament in the following January. She died at the Palace in 1558.

In the twelve years between King Henry's death at Whitehall and Queen Elizabeth's accession, a total of £3,654 was spent on Whitehall and the old Palace, and little new work was carried out. Elizabeth built the orchard, south of the Privy Garden, erected a landing stage and made improvements to the Privy Garden, adding flowerbeds, trees and herbs and later, carved heraldic beasts and garden seats.

The Queen also built three banqueting houses. The first, for the reception of the Duc de Montmorency's embassy in May 1559 was a 'floral improvisation', probably in the Stone Gallery. For his second embassy in 1572 to treat for the proposed marriage of the Queen to the Duc d'Alençon, a canvas-covered temporary structure was built in the Preaching Place, also covered with leaves and flowers. The third, erected 1581 to 1582 on the site of the present Banqueting House, was constructed of wooden poles and canvas, decorated with ivy, fruit and flowers. Although seemingly fragile it lasted for twenty-five years, and the first two masques of Inigo Jones were performed there. According to Holinshed, the walls of this banqueting house were closed with canvas and painted outside with a substance called rustic, much like stone. In 1581 Queen Elizabeth held a tournament in the Tilt Yard in honour of the French ambassadors and their retinue, with magnificently caparisoned jousters, ushers and pages.

Shakespeare's *Love's Labour's Lost* was presented before the Queen on 26 December 1598, probably in the Great Hall. Other Shakespeare plays performed there included *The Merry Wives of Windsor*, *The Two Gentlemen of Verona*, *The Comedy of Errors*, *The Merchant of Venice* and some of the history plays. After James I acceded to the throne an annual performance in Whitehall for All Saints' Day (1st November) was arranged.

Elizabeth died at Richmond in 1603 and her body was brought by barge to Whitehall for the funeral which took place at Westminster Abbey on 28 April 1603. But that same day, 'by ten o'clock the King [James I] was proclaimed at Whitehall upon the Green, right against the Tilt Yard'.

The Stuarts

The reign of James I heralded a halcyon period of royal patronage and love of the arts. Architects and sculptors, artists and woodworkers came to London to adorn the royal palace and the King amassed a magnificent collection of paintings, as did his son, King Charles I, after him. One of the most significant figures of that period was Inigo Jones (1573–1652), who was appointed Surveyor to the Prince of Wales in 1611, and became Surveyor of the King's Works in 1615. Most of the Surveyor's duties were administrative and included preparation for the King's visits to his palaces, supervision of repairs and alterations, and oversight of financial matters. Under him were the paymaster, financial comptroller, masons, carpenters, and similar purveyors of services.

Inigo Jones was an expert producer of masques and between 1605 and 1640 was responsible for staging over fifty 'masques and mummeries', many in collaboration with the dramatist Ben Jonson. In Queen Elizabeth's time the masque was an allegorical representation of monarchy and its attributes. The Stuart masque was elaborated further and included a spoken anti-masque with comic elements, performed by actors, followed by the masque itself which would be danced by members of the Court, and symbolised an ideal world that superseded the previous imperfect one. These masques were originally performed in the Great Hall with the King watching from the dais and the action in front of the Minstrels' Gallery. This arrangement was also used in the banqueting houses.

King James I pulled down the 'old rotten sleight-builded' banqueting house in 1606 and rebuilt it 'very strong and statelie'. Rebuilding began in 1606 and was finished in 1609, but after only ten years the new banqueting house was burnt down in January 1619, owing to the negligence of two men who were appointed to sweep the room. A letter from Gerard Herbert paints a vivid picture of how they,

'having candles, firing some of the oily clothes of the devices of the mask . . . that fire inflaming suddenly about and to the roof, which the two men not able to quench [it] and fearing to be known that they did it, shut the doors, parting away without speaking thereof, till at last perceived by others, when too late and irrecoverable. The two, since confessing the truth, are put to prison.'

9 *Portrait of King James I (1566–1625), who reigned from 1603 to 1625. Taken from Arthur Wilson's* The History of Great Britain, being the life and reign of King James the First, *1653.*

The Lord Chamberlain ordered some other buildings to be knocked down to prevent the fire spreading, and so saved the Palace. But many state papers stored in the basement were lost, and some of the royal apartments and a staircase damaged. The estimate for immediate rebuilding came to £9,859.

Inigo Jones was entrusted with the design of a new Banqueting House. Work began on 1 June 1619 and was completed in 1622 at a cost of over £15,000. The building was in Palladian style and must have stood out amid the rambling and assorted Tudor buildings of the Palace. It was built on the same site and was almost the same size as its predecessor. There was a gallery on the north, east and west sides and the King's dais was at the south end. The Banqueting House was divided into seven 15-foot bays by Ionic attached columns below, and composite pilasters above. It was in the form of a double cube with a huge ceiling (110' × 55') upon which Rubens' magnificent nine paintings depicting the peace and prosperity of James I's reign were installed in 1635. Different coloured stone was used for the basement, for the walls of ground and first-floor levels, and for the columns, entablatures and balustrade.

10   *During James I's reign the examination of Guy Fawkes took place in Whitehall. When asked what his intentions were in regard to the many barrels of gunpowder that had been discovered, he is said to have replied: 'One of my objects was to blow Scotchmen back into Scotland.' This reconstruction of the scene is from a painting by the mid-Victorian artist Sir John Gilbert.*

The first masque staged in the Banqueting House was Jonson's *Masque of Augurs* on Twelfth Night 1622, when the building was still not quite finished. Another notable masque was *The Triumph of Peace*, performed in 1633 in honour of the birth of the Duke of York (later James II), when the

> 'Banqueting-house at Whitehall was so crowded with fair ladies, glittering with their rich clothes and richer jewels and with lords and gentlemen of great quality, that there was scarce room for the King and Queen to enter in.'

The Banqueting House was also used for ceremonial occasions, reception of ambassadors, ratification of treaties, and state banquets.

Charles I

King Charles acceded to the throne in 1625, and it was during his reign that the old octagonal Cockpit was converted into a theatre designed by Inigo Jones in 1624. The interior was kept in the shape of an octagon, but a semi-circular stage was added. The new theatre was used mainly for masques, but other types of performance could also be given. In 1637 a new timber-framed hall was built in the Preaching Place for the enactment of masques and, together, with the Banqueting House, became the chief venue for elaborate performances. This Masque House was built as an alternative to the Banqueting House because it was realised that smoke from the torches used during masques could damage the Rubens ceilings. (However, within a few years it was destroyed under the Commonwealth. The *Journal of the House of Commons* for 16 July 1645 'ordered that the boarded Masquing House at Whitehall . . . and the Courts of Guard be forthwith pulled down and sold away'.)

In the late 1630s King Charles conceived the idea of rebuilding Whitehall 'new again in a more uniform sort' and transforming that disorganised huddle of courtyards, alleyways and large and small buildings into a stately and well-proportioned palace. Inigo Jones, and his pupil and colleague, John Webb, produced a series of elaborate designs for a new Whitehall Palace laid out in classical style. Drawings of these survive, and had the palace been built, it would have been on a vast and impressive scale, erected round a series of quadrangles and extending from the river

11 *King Charles I (1600–49) (Engraved by George Vertue from a portrait by Van Dyck in Hampton Court.)*

to St James's Park, incorporating the Banqueting House and building over The Street, which would have run straight through the middle of the main courtyard. The proposed palace would have had a river frontage of nearly 900 feet. A later design by John Webb was for an equally large building but one set back from the river and further into the Park.

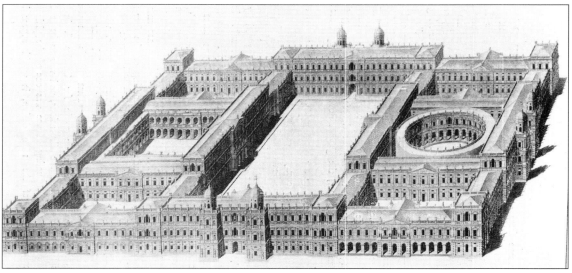

However, neither was built, for the King had by then weightier matters on his mind than redesigning his palace.

Civil War

The history of old Whitehall is dominated by the trial and execution of King Charles I. What led up to that event has been pondered over and written about ever since, though sharply differing views are expressed. Trouble between the King and his Parliament began when the Commons put forward the Petition of Right in 1628, demanding an end to martial law and its use against civilians, an end to arbitrary imprisonment and an end to taxation not sanctioned by Parliament. The King was forced to agree to this, but early the next year he ordered the Speaker to adjourn the House. Between 1629 and 1640 he ruled without a Parliament, using Archbishop William Laud and Thomas Wentworth, Earl of Strafford (previously a leader of the opposition), as his agents to enforce policies 'by the King's authority'. King Charles's religious policy was carried out through the Star Chamber and High Commission. Laud (created Archbishop of Canterbury in 1633), and William Juxon, Bishop of London, were leading members of the King's Council.

The King went north in March 1639 to fight against the Scots, who had risen against him, leaving his 9-year-old son Charles at Whitehall. In April 1640, King Charles called together a new Parliament, known as the Short Parliament, but once again its members demanded redress for their grievances. When it became clear that its leader, John Pym, was preparing a petition against war with Scotland, Parliament was again dissolved. Still trying to raise money, Charles opened the Long Parliament on 3 November 1640 (so-called because it sat for almost twenty years). Late in 1641 Parliament's manifesto, the Great Remonstrance, was passed by eleven votes. Soon afterwards the King left Whitehall, not to return until his trial and execution.

For a while in the 1640s Whitehall Palace lay empty and desolate. A contemporary pamphlet vividly describes what the atmosphere was like in

'a Palace without a presence! A White-Hall clad in sable vestments! . . . You may walk into the Presence Chamber with your hat, spurs and sword on, and if you will presume to be so unmannerly you

12 *Inigo Jones's designs for a new Whitehall Palace, 1639. (Engraved by D. M. Muller, published 1748 and 1749.) Two views – one a bird's eye view of the interior courts, the other, the river frontage. The designs were asked for by King Charles I, but the Palace was never built. The drawings were, however, recalled by John Brydon when producing his designs at the end of the 19th century, for the new Government Offices, Great George Street.*

13   *The execution of King Charles I in front of the Banqueting House, Whitehall, January 1649. (Engraved from a painting by Sir Godfrey Kneller). The portraits that border the picture are of the King's supporters who died in his cause.*

may sit down in the chair of state . . . There is no press at the wine cellar doors and windows, no gaping noise among the angry cooks in the kitchens, no waiting for the opening of the postern door to take water at the stairs, no racket nor balling in the tennis court, no throng nor rumbling of coaches before the court gates, but all in a dumb silence, as the palace stood not near a well peopled city, but as if it were the decayed buildings of ruined Troy.'

In 1643 Parliament set up a battery between the Banqueting House and Holbein Gate, anticipating an attack by Royalist forces. The gun platform remained for 80 years, until in 1723 the King Street Gate was demolished and the wall of the Privy Garden set back to the Banqueting House frontage.

The Committee of Whitehall carried out a purge of the Palace in 1644 of 'all papists . . . all women whose husbands are now or have been, in service against the Parliament . . . all other ill-affected persons, and persons of scandalous conversation . . . '. That same year the stained glass in the Chapel Royal adjoining the Great Hall was smashed and replaced with clear glass; sculptures and pictures were defaced, the cross taken down and the organ removed.

Charles surrendered in 1646 and was taken prisoner by the New

Model Army which then captured London and installed its commander, Sir Thomas Fairfax, as Governor of the Tower, with Oliver Cromwell as deputy. The King escaped to the Isle of Wight the following year and the second civil war began in 1648. Also in 1648 troops were quartered in Whitehall Palace and a number of the hangings in the Palace with 'superstitious and idolatrous pictures in them' sold to defray expenses for the army.

King Charles was brought to St James's Palace on 19 January 1649 and put on trial in Westminster Hall for treason against Parliament and England. By then Cromwell was determined to 'cut off his head with the crown upon it', and the king was sentenced to death on 27 January. He was brought from the palace on the 30th of January by sedan chair across the park and up the stairs leading to the Tilt Yard Gallery, over the Holbein Gate and so to the 'green chamber' between the King's closet and his bedchamber, where he rested briefly.

The death warrant specifically commanded that the execution should take place 'in the open street before Whitehall' and contemporary accounts mention the provision of a special means of access from the Banqueting House to the scaffold. Sir Thomas Herbert, who attended the king faithfully during his last days, writes that a wall was purposely broken down at the north end of the room, while other contemporary references mention a window being specially enlarged, or to the King stepping through a window in a small building butting on to the north side of the Banqueting House.

Edgar Sheppard, in his history of the Old Royal Palace, inclined to the latter view, citing the words of Sir Reginald Palgrave, writing in a letter to *The Times*, 17 May 1890:

'Charles walked down the length of the Banqueting House until he reached the north end wall, and before him was a doorway cut through the wall, giving entrance into a narrow room beyond, and then, when he stood within that room, the daylight streamed in upon him through the dismantled window-opening, and he saw the way to death . . .'

But a letter from one of the three Scottish Commissioners written on the day itself states:

'This day, about two of the clock in the afternoon, His Majesty was brought out by the window of the balcony of the Banqueting House of Whitehall, near which a stage was set up, and his head struck off with an axe . . . '

Many who knew the King, as well as members of the public, watched the execution from the roofs of adjacent houses. A friend of Sir Philip Warwick, whose *Memoirs*, published in 1701, spoke so graphically of Charles I's death, related that it was a very cold day and the King wore an extra shirt so that he should not shiver and be thought afraid. He walked out of the Banqueting House 'with the same unconcernedness and motion that he usually had, when he entered it on a masque night'. Beforehand he had drunk a glass of claret and eaten a piece of bread lest he faint on the scaffold. He addressed a few words to the executioner and spoke to Bishop Juxon who had been with him constantly for the past days, saying 'I have a good cause and a gracious God on my side'. Juxon replied: 'You have now but one stage more; the stage is turbulent and troublesome, but it is a short one; it will soon convey you a very great way; it will carry you from earth to heaven.' The King laid himself upon

14   *Charing Cross from Northumberland House. Watercolour dated 1807, possibly by G. Shepherd of a scene some years earlier. 'I think the full tide of human existence is at Charing Cross', said Dr Johnson. The picture shows the statue commemorating King Charles I, commissioned by the Lord High Treasurer, Sir Richard Weston and sculpted by Hubert Le Sueur. It was erected in its present position in 1676 on the site of the old Charing Cross where those who had signed the King's death warrant were executed in 1660.*

the block; after a brief interval he stretched out his hands as a signal to his executioner, and the axe fell.

According to the historian Clarendon, 'His body was immediately carried into a room at Whitehall, where he was exposed for many days to the public view, that all men might know he was not alive.' The King faced his death with undoubted dignity. Even the Puritan poet Andrew Marvell was moved:

'That thence the royal actor borne
The tragic scaffold might adorn:
While round the armed bands
Did clap their bloody hands.
He nothing common did or mean
Upon that memorable scene.'

An Horatian ode upon Cromwell's return from Ireland

The Statue of Charles I

The statue of the King was sculpted by Hubert Le Sueur, a Huguenot who settled in England in 1610. It was commissioned by Sir Richard Weston (later Lord Portland), Lord High Treasurer, in 1630 and cost £600. The statue was cast in 1633, but not erected in London before the Commonwealth. Parliament then passed it to a brazier, one J. Rivett, with orders to break it up, but he hid it and according to tradition, produced from his own stock bronze knives and forks to sell to Royalists as souvenirs supposedly made from the statue of the King. The statue was recovered after the Restoration and was erected in 1676 in its present position on the site of the old Charing Cross where those who had signed the King's death warrant and were still alive in 1660 had been executed.

The pedestal is attributed to Christopher Wren and was carved by Joshua Marshall, the King's Master Mason. At this period Charing Cross was a small open cobbled area, flanked by the King's Mews to the north, to the east by Northumberland House and south by Scotland Yard and Whitehall. A pillory stood at Charing Cross and punishments differed in severity according to the popularity of the victim. Daniel Defoe was put in the pillory for libelling the Government in 1703, but the crowd decorated it and gave him an ovation. However, John

15   *King Charles I
(1600–49). Equestrian
bronze by Hubert Le Sueur,
sculpted in 1633, with a
pedestal designed by
Christopher Wren. Drawing
by Howard Penton, 1902.*

Middleton, pilloried in 1723 for perjury, was so badly treated that he died before his release.

In February 1769 the Board of Works fixed six globe lamps to the iron railings around the statue for the safety of passing carriages. During the changes made to Charing Cross in the next century (the King's Mews and several other buildings were demolished to allow for wider roadways when Trafalgar Square was laid out) the paving round the pedestal was enlarged and six lamp standards replaced the former gas lamps. Repairs to the statue were carried out in 1855–6 and the railings removed in 1860. With the demolition of Northumberland House in 1874, all traces of the old Charing Cross (except the statue of Charles I) had disappeared.

During the First World War, the statue and pedestal were protected from air attack by being entirely covered by layers of sandbags supported on a wooden framework, the whole then encased in corrugated iron. A similar procedure was carried out in October/November 1939, but in 1941 a suggestion was made in a letter to *The Times* (30 May) that this 'effigy of a man who was liquidated because of his attachment to a complex of many ancient and some gracious things, in face of the realities and inevitable ruthlessness of a military dictatorship and the necessities of a changing order' should be removed to a place of safety for the duration. The statue was accordingly sent to Lord Rosebery's home at Mentmore in June 1941. A defence post round the pedestal was erected by the War Department later in the year, commanding a prospect of the Strand and Whitehall.

After the war, repairs were carried out and the George medallion hanging from the collar replaced. The history of the George appears in various accounts. When the King had given away his jewellery to his children, he is said to have retained only the George and handed it to Bishop Juxon saying: 'Remember'. The faithful Sir Thomas Herbert described it as 'cut in an onyx with great curiosity, and set about with twenty-one fair diamonds, and the reverse with like number'.

Many wreaths are still laid where the statue stands and a service is held by the Society of King Charles the Martyr on 30 January each year to commemorate the anniversary of Charles's death. Fittingly, in 1992, the Eucharist was celebrated at the Banqueting House. Those attending, had they wished, could have looked out of the windows on to the very site of the King's execution.

Oliver Cromwell

Following Charles I's execution in January 1649, the House of Lords and the monarchy were abolished. Parliament began to disperse the magnificent royal art collection and the bulk of the Palace furnishings. King Charles's art treasures included a number of Titians, Holbeins, Correggios, a Van Dyck portrait of the King, and a Raphael. An entry in the *Journal of the House of Commons* for 11 March recorded that 'it be referred to the Committee of Whitehall to consider what goods are set aside for the use of the Commonwealth and Parliament . . . ' Many chiefs of the new Commonwealth lived in the Palace and retained some of the furniture for their own use. But, according to Christopher Wren: 'What followed was all darkness and obscurity, and 'tis even a wonder they left a monument of the beauty [the Banqueting House itself] 'twas so agreeable to their natures to destroy'. They melted down gold and

16   *Oliver Cromwell (1599–1658), Lord Protector. (Engraved by George Vertue from a 'most excellent limning, done by Samuel Cooper'.)*

plate, sold jewels and the royal armour, and disposed of hangings and other furnishings.

In 1653 Cromwell was declared by the Council of Officers to be Lord Protector of the Commonwealth of England, Scotland and Ireland, and of its Dominions and Territories. On 16 December 1653 he rode to the investiture ceremony and then returned to Whitehall. He did not, however, continue the dispersal of furniture and decoration from the Palace. On the contrary, many of the royal furnishings were recovered 'for refitting the rooms at Whitehall'.

In 1650 Cromwell had taken up residence in Cockpit Lodgings and in 1654 he moved to the Palace itself. An entry in *Severall Proceedings of State Affaires* for 13 April 1654 records: 'This day the bedchambers and the rest of the lodgings and rooms appointed for the Lord Protector in Whitehall were prepared for his Highness to remove from the Cockpit on the morrow.' The Banqueting House was used by the Lord Protector for audiences and receptions, as it had been by his predecessors, and on these occasions the walls were hung with tapestries once more.

John Evelyn mentions in his *Diary* for 11 February 1656: 'I ventured to go to Whitehall, where of many years I had not been, and found it very glorious and well furnished, as far as I could safely go, and was glad to find they had not much defaced that rare piece of Henry VII etc done on the walls of the King's Privy Chamber' [see p. 7]. An unsuccessful attempt was made in January 1657 by Miles Sindercombe, a one-time quartermaster cashiered by General Monck, to set fire to the Chapel Royal and murder Cromwell in the ensuing confusion. Happier events were the marriages of Cromwell's daughters at Whitehall 'celebrated with all imaginable pomp and lustre'.

Cromwell died at Whitehall Palace on 3 September 1658. The following year his widow returned to live at the Cockpit, and Whitehall was put up for sale. The *Journal of the House of Commons* for 16 May 1659 records 'that Whitehall with all and every the appurtenances be forthwith exposed to sale, and improved to the best advantage of the Commonwealth, for and towards the satisfaction of the great arrears and pay due unto the army'.

The sale never took place. In February 1660 the Prince's Lodgings in Whitehall were assigned to General Monck. The Long Parliament sat for the last time in March, and a new Parliament called for the monarchy to be reinstated, and ordered that the Palace should be suitably restored for the king's forthcoming return. Inigo Jones's colleague John Webb was in charge of preparations at Whitehall, and Balthazar Gerbier designed the triumphal arches for the royal procession from London Bridge to the Palace.

On 29 May 1660 King Charles II rode in triumph 'in military fashion' through London to Whitehall by way of the City and Charing Cross, where he was received in the Banqueting House by both Houses of Parliament. Evelyn wrote in his *Diary* that the way was 'strewed with flowers, the bells ringing, the streets hung with tapestry, fountains running with wine'.

Restoration of the monarchy also meant restoration of the former departments of the royal household, including the Office of the King's Works. Several of Charles I's officials had lived through the Commonwealth and reclaimed their posts, although Inigo Jones himself had died in 1652. In 1669 Dr Christopher Wren was appointed Surveyor of the King's Works; his tenure of the post would be the longest in its history, lasting until 1718, though ending unhappily. Towards the end of his rule, his authority was split among an enlarged Board and he had no power to overrule the others or give a casting vote. He was dismissed in 1718 and his title given to William Benson.

Charles II

During the reign of Charles II a great deal of maintenance and refurbishment was carried out at Whitehall. The King, like his father, was much taken with the idea of a complete rebuilding of the palace. John Webb and Christopher Wren both produced proposals and designs, more modest than the schemes of the 1630s and 40s. Even the King himself, said Evelyn, sketched a design for a future Whitehall. However, none of the plans were proceeded with, mainly through lack of money. Christopher Wren's scheme had included provision for building over Whitehall itself, and making the Banqueting House the centre of a single massive building.

Instead, much costly renovation of the existing fabric was carried out. Charles II had the state rooms repainted and gilded, and many of the pictures, embroideries and furnishings that had been dispersed during the interregnum were recovered. A large quantity of material was retrieved from Cromwell's widow. Plate, hangings and pictures were daily being brought in, according to Evelyn.

The Privy Garden at that time was laid out in sixteen grass squares, each containing a statue. The statues had probably come from St James's Palace in the 1650s and had been severely damaged during the last years of the Commonwealth. They were removed after Charles II came to the throne and either repaired or replaced. Repairs were also carried out on the sundial standing towards the northern end of the garden. The Privy Garden was, as its name implied, a private place, hidden from The Street by a high wall, from the river by the Stone Gallery and royal apartments, from the court by attendants' lodgings and from the Bowling Green by a line of trees.

The King's private apartments were redecorated and in April 1662 work began on the Queen's privy lodging in readiness for the arrival of his intended wife, Catherine of Braganza. Accommodation was needed for other members of the Royal Household too, including the King's brother, James Duke of York and his wife, and the King's cousin, Prince Rupert. A clutch of the King's mistresses, among them Lady Castlemaine, the Duchess of Portsmouth, Duchess Mazarin, Miss Stuart and Winifred Wells, were also housed at Whitehall.

17   *Sundial in the Privy Garden. Inscription reads: 'Pyramidical dial in the King's Garden, Whitehall, erected in 1669 by Father Hall SJ.' The dial bore portraits of King Charles II, the Queen, the Duke of York and Prince Rupert. Ironwork branches supported glass bowls which displayed the time.*

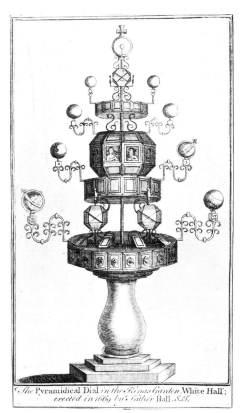

The Pyramidical Dial in the Kings Garden, White Hall; erected in 1669 by Father Hall, S.J.

The entrance gateway to the Banqueting House was enlarged and a brick gallery and staircase built from the entrance to the guard chamber. In what had been the Tilt Yard Charles built quarters for his Horse and Foot Guards in 1663–34. A fire nearly consumed the new building on 9 November 1666 and disaster was only averted because it was 'so close under his Majesty's own eye' that the blaze was put out immediately with little loss.

Very soon after the Restoration an organ was again installed in the Chapel Royal that adjoined the Great Hall on the east. Pepys wrote on 17 June 1660: 'This day the organs did begin to play at White Hall.' The ancient custom of touching for the King's Evil was revived:

'His Majesty sitting under his state in the Banqueting-house, the chirurgeons cause the sick to be brought, or led, up to the throne, where they kneeling the King strokes their faces or cheeks with both his hands at once and when they have all been touched, puts angel gold strung on white ribbon round their necks.'

The custom was discontinued by King William III, although Queen Anne tried to revive it. The Maundy Thursday ritual, with the King washing the feet of the poor, lasted till the reign of King James II. The custom of distributing silver maundy money was begun by Charles II.

A French physician and translator, Samuel Sorbière, visited England about 1665 and mentioned Whitehall in his account of *A Voyage to England*. He wrote that the Banqueting House 'looks very stately, because the rest of the Palace is ill built and nothing but a heap of houses, erected at divers times and of different models, which they made contiguous in the best manner they could for the residence of the court'.

The old game of tennis was popular at Whitehall under the Stuarts in the 17th century. The older form of the game had been enthusiastically pursued by Henry VIII who had built courts at Hampton Court and at Whitehall Palace. Originally four tennis courts were in use at Whitehall Palace: two Close Tennis courts, the Small Open Tennis Court and the Brake or Great Open Tennis Court. During 1604–5 the Small Close Tennis Court had been adapted as a kitchen and other offices for Princess Elizabeth, daughter of James I.

The Great Close Tennis Court was built of brick with octagonal turrets; it was massive (83' 6" × 26'), and looked rather like a banqueting hall or chapel. The original height was 65 feet and the upper part of the

18 *King Charles II (1630–85). (Engraved by George Vertue, from a painting by Sir Peter Lely.)*

turrets at the four corners were faced with flint and stone chequer-work, and originally capped with elaborate stone cupolas. Most of a corner turret still remains and has been restored, but the other three were destroyed, as was the Whitehall front (except for a small section) when Charles Barry extended the old Treasury Buildings between 1846 and 1847.

In 1662 a new covered court was built on the site of the Brake – the ground adjoining the Cockpit. Pepys mentioned in his *Diary* for 26 July 1662: 'Here I find that my Lord has lost the garden to his lodgings, and that it is turning into a tennis court'. King Charles II was anxious to lose weight and had himself weighed before and after play. Pepys records that after one session, the King had lost 4 ½ lbs.

The Small Close Tennis Court may have been intended for hand ball, and its remains may still be seen from the windows in the south wall of what is now part of the Cabinet Office. The Brake or Great Open Tennis Court was on the south side of Cockpit Passage, parallel to The Street, and a Small Open Tennis Court stood west of Holbein Gate. Cockpit Passage was a two-storey structure, the first floor of which consisted of a 130-feet long gallery where courtiers could watch the sports from large windows along the south side. It gave access from The

Street to various buildings and court lodgings round them.

In 1663, when construction of Charles II's tennis court was in progress, the Great Close Tennis Court with its adjoining buildings was converted into lodgings for the King's natural son, the Duke of Monmouth, although its street façade survived until 1846, when Charles Barry extended the old Treasury Building. The lodgings comprised the north part of the block on the south side of Treasury Passage and west of the new tennis court. Later the lodgings spread into part of the corresponding block on the north side of the Passage. After the Monmouth rebellion in 1685 they were taken over by Lord Dartmouth, Master of the Horse, and later passed to successive Lord Chamberlains of the Household.

During the 17th century the western side of Whitehall Palace gradually lost its sporting prominence. The orchard south of the Privy Garden had been converted into a bowling green soon after the Restoration. This orchard and garden had originally been the property of the Lamb Inn in King Street and was acquired to enlarge the grounds of Whitehall Palace in about 1545. (Lamb Alley would originally have run along the south side of the Privy Garden, with a wharf at the end – very useful for bringing in equipment when building Henry VIII's Palace.)

The Volary Building, erected on the river side in the 1660s, contained the King's apartments. Its garden housed his aviary and was between the river and the Stone Gallery. New lodgings for the King were built in 1667 with a new Volary Court lying between the apartments of King and Queen.

The old Cockpit Theatre was refurbished in 1660 and men worked overtime to ready it for the first performance on, 19 November, of Ben Jonson's *The Silent Woman*. In 1665 the much larger Great Hall, which stood between the river and The Street, and had often been used as a temporary theatre, was adapted for permanent use as a playhouse. The Cockpit Theatre eventually fell into disuse and was pulled down, probably at the end of 1675.

The cockpit building was replaced by Lord Treasurer Danby's house in 1676 – a nondescript four-storeyed brick edifice. The Cockpit Lodgings were partly occupied by the Duke of Albemarle (formerly General Monck) who had moved into Cockpit Lodgings at the Restoration. He died there in early January 1670 and his apartments were then renovated for the reception of the Prince of Orange later that year. After Albemarle's death, the lodgings were assigned respectively to the

19 *Two views in St James's Park looking towards Whitehall. (Engraved by Samuel Rawle about 1680 and published in June 1804 by J. T. Smith, reproduced in his* Antiquities of Westminster, 1807.*) Top shows an avenue of trees with, in the background, the turrets of Northumberland House, Wallingford House, the old Horse Guards, the Banqueting House, the Holbein and King Street Gates, the Cockpit and Westminster Abbey. The second picture is an engraving from an oil painting. The figure in the foreground, striding towards the right with his hat on and hands behind his back, is thought by many to be King Charles II. Behind are the buildings of Whitehall: on the left, the roof of the Great Hall destroyed in the fire of 1698, then the old Horse Guards, the Banqueting House with the Tilt Yard in front, the Holbein Gate, and further to the right the turreted Old Tennis Court.*

20   *A reduced copy of Fisher's ground plan of Whitehall Palace, surveyed by John Fisher in 1670, engraved by George Vertue in 1747. The plan shows the Palace from the Bowling Green to Scotland Yard, and from St James's Park to the Thames. Although the date given on the original plan is 1680, a number of discrepancies show this to be incorrect. For instance, the plan includes the Cockpit, which was demolished in 1675 and the Bowling Green, which became part of the Privy Garden in 1675. It provides a good idea of the warren of small offices and apartments that made up the ground floor of the royal palace, but of course gives no information about the upper galleries and chambers.*

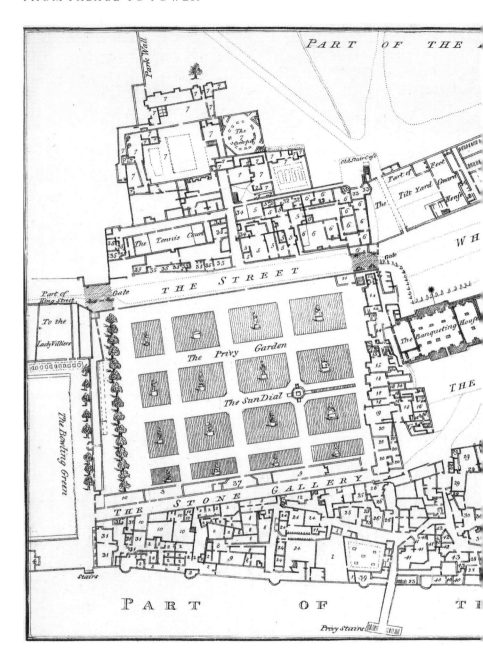

Duke of Buckingham (west, near the park), the Duke of Monmouth (east), with the central section being allotted to the Earl of Danby.

This central portion was bought back by King Charles for his niece Anne, Princess of Denmark, sister of Mary of Orange, and later Queen Anne, in 1684. She rented it from the King at 6/8d (about 33

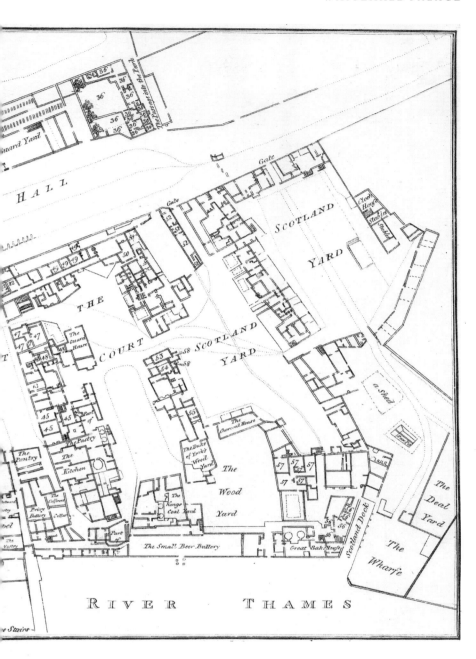

pence) per annum. In November 1688 the Princess is said to have escaped secretly from her apartment on hearing that her husband had gone over to the Prince of Orange's side. After the accession of William and Mary to the throne, Princess Anne returned to Cockpit Lodgings.

On the 2nd of February 1685, Charles II was 'surprised in his bedchamber with an apoplectic fit' and died on 6 February: 'a prince of many virtues and many great imperfections'. John Evelyn recalls the last Sunday of the King's life memorably in his *Diary*:

> 'I can never forget the inexpressible luxury and profaneness, gaming and all dissolutenesss, and as it were total forgetfulness of God . . . which this day se'nnight I was witness of, the King sitting and toying with his concubines, Portsmouth, Cleveland and Mazarin, etc., a French boy singing love-songs in that glorious gallery, whilst about 20 of the great courtiers and other dissolute persons were at basset round a large table, a bank of at least £2000 in gold before them; upon which two gentlemen who were with me made reflections with astonishment. Six days after, was all in the dust.'

21   *King James II (1633–1701). Bronze figure in Roman dress, by Grinling Gibbons, 1686.*

James II

Charles was succeeded by his brother, the Duke of York, who as James II reigned only for four short years, but came to the throne determined to restore Catholicism in England. Evelyn's *Diary* entry for 5 March 1685 notes: 'To my grief I saw the new pulpit set up in the Popish Oratory at Whitehall for the Lent preaching.'

During James's reign the buildings on the east side of the palace were pulled down and three new blocks, designed by Christopher Wren, were erected. These extended along the north side of the Privy Garden and from the Banqueting House to the Presence Chamber. They included state apartments and a lobby, and staircase building giving access to a Catholic chapel, also by Wren. The chapel was next to The Street and contained carvings by Grinling Gibbons and a magnificent marble altarpiece by Arnold Quellin. Evelyn remarked of the chapel on 29 June 1686: 'I went to hear the music of the Italians in the new chapel now first opened publicly at Whitehall for the Popish service. Nothing can be finer than the magnificent work and architecture at the end.'

New lodgings for the Queen were also built on the river side of the Palace and designed by Wren in classical style. The rebuilding probably improved the overall plan from that 'heap of houses' described by the French physician and traveller, Samuel Sorbière. According to Evelyn, writing in his *Diary* for 18 December 1685, the Banqueting

House was used to store goods and furniture in the interim, and receptions and audiences took place instead in the Queen's Presence Chamber.

The gun platform which had been demolished in July/August 1685 was rebuilt in 1688 and can be seen in Terasson's view of the Banqueting House, dated 1713 (see plate section). James, 'being extremely restless and uneasy', ordered a weathercock to be erected on the north end of the Banqueting House, above the entrance, on 23 October 1688 so that he might 'learn by his own eyes whether the wind is Protestant or Popish', and whether it would hasten the approach of the Dutch fleet under Prince William of Orange. Eventually it proved to be a Protestant wind that brought the Prince of Orange to England and the throne.

King James abdicated in December 1688 and 'stole away from Whitehall by the Privy Stairs' casting the Great Seal into the river,

22 *The reception of the Protestant Prince of Orange on his entry into London. Prince William and his wife Mary, daughter of King James II, were jointly offered the Crown of England in Whitehall at the Banqueting House in February 1689.*

although it was recovered by fishermen and restored to the Government. James lived on in exile for more than a decade, outliving his daughter Mary, and dying in September 1701 at St Germain.

A bronze statue of the King in Roman dress, by Grinling Gibbons, was set up on 31 December 1686 in Pebble Court. It escaped the Great Fire of 1698 that destroyed Whitehall Palace and was not moved until 1897 when it was taken to the garden of Gwydyr House. A small extension had been built into the garden at the south and a correspondent wrote to *The Times* for 19 March 1896:

'It is proposed to remove to the front of this garden facing Whitehall the admirable bronze statue of James II by Grinling Gibbons, which is at present rather hidden away in the court behind the Banqueting House. There is no particular reason why it should remain in its present position, for the idea that the King is represented as pointing to the spot where his father was executed is without foundation, and on the other hand, the excellence of the work is a strong reason for placing it where it will be better seen'.

A later sojourn in St James's Park from 1903 onwards was followed by the erection of the statue on a modern base, in its present position in front of the National Gallery, in 1948.

23   *Queen Mary II (1662–94), wife of William of Orange (William III). (Engraved from a painting by Sir Godfrey Kneller.) 'She came into Whitehall laughing and jolly as to a wedding, so as to seem quite transported. She rose early the next morning, and in her undress . . . went about from room to room to see the convenience of Whitehall.' John Evelyn: Diary, 21 February 1689.*

William and Mary

The last great ceremony which took place in the Banqueting House was when the crown was offered to the Prince and Princess of Orange by the Grand Convention of the Lords and Commons, with a Bill of Right limiting their powers. No monarch would ever in future be allowed to keep an army in peace-time or suspend the law of the land without the consent of Parliament. Nor would he or she be able to rule without a Parliament.

On 13 February 1689 'the Lords and Commons of England . . . went in a body with their speakers and maces to Whitehall to pray the Prince and Princess of Orange to accept of the Crown'. William and Mary 'were graciously pleased to signify their approbation and consent to accept the crown accordingly, whereupon there were loud shouts for joy both in the Banqueting House and in all the courts of Whitehall'

[Reported in the *Universal Intelligencer*, February 1689]. William and Mary were proclaimed King and Queen immediately thereafter.

Under the new King and Queen, Whitehall Palace lost a large part of its power and influence. King William suffered from asthma and sometimes from the ague, both of which were exacerbated by the damp riverside situation. He found the Palace uncongenial and took up residence for the most part at Kensington Palace. Queen Mary spent more of her time at Whitehall.

A new building for the former Queen's apartments had been started by Christopher Wren in February 1688 but was not finished until the following March, after the arrival of William and Mary. In 1691 a terrace garden for the Queen was begun as part of a scheme of improvements planned after the fire of that year. The Privy Stairs were demolished for this terrace, which projected into the river about 70 feet and was about 285 feet long. The annalist and bibliographer Narcissus Luttrell's *Diary* for 31 August 1693 notes that: 'The Queen's terras walk at Whitehall, facing the Thames, is now finished, and curiously adorned with greens, which cost . . . about £10,000'. The remains of the terrace can still be seen facing the river at the back of the Ministry of Defence main building in Whitehall.

Fire was an ever-present danger in the crowded and ramshackle buildings of Whitehall Palace and it finally erupted on 9 April 1691: 'this night a sudden and terrible fire burnt down all the buildings over the Stone Gallery at Whitehall to the water-side', wrote the diarist John Evelyn. The fire began in the apartments formerly belonging to the Duchess of Portsmouth (which had, Evelyn sourly observed, 'been pulled down and rebuilt no less than three times to please her') and was caused, so it was said, by a careless maid. It took 48 hours to extinguish the flames.

Queen Mary died unexpectedly from smallpox on 28 December 1694 at Kensington Palace. Her body was removed to Whitehall and Wren was put in charge of the decoration of the Banqueting House for the lying-in-state, and also designed the catafalque. The public were not allowed in to the Banqueting House to see the body of their dead Queen until 21 February 1695. The historian Macaulay related that: 'While the Queen's remains lay in state at Whitehall, the neighbouring streets were filled every day, from sunrise to sunset, by crowds which made all traffic impossible.' Railings from Whitehall to Westminster Abbey were draped in black cloth and the paths were gravelled for the funeral, which took place on 5 March 1695. Purcell wrote the funeral music, very soon before he himself died.

Evelyn mentioned in his *Diary* for 27 February 1695 that the King had conceived a design to buy the whole of King Street and build it 'nobly', it being the street leading to Westminster. But the plan came to nothing, possibly because of the great expense of the Queen's funeral, which cost £50,000.

The Great Fire on 4 January 1698 which began at the King's apartments when he was not in residence, was very much more devastating than that of 1691. It spread over the whole of Whitehall Palace, consuming the riverside buildings, the Privy Gallery, the Guard Chamber and Presence Chamber, the old chapel and all the buildings erected by King James II. At one time it seemed to die down, but it started up again next to the Council Chamber and was not finally extinguished until the following morning. In the debris a looter is said to have picked up a gold bust of Cardinal Wolsey – an ironic end to what Wolsey had begun over 160 years before.

On the river side of the palace every building was consumed by the flames except for the Banqueting House, the south side of the Volary Building, and the south end of the remains of the Stone Gallery, which were spared. About a dozen people were killed, but according to the engraver and antiquary George Vertue, all the pictures, tapestry and furniture were saved.

The Great Fire is reputed to have been caused by a Dutch laundress who had carelessly left some linen to dry over a charcoal fire, which spread to hangings and furniture. A contemporary report included in the Harleian Manuscript and reprinted in the *Wren Society*, vol. vii for 1930, relates:

'In an instant . . . the merciless and devouring flames got such an advantage, that, notwithstanding the great endeavours used by the water-engines, numerous assistance, and blowing up houses to the number of about 20, it still increased with great fury and violence all night, till about eight of the clock next morning, at which time it was extinguished after it had burnt down and consumed . . . about one hundred and fifty houses . . . Such was the fury and violence of this dreadful and dismal conflagration, that its flames reduced to ashes all that stood in its way from the Privy Stairs to the Banqueting House, and from the Privy Gardens to Scotland Yard, all on that side, except the Earl of Portland's House and the Banqueting House, which were preserved, though much damnified and shattered . . . '

Many people commented on the fire. Macaulay related that before midnight the King's and Queen's apartments, the Wardrobe, the Treasury, the Privy Council Office, and the Office of the Secretary of State had been destroyed. The courtier, Sir James Ogilvie, wrote to the Earl of Marchmont on 5 January: 'All the palace of Whitehall, at least what was built by King Charles the Second and King James, is burned down'. One Andrew Kineir wrote: 'All the royal apartments with the King's Chapel and Guard Hall, the Duke of Shrewsbury's Office, the Treasury Office, Council Chamber, the late King's new chapel, the long galleries . . . with several other lodgings are all consumed . . . ' Evelyn, who usually had so much to say on every topic, was shocked into brevity in his *Diary* entry for 2 January: 'Whitehall burnt: nothing but walls and ruins left'.

King William visited the scene and according to Narcissus Luttrell's account, 'seem'd much concerned, and said, if God would give him leave, he would rebuild it much finer than before' (although an account exists of him writing in a letter to a friend that the accident 'affected him less than it might another, because Whitehall was a place in which he could not live'). Christopher Wren produced new designs for the rebuilding, incorporating the Banqueting House, but in the end nothing came of the elaborate baroque plans, perhaps because of the expense or lack of inclination on the part of the King. The Court removed to St James's Palace.

However, within days of the fire the Banqueting House was being fitted up as a chapel and by Christmas Day 1698 the new Chapel Royal was ready for its first service. New fittings included an organ against the west wall, the altar at the north end and the pulpit at the east. Box pews faced each other on either side of a narrow aisle.

Many of today's Government buildings were first erected on their present sites after the fire and for many years the nobility were encouraged to build their town houses on the site of Whitehall Palace itself.

24 *View of the Royal buildings for his Majesty's Horse and Foot Guards . . . . the Banqueting House White Hall, 1753. (Engraving by John Boydell.) The Royal procession with King George II's coach is passing through the new Horse Guards archway on its journey down Parliament Street for the opening of Parliament. From the left, we see the Banqueting House, Parliament Street, the Holbein Gate and the new Horse Guards building, with its cupola.*

3
WHITEHALL AFTER THE FIRE: EIGHTEENTH CENTURY

'Cockfights were consecrated contests in this region before they were superseded by the more exciting struggles of political humanity at Westminster.'

Address by the President, the Earl of Rosebery,
at the 10th Annual Meeting of the London Topographical Society, 1909.

THE erection of Westminster Bridge (1738–49) changed the character of Whitehall. King Street was too narrow to take the increase in traffic and new laws were passed permitting the widening of existing streets or creation of new ones. Parliament Street was laid out in 1756 and ran through the old Privy Garden of Whitehall Palace. Much of the area was rebuilt: the burnt-out site of the Palace on the river side was sold off in plots to noblemen of the court and several large houses erected. The park side of the Palace was taken over for the offices of the Lord Chamberlain, Commissioners for Trade, the Treasury and the Privy Council.
During the 18th century, Downing Street was developed for official occupation, a new Treasury designed by William Kent, the Holbein and King Street Gates demolished, and a new Horse Guards building (also by William Kent) erected. A new and much criticised Admiralty was completed in 1726. Plans for improved layouts, new streets and buildings in Whitehall were invited from eminent architects towards the end of the century, and over the next thirty years the face of Whitehall began to change.

Changing thoroughfares and new houses

With the building of Westminster Bridge, begun in 1738 and after various vicissitudes, such as a sinking pier, opened in 1750, the whole area of Whitehall changed in character. Previously, the traffic going to and from Westminster and Charing Cross had to pass through King Street, which was extremely narrow – hardly more than 40 feet wide between the Holbein and King Street Gates. The Commissioners appointed under the Act for building the bridge were authorised to clear and rebuild the streets and passages on each side of the River Thames, to and from the bridge. Later laws allowed them to oversee the architecture of the street fronts and preserve their 'beauty' and 'uniformity'.

The Commissioners had powers to widen existing streets or lay out new ones, and acquired nearly all the property between King Street and the river and pulled it down. Courts and alleys leading from King Street eastwards to Cannon Row disappeared and Parliament Street – a 60-foot wide thoroughfare designed as a link between Whitehall and the

approach to Westminster Bridge in order to relieve King Street of some of its traffic – was laid out in 1756. Once Parliament Street, which ran through what had been the Privy Garden and the Bowling Green, was opened, King Street became a backwater.

The new street layout was very much more regular, as can be seen from contemporary maps. Improvement schemes for the area had been proposed by Thomas Lediard and James Mallors. Lediard, the bridge surveyor, had suggested the creation of an open space with trees, where the public could walk, but this idea was not taken up. However, many road improvements were carried out and resulted in rebuilding of much of the area, including the construction of Great George Street.

In 1752–3, James Mallors, builder of some of the Parliament Street houses, obtained an Act of Parliament authorising him to 'open a street from the west side of King Street . . . to the back part of the houses, gardens and yards on the west side of Delahay Street'. He was permitted to acquire ground and houses on a site bounded roughly by King Street, Gardiners Lane (west side), St James's Park and Bow Street. The site –

Richmond's House, burnt down in 1791 and not rebuilt. The clear space in the foreground is Whitehall itself.

26   *Old Westminster Bridge. Begun in 1738, the bridge was opened in 1750.*

originally occupied by Antelope Alley, Blue Boar's Head Yard, George Yard and Bell Alley, and parts of King Street and Delahay Street – now became Great George Street, and provision was made for 'good and substantial houses' to be built on each side. Acquisition and clearing of the existing buildings took about three years, and Great George Street appears for the first time in the rate book for 1757, by which date most of the houses had been built.

The narrow part of the street leading from Charing Cross to Whitehall was widened to at least 70 feet and the improvement completed by the end of 1758. The almost burnt-out site of Whitehall Palace on the river side was parcelled up into plots, leased on easy terms to noblemen of the court for private building. During the 18th century, several large houses were erected, including Carrington, Gwydyr, Montagu, Pelham and Pembroke Houses.

The park or west side of the Palace was also affected by the fire, but more insidiously. Office space was sorely needed, and within a month of the fire the Treasury established itself in temporary buildings on the Cockpit site in the house built by Lord Treasurer Danby. The Privy Council occupied the site of what had once been the Small Close Tennis Court and part of Downing Street. The bulk of Montagu Lodgings were later taken over by the Lord Chamberlain, the Secretary of State and the Commissioners for Trade and Plantations.

Downing Street

Towards the end of King Charles II's reign, Hampden House, west of King Street, the property of Elizabeth, mother of John Hampden (who had refused to pay 'ship money' – a tax to raise money for ships for the Navy – to King Charles I), and aunt of Oliver Cromwell, was pulled down and the property leased in 1682. The house and its grounds became the site of Downing Street. Two little lanes ran parallel to Downing Street – Duffin's Alley and Axe Yard, later the site of Fludyer Street, and one-time home of Samuel Pepys. There were also two public houses in the area: the Axe Brewhouse and the Cat and Bagpipes, on the corner of Downing Street next to King Street.

A reversionary lease had been granted to George Downing in 1644, with permission to rebuild in due course. The previous lease finally expired in 1682 and Downing took possession. George Downing had

27 *Fludyer Street was formerly situated south of Downing Street and extended from King Street to St James's Park. It was built about 1766 and named after Sir Samuel Fludyer (Lord Mayor of London in 1761).*

previously been strongly pro-Cromwell, but at just the right moment he crossed over to become a supporter of the restoration of the monarchy. He built Nos 10–12 Downing Street late in the 17th century as part of an overall scheme comprising a group of large houses, described in the 1720 edition of John Stow's *London Survey* as 'four or five very large and well-built houses, fit for persons of honour and quality, each house having a pleasant prospect into St James's Park with a terrace walk'. Parallel with Downing Street was Fludyer Street (built about 1766 and named after a former Lord Mayor of London). The Crown leased Fludyer's home in 1793 and later bought the freehold.

In 1738 Horatio Walpole, having obtained the lease of Clarendon House, applied for a new lease of the house and stables and for Nos 1, 2 and 3 Downing Street and the Axe and Gate Inn on the north side of Downing Street at the junction with King Street. In 1765 his son, Lord Walpole, took a 50-year lease of the properties, the inn and the Henry VIII Tavern.

No 10 Downing Street actually consisted of two houses; that at the front was a modest affair, but behind it, connected by a long passage, was a more substantial house, built originally by Charles II for the Earl and Countess of Lichfield (she being the King's daughter by the Duchess of Cleveland), on the site of the western part of Cockpit Lodgings in the 1670s. This house could be seen properly only from Horse Guards Parade. To the south of it lay Hampden House and garden, and this was the land acquired on a 99-year lease by Downing. The site of the

Lichfield's house had been occupied by Charles I as a child, then by his sister, Princess Elizabeth, Lord Rochester, the Earl of Pembroke, Cromwell, General Monck (later Duke of Albemarle) and the Duke of Buckingham.

The Lichfields were dismayed by their loss of privacy when Downing began to build his houses in 1682, and the Countess complained to her father. The King replied: 'I think it a very reasonable thing that other houses should not look into your house without your permission, and this note will be sufficient for Mr Surveyor to build up your wall as high as you please . . . '.

No 10 has belonged to the Crown since 1736. After its occupation by the Lichfields, Lord and Lady Overkirk lived there. In 1720 it was taken over by the Crown and fitted up as a residence for Count Bothmar, Hanoverian envoy in London. After Bothmar's death the house was offered by George II to Robert Walpole who in 1732 agreed to take over both the north and south houses to be combined as the permanent official residence for the First Lord of the Treasury. However, he did not actually move in until 1735. The architect William

28 *Downing Street. (Watercolour sketch by J. C. Buckler 1827.) At this time there was no access from Downing St to St James's Park and the cul-de-sac at the end was known as Downing Square. The first door on the right was the front door of No 10. 'There is a fascination in that little cul de sac; an hour's inhalation of its atmosphere affects some men with giddiness, others with blindness, and very frequently with the most oblivious boastfulness' – Theodore Hook.*

Kent, at that time Deputy Controller of the Board of Works, was responsible for extensive repair work and rebuilding in the 1730s. He drastically reconstructed the northern house, which contained the Cabinet Room and principal drawing rooms, and was originally built for the Lichfields on an L-shaped plan – the long 'arm' being along the Horse Guards Parade.

Kent built a new main staircase and removed the subsidiary ones. The Horse Guards frontage was given a central feature surmounted by a triangular pediment, and the entrance from Downing Street became a spacious hall. The Downing Street section seems to have been intended mainly for use as offices. A garden was adapted from part of the Horse Guards Parade which had been annexed and fenced in during Count Bothmar's tenancy.

Further alterations were carried out, probably by the architect Sir Robert Taylor, in the second half of the 18th century after the Board of Works had found the walls of the old part of the house decaying, floors and chimneys sunk and no party wall existing between No 10 and the house adjoining it on the west side. The foundations were improved, new kitchens provided, and the Cabinet Room was extended.

During the late 18th century Downing Street was increasingly taken over by officialdom. From 1783 to 1801 No 10 was occupied by the younger Pitt; and the Foreign Office moved into Downing Street in 1793 after a brief stay in the Cockpit.

Kent's Treasury

In 1660, King Charles II had allotted chambers in Whitehall Palace to the Treasury, in the section extending eastwards from Holbein Gate to the main buildings of the Palace, passing close by the southern end of the Banqueting House. These chambers are mentioned by Evelyn in his *Diary*, and in Macaulay's account of the Great Fire which destroyed most of Whitehall Palace in January 1698. In February 1698, King William III granted new chambers in the Cockpit to the Treasury.

The Board of Works reported in 1732 that that building used by the Treasury was 'in so ruinous and dangerous a condition that we don't think it safe for your Lordships to continue in it'. William Kent was instructed to prepare plans for a new Treasury, to face north on to Horse Guards Parade, and in 1733 his plans were approved at an estimated cost

29　*Kent's Treasury and the Horse Guards. The Treasury, designed by William Kent, was completed in 1736. Kent's design had consisted of a three-storey block with pavilions at either end, but only the centre section was built. The north front is of Portland stone and overlooks Horse Guards Parade. Kent's Treasury has 'that slightly unlikely wide-awake look that one sees in old prints', said Raymond Erith, architect in charge of the refurbishment of the Old Treasury and Downing Street in the 1960s.*

of £8,000. The old Cockpit Lodgings were pulled down, but the buildings on the site were still called by its name, and the King's speech used to be read to government supporters in what was called the Cockpit at least up to the death of Pitt the Younger in 1806. Until the end of the 18th century Treasury correspondence was signed: 'from the Cockpit'.

Kent's design for the Treasury consisted of a long three-storey block with pavilions at each end, but only the centre of the block was built, omitting the three bays at each end and the pavilions. The building was completed in 1736 at a final cost of approximately £18,000.

The old Treasury Building today still contains an impressive Board Room with some of the original furniture, including the King's chair where, it is said, he would sit when presiding at meetings of the Treasury Board. George III was the last King to do so. In this room the Board used to meet until the later years of George III's reign, but eventually Treasury business was settled by direct submission to the Chancellor. In the centre of the room is the huge carved table where the members of the Board sat. A bill of 1739 records a charge of 10/6d by Robert Sapp, upholsterer, for 'cutting the table in the Board Room lower' and of five guineas for making seven wainscot drawers for the table. The room also contains a handsome astronomical clock made by Charles Clay, who was appointed to maintain official clocks for the

Board of Works in 1721. He died in 1739 and in 1742 his widow was granted an annual payment of £4 for keeping the clock in order.

Part of the old Cockpit building existed well into the 19th century, although cock-fighting itself probably ceased there in the 1660s. The property to the east of the Cockpit, comprising a small group of buildings, was leased to the Earl of Dorset in 1725. By 1755 the rear part of Dorset House had been rebuilt and in 1808 the lease reverted to the Crown for use as offices by the Secretary of State, the Home Department and the Indian Board of Control.

After the fire of 1698, the Privy Council was housed in that part of the Monmouth apartments that was on the south side of the Treasury Passage. The Montagu Lodgings (Montagu was one-time Master of the Great Wardrobe) adjoined the tennis court near the Cockpit; the northern part was used from 1768 onwards by the Board of Trade, while the southern was used as the State Paper Office.

By the early 18th century, the Cockpit area accommodated several government offices – the Treasury, the Secretary of State for Scotland (after union with Scotland), and the Board of Trade. A coffee house established with an entrance off Cockpit Passage was soon doing good business and functioned throughout the 18th century.

Home Office and Dover House

The Home Office came into existence under the Rockingham administration in March 1782, when the Secretary of State for the Southern department became Secretary for the Home Department, including Ireland and the Colonies. When the Board of Trade was abolished in 1782, the new Secretary of State for the Home Department took over its offices and much of its work. In 1786 a reconstituted Board of Trade rose from the ashes of the old, but the Home Office stayed on the site of the Old Tennis Court until the mid-19th century.

Dover House, previously known as York House, and later Melbourne House, is on the site of the apartments occupied by the Duke of Ormonde, who was Lord Steward of the Household, and by Colonel Darcy, a Gentleman Usher of the King's Privy Chamber. The house lay on the old Whitehall Palace Tilt Yard ground and was probably on the site of the Small Open Tennis Court. After the Duke of Ormonde died in 1688, his grandson applied for a new lease in 1696 and was granted one

30 *The Home Office, old Board of Trade Building and Old Tennis Court, 1782 to 1845. In 1782 the Board of Trade was abolished and the Home Department took over its premises in the old Tudor Tennis Court of Whitehall Palace until it moved to Sir George Gilbert Scott's Old Public Offices in 1875. Dover House is on the right.*

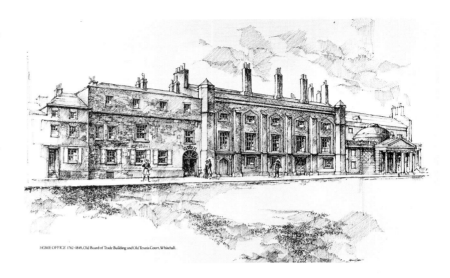

HOME OFFICE 1782–1845, Old Board of Trade Building and Old Tennis Court, Whitehall.

31 *John Maurer's view of 1753 shows the Holbein Gate and adjoining Van Huls' House built 1712, and Malmesbury House on the far right.*

for 42 years. However, he had Jacobite sympathies and joined the Old Pretender in 1715. He was charged with high treason and the lease granted to him was forfeited.

In 1716 the house was taken over by Hugh Boscawen, later Viscount Falmouth, the Comptroller of the Household of King

George I. He was granted permission to fit up the lodgings at his own expense, to enclose the galleries and pull down the Park Stairs; later, he was allowed to enclose a piece of St James's Park. After his death, his widow remained in the house and when she died, the lease was sold in 1754 to Sir Matthew Featherstonehaugh.

The house was later rebuilt by James Paine, a leading architect of the day. It was completed in 1758 and was set back from the street, being on the site of what had originally been the garden. Sir Matthew died in 1774 and the next tenant was the French Ambassador, the Marquis de Noailles, who returned home at the outbreak of war with France in 1778 during the American War of Independence. The house was subsequently occupied by Lord Amherst, Commander-in-Chief of the Army.

The premises were assigned to HRH Prince Frederick, Duke of York and Albany, in December 1787 on payment of £12,600. The house had originally been in the shape of an 'E' with the main rooms facing Horse Guards Parade, and the entrance and courtyard facing Whitehall. It contained a fine plaster ceiling by Paine in what is now the Minister of State's room. The prince at once had the forecourt filled in, adding 'a new central front, with a dome and portico with four Ionic columns extending across the footway next to Whitehall, and grand staircase in the Ionic order, after the designs of Henry Holland, the architect'.

Holland altered the old entrance hall and constructed a new entrance and circular hall. The Duke built his stables on the other side of the street, on the site of the old Lottery Office. In 1792 the Duke exchanged York House with Lord Melbourne's house in Piccadilly (now Albany); it was occupied by Melbourne until 1830 and was known by his name. It was then sold once more, to Mr Agar-Ellis, Chief Commissioner of Woods and Forests, who became Baron Dover in 1831.

Gates at Whitehall

With the increasing use of wheeled traffic, the two gates across Whitehall were inconvenient. In 1718 a committee was appointed to consider ways of easing the passage to MPs when going to and from the House. Officers of the Works felt that 'the Gate next to the Banqueting House [the Holbein Gate] cannot be made wide enough for coaches to pass, but must be taken down to give sufficient room', whereas they

32 & 33   *The Holbein and King Street Gates straddled Whitehall and differed greatly in style. The Holbein Gate (not built by Hans Holbein), stood at the north entrance to King Street. Erected in 1531–2 it was composed of chequered flint and stone with octagonal turrets at each corner. The upper storey was used as the Paper Office from 1672 onwards. The Holbein Gate was demolished in 1759 together with the adjoining house belonging to Van Huls, Clerk of the Queen's Robes and Wardrobes. King Street Gate was to the south – a rectangular two-storey building and used from the early 17th century for lodgings rather than as a passageway to the Cockpit side. It was demolished in 1723.*

thought that the King Street Gate could be enlarged, at a cost of £150. Both gates were demolished during the 18th century.

Sir John Vanbrugh, Comptroller of the Board of Works (1702–13, 1715–26), was a distinguished architect and playwright, and author of, among other titles, *The Relapse* and *The Provoked Wife*. He was determined that the Holbein Gate should be preserved, and suggested that the buildings extending eastward from the gate to the Banqueting House should be taken down instead and a new wider road be made by including part of the Privy Garden. Although the Treasury accepted his proposals nothing more was done until 1723 when instructions were given to the Surveyor-General to pull down the King Street Gate and to set back the wall of the Privy Garden, just as Vanbrugh had proposed.

The Gate was at this time part of the Earl of Clarendon's House which was 'resumed' by the Government for £6,000 and divided in two by the gate's destruction. The river side was refurbished for the Commissioners of Trade & Plantations, and the park side allocated to Horatio Walpole, Auditor and Surveyor General of HM Revenues in America, who had petitioned for Clarendon House to be granted to him and his successors in office. At the same time the gun platform next to the Banqueting House was removed, and the arch of the Holbein Gate opened up. The cost of the entire operation was £3,945.

The Holbein Gate with the adjoining house belonging to William Van Huls, Clerk of the Queen's Robes and Wardrobes, remained as a partial obstruction to the road for over 30 years more, until in 1755 the Treasury asked the Board of Works to consider moving it elsewhere. The cost of removal was too much for the Treasury and following a further complaint from Sir Matthew Featherstonehaugh that it was hindering his building work on the premises now known as Dover House, the State Paper Office in the room upstairs was removed in 1756. On 21 June 1759 the Board of Works was authorised to demolish the Holbein Gate and the adjoining house belonging to Van Huls. Some of the stonework and ornamental features were taken by the Duke of Cumberland who talked of erecting the Gate at the end of the Long Walk at Windsor, but this project was never carried out.

Whitehall or Court Gate survived the fire of 1698 and stood until 1765 when it was in such a state of decay that it too had to be demolished.

The Horse Guards and Paymaster General's Office

A Guard House built in the Tilt Yard for the defence of Whitehall in 1649 survived the Commonwealth and was added to at the Restoration, at which time the Horse Guards and Foot Guards were

34 *The Old Horse Guards 1674, engraved by P. Mazell from a painting by Hendrick Danckerts, who was invited to England by Charles II. The Banqueting House is on the left, and in front are several low buildings next to and within the Tilt Yard. To the right is the gateway to the Tilt Yard and the Park Stairs up to the Gallery. Behind is the Holbein Gate. In the centre is the turreted Tudor Tennis Court and, further right, the Cockpit with its octagonal roof and battlemented walls. In the foreground is King Charles II with his dogs and courtiers.*

created for the personal protection of King Charles II. Preparations for a much larger building to accommodate them began in 1663. The ground floor was mainly given over to stabling and the first floor consisted of rooms for the Judge Advocate-General and the officers. This building, of red brick and Portland stone, had a layout similar to that of the later Horse Guards so familiar today; there were two sentry boxes at the Whitehall entrance as there are now. Above the central arch was a large chapel, which was also used for court-martial proceedings. It cost approximately £4,000 and was looked after by its own surveyor.

By the end of the 1680s, the duties of the staff at the Horse Guards had been greatly increased and there were new offices of Adjutant General and Quartermaster General in operation. The Horse Guards was by then virtually the War Office of Government. More space was needed for the new departments in operation, rooms were subdivided, and other alterations made which weakened the structure. The old Horse Guards was not solidly built; the north and south walls of the central pavilion stood on wooden girders which eventually bowed under the weight of the building and it was only kept from collapse by being propped and shored up.

In the early 18th century much of this accommodation was used by people other than the Horse Guards – including the Paymaster General. In 1713 senior officers complained to the King that their work was being hampered by the inadequate and cramped offices they had to work in. But the country was heavily indebted by war, and little was done except for the demolition of the north wing in 1732 to build a new office for the Paymaster General. This office also housed the Commissioners of the Royal Hospital in Chelsea.

By 1745 the building was in a dangerous state and a memorial [petition] was presented to the Secretary of War by the Colonels of the two troops of Horse Guards and the Judge Advocate-General, saying that the building was in a 'very rotten and decayed condition'. It was too unsafe even for the King's coach to pass under the gateway and men on duty were in constant fear that the building would fall down and the chimneys catch fire. Plans were put in hand for a new building and by 1750 the old one had been demolished.

The new Horse Guards group of buildings was designed by William Kent, architect of the Treasury Building, who died in 1748 before he could submit the plans for approval. The Board of Works submitted them in 1749 and the building's eventual erection was

Plate 1   *Whitehall and the Privy Garden looking north, with Montagu House and the Thames. (Painting, oil on canvas, by Canaletto, probably 1751.) Whitehall and the Privy Garden are on the left; to the extreme left scaffolding has been erected for the building of the first Parliament Street houses. The stables of Richmond House are in the centre foreground; behind them is Montagu House. At the end of Whitehall the Holbein Gate may be seen, and behind another building, the Banqueting House.*

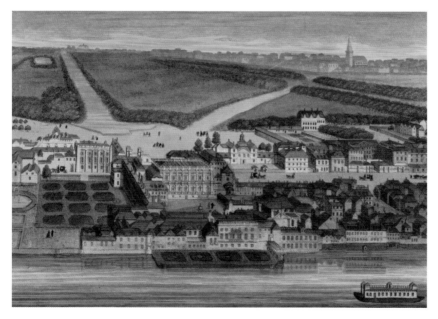

Plate 2   *The Palace of Whitehall as it appeared about the reign of James the second. (After an original drawing in the possession of Thomas Griffiths. Ascribed to Leonard Knyff, published 1808, and reproduced from* Londina Illustrata*.) Knyff's bird's-eye view shows the new Admiralty buildings erected 1694–5 on the site of Wallingford House, and the alterations made at Whitehall Palace by James II, such as the new Privy Garden range, the Catholic chapel and Council Chamber. Although the picture is captioned as the view as it appeared about the reign of James II it is probably about ten years later, dated by the vacant space between the Stone Gallery and the Thames, which indicates damage caused by the fire of 1691. Queen Mary's Terrace was not built until 1693.*

Plate 3   *Her Majesty's Royal Banqueting House of Whitehall, 1713. Engraved by H. Terasson. (J. T. Smith's* Nouveau Théâtre de la Grande Bretagne [Britannia Illustrata], *volume 3, 1724.) An annex at the north end encloses a staircase to the floor and gallery. When Inigo Jones originally built the Banqueting House, there was no inner staircase. King Charles I is believed to have walked out to the scaffold from the window in this annex.*

Plate 4   *Coronation procession of King George IV up Whitehall to the House of Peers in January 1821, showing the principal buildings from the Admiralty to Parliament Street. (Coloured aquatint panorama, published by G. Humphrey in 1822.)*

Plate 5 *Commander-in-Chief's Levée Room, the Horse Guards. (Engraved by T. Turnbull from a drawing by T. H. Shepherd, c. 1845.) The room is in the central archway overlooking Horse Guards Parade and the picture shows the Duke of Wellington, who held office as Commander-in-Chief from 1842 to 1852, with the widow of a fallen officer who is asking for help for her son. The portraits on the wall are of King George III and Queen Charlotte.*

Plate 6 *Admiralty Board Room. This has remained almost unchanged for 250 years and is still used for Board meetings. The walls are lined with oak; the wind dial over the marble mantelpiece dates from between 1707 and 1714 and was probably preserved from the former Admiralty building. The carved festoons over the mantelpiece are of fruit, flowers, fishes and nautical instruments and were attributed to Grinling Gibbons. The end of the table was cut out to accommodate a rather corpulent First Lord.*

Plate 7 *This 1923 painting by Fred Taylor gives an unusual aerial view of Whitehall before the present Ministry of Defence main building was built and when the houses in Whitehall Gardens, including Montagu House, were still standing. It also shows the circular and square courtyards of the Government Offices, Great George Street, and Horse Guards Parade empty of parked cars.*

Plate 8   *Programme for a charity concert held in 1814 in the Chapel Royal (the Banqueting House) in aid of the Germans who had suffered during the Napoleonic Wars.*

Plate 9   *The old Board of Trade Board Room. (By Thomas Rowlandson, 1809, published in Ackermann's* Microcosm of London.*) The decorative ceiling contains the letters JAMB below a ducal coronet – the initials of James and Anne, Duke and Duchess of Monmouth and Buccleuch. The room, according to Ackermann, was formerly the Duke of Monmouth's bedchamber, but this theory is disputed in the* Survey of London.

Plate 10 *Horse Guards, c.1837. (By T. Clark, published in J. Woods's* History of London, *1838.) The Horse Guards is seen from the Parade Ground, with the Admiralty to the left.*

Plate 11 *View of Lord Carrington's house, Whitehall, showing a corner of the Banqueting House. (By E. Angell Roberts, 1899.) Carrington House stood on the site of what is now the Old War Office.*

Plate 12   *The first floor of the refurbished Grand Staircase in Sir George Gilbert Scott's Foreign Office. The dome is decorated by female figures representing countries which had diplomatic relations with Britain in the 1860s. The dome and the stencilled walls and ceilings were by the church decorators Clayton and Bell, and the two ormolu and bronze chandeliers were made by Skidmore's Art Manufacturers Company of Coventry.*

Plate 13 *Exterior of the Foreign Office from the Park side. The building, started only a year after the virtual completion of Barry's and Pugin's Palace of Westminster in 1860, must at the time have appeared to the general public as yet another symbol of Victorian confidence.*

Plate 14 *Richmond Terrace, Whitehall, 1827. (By T. H. Shepherd and engraved by M. S. Barenger, published in Elmes's* Metropolitan Improvements: London in the Nineteenth Century, *(1827–30.) The Terrace occupies part of the site of the orchard of Whitehall Palace, which was later the site of Richmond House. In 1822 the lease was bought by the Crown and eight houses erected by a local builder.*

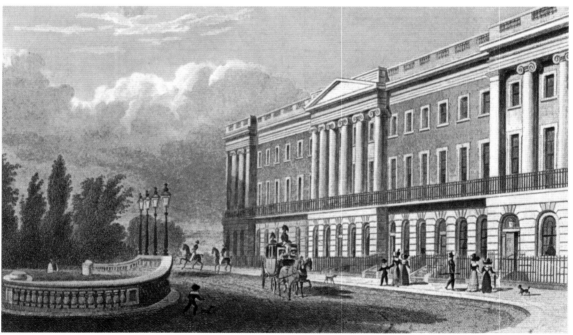

supervised by John Vardy, Kent's assistant. The group was of a formal and symmetrical design, with a central block three storeys high with pavilions going up to four storeys, a central cupola and triple Venetian windows. This central block had a frontage to the courtyard on the Whitehall side with a pediment on which was carved the royal arms and supporters. The returns on either side of the courtyard were lower and terminated in two-storey return wings. In the centre was an archway for carriages and two for those on foot. When the building was ready for occupation, as was common at the time, it was lit by candles, had open fires and no running water. Chamber pots were provided for the occupants. When passing under the central archway, the visitor can look up and see the initials 'SMF' and 'St MW' on the ceiling. These stand for St Martins-in-the-Fields and St Margaret's, Westminster. The parish boundary passes from east to west through the centre of the building.

The ground floor consisted of stabling and quarters for the Guards, stores and offices. The western or park side is more particularly attributed to Kent, and the buildings and façade on the Whitehall side to Vardy. The building was designed as a series of suites, all self-contained, and the finest rooms were that of the Commander-in-Chief, formerly the levee room, over the central carriageway and overlooking Horse Guards Parade, the Library and the vestibule. The Commander-in-Chief's room was panelled, with a Venetian window and marble fireplace. The three-storey octagonal hall rose to the height of the clock chamber in the cupola.

The central building and north wing were completed in 1753 and in 1755 the Household Cavalry moved in, but the south wing was not begun until 1754. Units of Foot Guards moved into the southern wing in 1756 and the building was finally completed in 1759. The estimate of £31,748 had been somewhat optimistic and the final cost was probably over £65,000.

The maintenance of the Horse Guards building was the responsibility of the Secretary for War and his appointed surveyor until, in 1817, the surveyorship was abolished and the building was handed over to the care of the Office of Works.

The Paymaster General's Office stands on a site where once was part of the Tilt Yard and afterwards stables and barracks built for the Horse Guards during King Charles II's reign. The north wing of the old Horse Guards building was in use in 1726 as the Office of the Paymaster General to the Forces, and from the beginning he was provided with a house as well as offices. The premises were entirely rebuilt in 1732–3 by John Lane, surveyor to the Horse Guards. The account for a total of £3,842 10s 11d for pulling down, rebuilding and repairing the 'Office of our Paymaster General of our Forces and the house thereunto belonging' was approved in June 1733.

It is possible that some parts of the King Charles II buildings were embodied in Lane's building. It was a three-storey edifice, with a brick frontage to Whitehall and a large central gable set within a pitched roof. The rear of the building overlooked a walled lawn.

Admiralty and Admiralty House

The Admiralty was built on the site of Wallingford House which in its turn had stood immediately to the north of the Tilt Yard. The house had since 1622 been owned by the King's favourite, George Villiers, Duke of Buckingham, after he had been appointed Lord High Admiral in 1619. He established a Council of the Sea which later became the Board of Admiralty. Buckingham's body lay in state at the house after his assassination in 1628.

It was commonly said that it was from the roof of this house that Archbishop Usher watched King Charles I being led out to the scaffold in front of the Banqueting House in 1649. However, the writers of the *Survey of London* believe it to have been from the roof of another house in Charing Cross (now known as part of Whitehall). Later, after Oliver Cromwell's death, the General Council of Officers of the Army, otherwise known as the Wallingford House party, was thought to have

35 *The Admiralty, designed by Thomas Ripley, was completed in 1726. The left-hand picture shows his plain stone wall concealing the courtyard from the street, but this was generally thought ugly, and it was replaced in 1760 with a 'handsome screen' by Robert Adam (right). This was set back further into the courtyard to allow for street widening and has an archway topped with a parapet; on either side is the carved figure of a winged sea horse. Niches in each wing were intended to contain statuary. The screen was altered, not for the better, by George Kedwell Taylor (civil architect to the Navy) in 1827–8, and was restored by the Office of Works in 1923.*

met at Wallingford House in an attempt to thwart General Monck's plans to restore the monarchy. The house reverted to the second Duke of Buckingham after the Restoration.

Wallingford House was demolished and the first purpose-built Admiralty building erected in 1694 to 1695 on the same site by John Evans at a cost of over £18,000. By 1720 the Admiralty had acquired the freeholds of all the other houses, mostly used as shops, that occupied the site, and was granted part of Spring Gardens for use as a garden. In 1723 the building was demolished because it was in such bad condition.

The new Admiralty building was designed by Thomas Ripley, one-time carpenter and coffee-shop keeper, later Clerk of the Works at the Mews. In 1721 he succeeded Grinling Gibbons as Master Carpenter and became Comptroller of the Works in 1726 upon the death of Sir John Vanbrugh. Ripley's building was completed in 1726, with the addition of the young Robert Adam's stone screen in 1760. The new Admiralty was not generally admired, the traveller and writer Thomas Pennant, calling it: 'A clumsy pile, but properly veiled from the street by Mr Adam's handsom skreen.' Thomas Shepherd was equally damning, describing it as 'A massy building of brick and stone. It has two deep wings and is entered by a lofty portico, supported by four very tall stone columns with Ionic capitals . . . but this portico, which was intended as an ornament to the building rather disgusts than pleases, in consequence of the immoderate height of the columns . . . '

To do him justice, Ripley was working under severe restrictions. The site had a narrow frontage and had to contain within a single building a number of separate residences for the Lords Commissioners, as well as working space for staff. Each residence had its own entrance on to the courtyard and link extinguishers beside each door remained there until the Second World War. (These items, which look like inverted horns, were for visitors to extinguish their flaming torches used to light the way in the dark).

A contemporary story has it that Ripley decided to copy St Paul's Cathedral by using columns four feet in diameter, but when they had been built up to the capitals it was found that the pediment would come right in the middle of the upper windows which had already been installed. Ripley had the whole work covered over while he pondered what to do next. In the end he built the columns up to the right height with garden rolling stones, but in the process spoilt the proportions of his scheme.

The building does, however, have a magnificent Board Room that is a survival of the first Admiralty and has remained unchanged for about 250 years. The fireplace bears the arms of King Charles II and the limewood carvings of fruit, flowers and nautical instruments are attributed to Grinling Gibbons. The nautical instruments represent those in use in the Navy during the 16th and 17th centuries, and include a globe, telescope, fore-staff for measuring altitudes and the sun, a pair of compasses, a sea astrolabe and ordinary nocturnal. The carvings at the top of the fireplace symbolise the Admiralty anchor, the sword of victory and

36   *The Telegraph, erected on the roof of the Admiralty in 1796, received urgent messages from the coast. It is said that a message from the Board Room could reach Portsmouth in under an hour.*

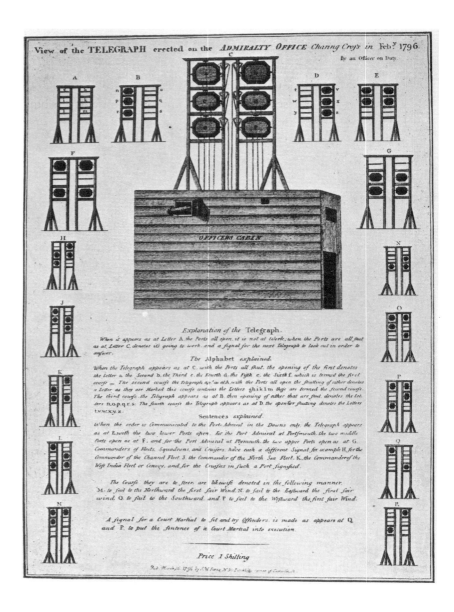

the trumpet of fame. In the centre is an ancient sign, the 'eye of glory', which can be seen on the Pyramids and was also used by the Stuarts to signify their belief in the divine right of kings.

The round wind dial over the fireplace still works and came from the earlier Admiralty. It dates from 1708 and is actuated by a metal weather vane on the roof. The table and chairs date from about 1788. The head of the table is cut out to accommodate a rather stout First Lord (George Ward Hunt, 1874–7) who weighed 24 stone. Smoking in the board room has long been forbidden – even Churchill observed this ban when he was First Lord. In 1796 a crude semaphore apparatus was installed for receiving urgent messages from the coast relayed by teams of signal men at prominent points. Twenty years later, a new and improved version was set up on the roof.

Admiralty House, next door, is on the site of Little Wallingford House and Pickering House, later known as Kinnoull House. It was built by Samuel Pepys Cockerell, surveyor to the Board of Admiralty, in 1786 as a residence for the First Lord of the Admiralty. The building is set back a little way from Whitehall and is in brickwork with stone dressing and of rather plain appearance, with a central Venetian window. Until this building was completed, the First Sea Lord and other Lords of the Admiralty lived in the Admiralty building itself and used the Board Room as their office and, indeed, sometimes their dining room.

Scotland Yard and the State Paper Office

In the 17th and 18th centuries Scotland Yard was part of Whitehall Palace. It provided sanctuary to debtors under the protection of the Board of Green Cloth until 1780. Numerous offices and official residences were grouped round three courts: Great, Middle and Little Scotland Yard. The Office of Works itself occupied a large part of Great Scotland Yard and there the Surveyor, the Comptroller, the Master Carpenter and the Clerk of Works for Whitehall had their offices. A large storehouse ran along the west wall of the gardens of Northumberland House and was the cause of some acrimony with the Duke. A long wharf was used for landing building materials.

The office of the Board was largely rebuilt in 1716-17, being in a dilapidated condition, but was pulled down in 1796. All the houses attached to the Board in Scotland Yard were involved in a

37   *Northumberland House, Charing Cross (after Canaletto, by T. Bowles, published 1753). The original painting was owned by the Duke of Northumberland.*

comprehensive scheme for the improvement of Whitehall which began in the 1790s and affected Whitehall Place, Whitehall Gardens and Richmond Terrace

In the 18th century the State Paper Office had been lodged in rooms on the top storey over the Holbein Gate; it had probably been there as early as 1672. In 1756 it was moved to 'a room over the passage that goes from the Treasury to the Secretary of State's Office', three years before the Holbein Gate was demolished. And in 1774 it was moved again to the southern portion of the Montagu Lodgings.

From 1788 onwards, the papers belonging to the State Paper Office were stored in a building between Middle and Little Scotland Yard. Ultimately their resting place was in the Public Record Office in Chancery Lane (completed in 1858).

Private houses belonging to the nobility

Cadogan and Cromwell Houses. In 1721 Sir George Byng (later Viscount Torrington and First Lord of the Admiralty) applied for a grant of a piece of waste land between Whitehall Court and the site of Malmesbury House. (He was father of the ill-fated Admiral Byng executed in 1757 for neglect of duty, 'pour encourager les autres'.) The ground is said to have comprised 'part of an old cellar and an old building called the cowhouse and some other small parts of ruins thereto adjoining'. The old cellar referred to was the Tudor wine cellar, originally belonging to Cardinal Wolsey, which had not been totally destroyed in the fire of 1698.

The Board of Green Cloth (responsible for the administration of the Household) had written to Sir Christopher Wren, Surveyor of the King's Works, on 25 November 1698 thus:

> 'Mr Dalton and the rest of the officers of his Majesty's great cellar have represented to us that a part of His Majesty's great cellar which was preserved from the late dreadfull fire at Whitehall, doth lye exposed to raine, and the wine lodged therein may receive much damage if timely care be not taken. We therefore desire you will give speedy order for making such a cover to the said cellar as may preserve it and ye said wine from the danger of the weather.'

The lease to Byng was granted in June 1722 for 31 years. In 1739 his son obtained a reversionary lease for another 36 years, and 20 years later the son's widow applied for a further extension and inclusion of a small strip of land between her house and ground leased to Lady Catherine Pelham. The lease was granted and subsequently acquired by Charles Cadogan.

The property was divided into two some time after 1768, the other half being known as Cromwell House. The premises above the wine cellar were erected in about 1722. The entrance to the part known as Cromwell House was approached by steps from Whitehall Yard. The Trial of the Pyx, a ceremony dating back to the time of Edward I, in which the coins issued by the Mint were tested for weight and fineness, at one time took place in room 79 of Cromwell House. By 1803 the house was being used as the office of the Comptroller of Army Accounts.

Carrington (originally Gower House). Lord Newburgh was granted a lease in 1721, but his house next to the Banqueting House was demolished when in 1765 Lord Gower leased some land in Whitehall on the site of the Palace Wardrobe, immediately facing the Horse Guards. Gower asked Sir William Chambers to design a plain house in Palladian style which, shortly afterwards, was built on an L-shaped site. Chambers decided to put the entrance at the rear elevation into Whitehall Yard.

38 *Rudolph Ackermann's view of Whitehall Yard in 1811 shows, on the extreme left, Carrington House (formerly Gower House). The white building on the right is Vanbrugh House, built at the beginning of the 18th century, and home of Sir John Vanbrugh, architect and dramatist and for two periods of eleven years each, Comptroller of the Board of Works.*

The house was set back from Whitehall by a moated railed area, and was distinguished by a magnificent Italianate staircase. It was bought by Lord Carrington who obtained a new lease in 1807, but was demolished in 1886. The Old War Office now stands on this site.

Fife House. In 1764 the 2nd Earl of Fife leased a piece of land at the east end of the Yard where Whitehall Palace's kitchen quarters had been. The land comprised the Pantry, Privy Buttery and part of the Pastry. Later, in 1769, he added the site of the kitchen and small beer cellar, and built a three-storey house. During his occupation he also constructed two embankments on the foreshore, adding the land to his garden – an expensive business, seemingly, for on 4 February 1803 he wrote to the Society of Arts: 'Fife House, Whitehall, is a crown lease. I have made two different embankments, which in the building have cost me many thousand pounds. The first embankment was made about five years after my entry on the lease, and the other 12 years after; they were made at a great expense.'

Gwydyr House. In 1770 Peter Burrell, Surveyor General of Crown Lands, obtained a lease of a piece of 'void and useless' ground adjoining the Lamplighter's Office, to be used as an office, and began to build. However, the work was eventually abandoned because of complaints by the 'nobility and gentry' living in the Privy Garden saying that a house in that position would deprive them of 'free air, light and agreeable prospect'. After further negotiations he was granted some land further north plus part of the Privy Garden. The house was built by John Marquand in 1772 at a cost of upwards of £6,000. It was built of brick with stone dressings, had five bays and was three storeys high with a semi-basement and an attic above the cornice, added at a later date. This fine 18th-century building has been preserved outwardly almost unchanged, although the exterior has recently been cleaned.

Harrington House. Harrington House stood in Craig's Court which was laid out towards the end of the 17th century and is still in existence north of Scotland Yard. Joseph Craig was a builder who died in 1711 and his house remained empty until 1714 when the Earl of Mar, newly-appointed Secretary of State and with no available apartment in the Cockpit, was told to take 'some convenient house in the neighbourhood of Whitehall' for his office. After the Earl's tenure, the Duke of Montrose took up residence, then Sir Richard Howe, and the Earl of Essex. In 1925 the site was bought by the Postmaster General and became a telephone exchange.

Malmesbury House. In 1721 Major John Hanbury, MP for Monmouthshire, applied for the lease of a vacant piece of land next to Pembroke House, extending north towards the building known as the Cowhouse and fronting the Privy Garden. This was then in the possession of Christopher Shrider, Organ-maker to His Majesty, and used by him as a workshop. The building adjoined on the south the entrance to Pembroke House and on the north was connected with Cromwell House and abutted against the old Tudor wine cellar. The house was built about 1725.

Montagu House. The house was built in 1733 by John, 2nd Duke of Montagu, who had leased a site in 1731. He erected 'a large and substantial house with outhouses and appurtenances thereto belonging', the lease valued by the Surveyor General at £200 p.a. The house occupied the southern part of the old Whitehall Palace buildings including part of the site of the Stone Gallery, a portion of the Privy Garden, and certain private apartments in Whitehall Palace.

The site was extended about ten years later to include the adjacent Thames foreshore near Queen Mary's Terrace where, between high and low tide large quantities of mud and filth would collect, and

where an embankment was sorely needed. Work on this bank, however, which was carried out in co-operation with the Duke of Richmond, was not completed for several years. Montagu House devolved to the Dukes of Buccleuch through the female line in 1790 when the Dukedom of Montagu became extinct.

Pembroke House. In 1717 Henry, Lord Herbert, obtained a lease of part of the site of the old Palace of Whitehall where the Queen's Apartments had stood, and on it built 'a very good house' designed in Palladian style by Colen Campbell, Deputy Surveyor to the Office of

Works, and overlooking the river. This part of the Palace had been completely destroyed in the fire of 1698 and nearly twenty years later the ground was still 'almost covered with heaps of rubbish, part of the ruins of the said Palace'.

A new lease, including some additional land, was granted in 1730; and in 1744 the 9th Earl of Pembroke asked for a further lease to include part of Queen Mary's Terrace along the river. He then enlarged the house, but in 1756 his son said that he was taking it down and building a more substantial and spacious home to the design of Sir William Chambers at a cost of about £22,000. The new house was approached via an arched entrance with a courtyard between lodge and house. It was taken over for government offices in 1851 and later became used as the War Office. It was demolished in 1938 for redevelopment as part of the Whitehall Gardens site.

Portland House. The Earl of Portland had lodgings in Whitehall from 1689 onwards, by the Stone Gallery, and was staying there when the two Palace fires occurred in 1691 and again in 1698, which damaged his rooms. A fresh lease was granted to the widow of his son, by the then Duke of Portland, who lived at the house until his death in 1762. It was in this house that the Dowager Duchess created the Portland Museum, which housed the celebrated Barberini vase, later known as the Portland vase, among other art treasures. The house remained in the family until 1805 when the interest in it was surrendered to the Crown and the property demolished. The site later became part of Whitehall Gardens.

Richmond House and Loudoun House. Towards the end of the 17th century a house was built on the site of the Bowling Green, to the designs of Christopher Wren for the Secretaries of State for Scotland. It was divided into two houses and enlarged when the Earl of Loudoun and the Earl of Mar took up residence. Some time after 1766, the house was bought by the Duke of Richmond and was lived in by his brother. After Richmond House was burnt down in 1791, the then Duke of Richmond went to live there. The first Richmond House, lying along the river at the east end of the Bowling Green, was built and occupied by 1668. It was taken over for government use and became the official residence of the Earl of Nottingham, Secretary of State, in 1702. In 1710 the lease was bought for a second Richmond House which was built to the west, and in 1791 the leases of the premises and land reclaimed from the river were acquired by the Duke. Late that year Richmond House was accidentally burnt down and was not rebuilt. The remainder of the lease was purchased by the Crown in 1822 and plans were prepared for the erection of a terrace of eight houses – Richmond Terrace.

    Vanbrugh House. On the north side of Whitehall Yard, Sir John Vanbrugh's small dwelling was built at the beginning of the 18th century out of the ruins of the Palace, on the site of Sir George Carteret's lodgings (vice-chamberlain of the household). It was later enlarged by the addition of wings. It was unkindly immortalised in Swift's satirical verses about its odd appearance:

41   *A copy of a drawing of Whitehall Yard, taken from the picture by Paul Sandby, engraved by Edward Rooker and published in 1766. Mistakenly titled 'Scotland Yard', the picture shows part of the Banqueting House, Pelham House, the gateway to the street and behind a high wall, Vanbrugh House. This area is now the site of Horse Guards Avenue.*

'One asks the waterman hard by,
  Where may the Poet's Palace lie?
 Another of the Thames enquires,
  If he has seen its gilded spires?
  At length they in the rubbish spy
  A thing resembling a goose pye.'

    Vanbrugh, as well as being a playwright and Comptroller of the Board of Works for two periods of eleven years, was also the builder of Blenheim Palace. Of him was written as his epitaph:

'Lie heavy on him, earth, for he
laid many a heavy load on thee.'

Vanbrugh House was demolished in the late 19th century.

Banqueting House or Chapel Royal

From 1698 until it became a museum for the Royal United
Service Institution nearly 200 years later, the Banqueting House was
known as the Chapel Royal. An altar was erected at the northern end and
a magnificent organ built in to the west wall. On 20 March 1724, George
I is said to have ordered that the preachers in the chapel should be
twenty-four persons selected by the Dean of His Majesty's Chapel from
Oxford and Cambridge, with a salary of £30 per annum. The first
sermon was ordered to be preached on Sunday, 5 April – Easter Day –
when the King attended the opening ceremony. However, the chapel
appears never to have been consecrated.

The Chapel Royal/Banqueting House became increasingly
dilapidated and extensive repairs were needed during the eighteenth
century, particularly to the painted ceiling, the painted masks and
festoons around the room and the roof. Restoration was carried out by
William Kent, who had been appointed Inspector of Paintings in the
royal palaces in 1728. The paintings were restored by Cipriani in 1776–7.
In 1773 the Board of Works told the Treasury that the stone facing of the
basement 'was greatly decayed owing to its having been originally built
with soft stone' and was given permission to reface it with Portland stone.
This work was carried out in 1774 at a cost of £524. In 1785 Sir William
Chambers renewed the original balustrade.

Redevelopment of Whitehall

During the Napoleonic period of the late 18th and early 19th
centuries, the face of Whitehall began to change once more. In 1795 John
Fordyce, Surveyor General of Land Revenues, was authorised by the
Treasury to invite eminent architects to produce plans and elevations for
new streets and buildings in Whitehall and Scotland Yard, based on plans
of the old Whitehall Palace area, for a premium of £200. Many well-

42　'View in Parliament Street showing Whitehall, the Treasury, &c'. (Engraved by R. Roffe from a drawing by G. Shepherd, published 1810.) Although entitled 'Parliament Street', the picture in fact shows the area called Whitehall and Charing Cross.

known architects, such as Cockerell, Holland, Soane and Wyatt, declined to participate in such an amorphous and wide-ranging scheme, and eventually the project was given to the architects attached to the Land Revenue Office, Messrs Leverton, Marquand, Chawner and Rhodes. During the next 30 years their plans gradually took shape as private leases fell in.

Scotland Yard was redesigned, and Carrington House and Vanbrugh House were enlarged by their tenants, as was Fife House. Various government departments moved into new offices and others were accommodated in Whitehall Place and Whitehall Yard. Government departments that occupied the Scotland Yard area included the Land Revenue Office, the Office of Works, the State Paper Office, the Wardrobe Office, the Queen's Treasury, the Almonry Office, Transport Office, and two orderly rooms for foot guards.

A new Land Revenue Office was built on the site of the old Office of Works building in 1796, opposite the Admiralty at the corner of Whitehall and Caddick's Row (later Whitehall Place). The Office of Works was transferred to a house in Little Scotland Yard, much to the annoyance of Charles Craig, its resident clerk, who complained that 'the

inconveniency of the [new] situation is great, it standing opposite to an alehouse frequented by noisy low people, draymen and others, and there being behind it a long narrow passage, frequented by prostitutes, etc'.

In 1788 the State Paper Office occupied offices between Middle and Little Scotland Yards. The Queen's Treasury remained in its original building, and the new Stationery Office was moved to Whitehall from New Palace Yard in 1812.

In 1782 the old Office of Works was abolished by Burke's Civil Establishment Act 1782 (the same Act that abolished the Board of Trade and Plantations). In fact, rather than being abolished, the Office of Works was severely pruned and reorganised, and a slimmed down Department with the same name began operations the following quarter, in October 1782.

The Westminster Bridge Commissioners had leased the land between Parliament Street and Cannon Row to James Mallors, a builder, in 1753, on condition that he repaired and made fit for habitation four dwellings in Cannon Row and built other houses on the site. The houses in Parliament Street were first occupied in 1758. Some remained as private homes until the 19th century, while a number were used as offices by professional men.

43 *A view of the Privy Garden Westminster looking south. (By John Boydell, published in Boydell's Collection of Views, 1770.) Picture shows the rear of the Banqueting House and the statue of King James II.*

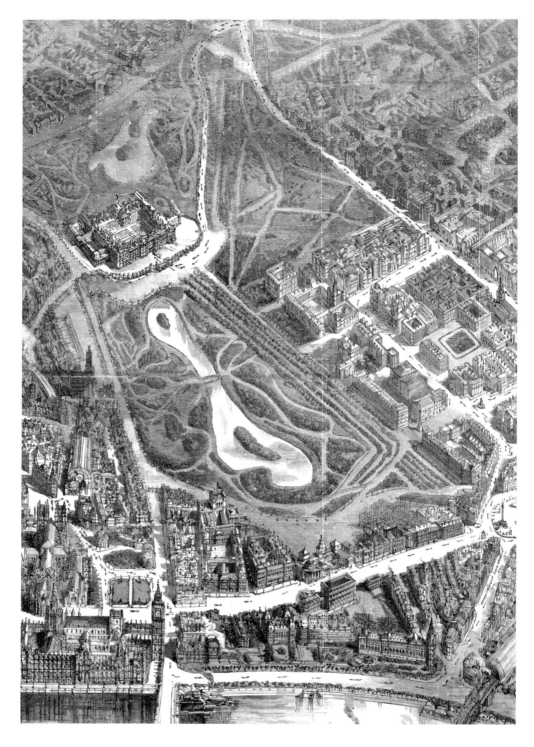

44   *Whitehall in 1887 (detail from a balloon view of Queen Victoria's Jubilee procession) showing the original houses on the GOGGS site, New Scotland Yard site and Whitehall Gardens before rebuilding.*

4
WHITEHALL IN THE NINETEENTH CENTURY

'I would rather see great men in little offices than little men in great offices.'

Sir John Trelawney MP

THE 19th century was the era of architectural competitions and new public buildings. By 1820 Whitehall Gardens and Richmond Terrace extended over the old royal Privy Garden and the Richmond House site. Middle and Little Scotland Yard disappeared and a new iron Westminster Bridge was opened in 1862. The Victoria Embankment was constructed in the mid-19th century and completed in 1870, and a road to reach it directly from Charing Cross driven straight through the Northumberland House site, compulsorily purchased by the government. Many grand schemes to redevelop the area were put forward and failed. However, individual buildings were restored or rebuilt, including a new block for the Foreign, Home, Colonial and India Offices, and Soane's design for the Board of Trade on the site of the old Treasury buildings. Extensions to the Admiralty were carried out at the end of the century and foundations for a new War Office laid in 1899.

Grand schemes

By 1820 the new layout on the east side of Whitehall was more or less complete. Whitehall Gardens and Richmond Terrace now extended over the Privy Garden and the Richmond House site. Whitehall Place had replaced Middle Scotland Yard, and by the beginning of the 19th century, Little Scotland Yard had also disappeared. In 1821 gas lighting for the streets was introduced into Whitehall and Charing Cross, and a new iron bridge to replace the dilapidated old Westminster Bridge, built in the previous century, was opened in 1862.

From 1832 to 1852 the Office of Works was combined with the Office of Woods, Forests and Land Revenues as an economy measure,

45 *General plan of Whitehall: first and second halves of the 19th century, from* The Builder, *January 1905. These show the changes that took place in the interim, such as site clearance for the Government Offices, Great George Street and the War Office, the removal of King Street, the erection of Scott's Old Public Offices, the opening of Horse Guards Avenue and the demolition of Northumberland House to make way for Northumberland Avenue.*

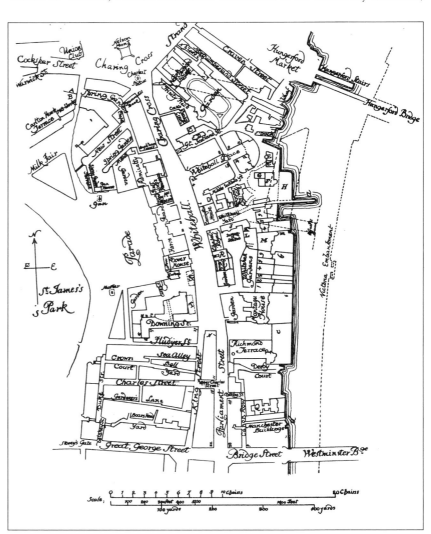

the enlarged department being administered by three Commissioners. However, in 1851 the offices were again separated and the senior of the three Commissioners, who was also an MP, became First Commissioner and political head of the new department, reporting directly to Parliament. The powers of the Office were codified by further legislation in 1874 and 1894, the scale and nature of the work changed, and the office took over general responsibility for accommodation from individual departments.

Many grand schemes to redevelop the area failed to reach fruition. For example in 1836, Decimus Burton was instructed to design new offices in the Downing Street area. Between 1836 and 1839 he produced a series of plans, finally recommending the provision of new

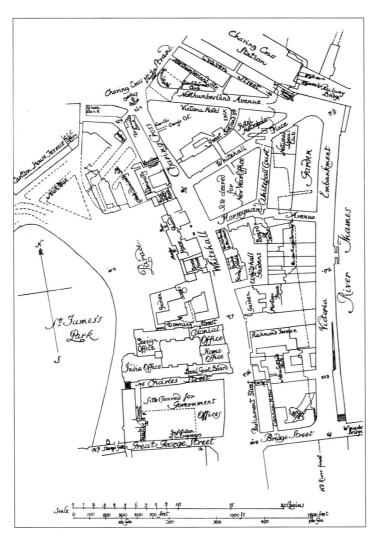

46 *Whitehall, Horse Guards, Government offices Date uncertain, probably between 1850 and 1865, as it shows the clearance of the first half of the Foreign Office building site. Wood engraving possibly taken from a mid-Victorian guidebook.*

offices for the Foreign Office and Colonial Office that encroached on the park. These offices were intended to form part of a general plan for Government buildings. A bill was introduced to purchase part of Fludyer Street, and Burton then incorporated the Fludyer estate into his plan and designed a Downing Square. According to *The Builder*, Burton's plans 'were duly printed and put away', possibly due to lack of funds. In 1854–5, Sir James Pennethorne, architect and surveyor, planned to erect a group of buildings on the west side around Downing Street to house the Treasury, Colonial Office, War Office and Board of Trade. He also drew up plans for building public offices on the east side of Whitehall, incorporating the Chapel Royal.

Sir Charles Trevelyan gave evidence to yet another Select Committee in 1856. He advocated building the public offices in groups and wished to make the Chapel Royal, i.e. Banqueting House, the focal point of several buildings on the east side, and to remove the Horse Guards so that Whitehall Palace might be opened to St James's Park and a broad street made through Whitehall Yard to the Thames.

Perhaps most elaborate of all was Sir Charles Barry's 'General Scheme for Metropolitan Improvements' which was unveiled in 1857 and proposed that all government and public offices should be massed together in one group of buildings between the park and Whitehall. He suggested that Whitehall be widened and a new embankment constructed. A central hall, 320 feet long and 150 feet wide with a glass roof, would link Whitehall to the Park and the State Paper Office would be removed.

Sir Andrew Clarke of the Admiralty submitted a plan in 1869 for the complete demolition of the west side of Whitehall, Parliament Street and King Street, to allow for a unified scheme for the Foreign and India Offices, the War Office and the Admiralty. Detailed plans for the concentration of Government offices were also produced by the architect Frederick Sang in the 1870s, with offices grouped around a large square. Luckily this scenario was never approved, for it would have involved the demolition of the Banqueting House.

None of these elaborate schemes were taken up. But in the early 1870s, Parliament approved the demolition of all the houses standing in front of the unfinished Home and Colonial Offices. The Parliament Street frontage was pulled down in March 1873 and the King Street side between 14 November and 5 December 1873.

By 1877 no grand scheme had been agreed, despite the number of designs drawn up. In that year three large-scale plans were submitted to the Select Committee of 1877 whose task it was to look into the concentration of certain public Departments. First, Sir Henry Hunt, adviser to the First Commissioner, and Surveyor for twenty-one years to the Office of Works, proposed that the War Office, the Admiralty and the Council Office should be accommodated on a block between Parliament Street, Great George Street, Charles Street and the Park; that the Board of Trade should be lodged between the Treasury Building and Horse Guards; and that Dover House should be pulled down. A new building for the Office of Works and the Office of Woods could be sandwiched between Horse Guards and the old Admiralty. The whole scheme was estimated to cost as much as £2.5 million.

Secondly, Algernon Mitford, Secretary of the Office of Works, suggested that part of the Great George Street site, from Parliament Street west, in the direction of the Park, should be purchased. After widening Parliament Street and so creating a magnificent approach to the Houses of Parliament, enough ground would be left for the new Admiralty to be built on the Great George Street site, between Charles Street and Parliament Square. Mitford also proposed that all the houses lying between the present Admiralty, including Drummonds Bank, should be purchased as the site for the War Office. He suggested that Dover House be demolished. Other public offices, with the Horse Guards as the centre, would be built on the west side of Charing Cross and Parliament Street.

Finally, Arthur Cates, a surveyor in the Office of Woods, proposed that one side of Whitehall Place and the houses in Whitehall Gardens as far as Montagu House be used as the site. He made use of the Fife House ground, and on it placed 'his' War Office, Admiralty and other departments. The cost was estimated at £850,000.

Even *The Builder* magazine came up with a plan of its own in which the Admiralty and War Office were to be built in blocks on the Embankment side of Whitehall, on part of the land on which Whitehall Palace had once stood. Inigo Jones's Banqueting House would then form part of a group of administrative offices facing the Horse Guards. A central archway opposite the main arch of the Horse Guards would lead to the War Office and Admiralty buildings, which would front to the river.

But in characteristically English manner no coherent plan was accepted. Changes and improvements took place piecemeal as so often before. A report on the saga of the Government Offices published in *The Builder* in 1882, condemned a scheme whereby the then First Commissioner of Works could carry out pet schemes of his own at the cost

'both of architectural propriety and of money. The present holder of the office appears to labour under a dangerous amount of ill-directed zeal; and if things go on this way, there is no knowing what

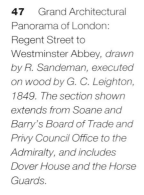

47   Grand Architectural Panorama of London: Regent Street to Westminster Abbey, *drawn by R. Sandeman, executed on wood by G. C. Leighton, 1849. The section shown extends from Soane and Barry's Board of Trade and Privy Council Office to the Admiralty, and includes Dover House and the Horse Guards.*

costly mistakes may not be made before another turn of the political wheel brings in another amateur architect to pull the metropolis about as he pleases'.

Looking back from the vantage point of 1905, a writer in *The Builder* was particularly dismissive of the various proposed schemes, stating that the entire story of the government offices 'will be found in volume after volume of reports, evidence, projects and plans – testifying to the procrastination, near-sighted, albeit wasteful, economy, departmental jealousies and partisanship of the government and their non-professional advisers.'

State Paper Office

Since 1788 the papers belonging to the State Paper Office had been housed in a building between Middle and Little Scotland Yard, but when part of this building collapsed early in 1819, the records were dispersed: those dating from 1688 to 1783 to a damp house in Great George Street; those dating from the reign of King Henry VIII to that of Charles II in the Middle Treasury Gallery.

In 1824 the Home Secretary, Peel, urged the Treasury to plan for a new building for the state papers. Although nothing came of this at the time, Sir John Soane was asked in 1829 to design a State Paper Office on the site of Lady Suffolk's house on the corner of Duke and Delahay Streets.

The new building was in Italian palazzo style imitated, Soane said, 'from the architecture of Vignola, Palladio, Inigo Jones, Sir

48 *The old Foreign Office, crammed into houses in Downing Street and Fludyer Street, was in such disrepair that it had to be shored up. For many years the Office had 'a most unsightly, not to say undignified appearance'.*

Fludyer Street

Foreign Office

Colonial Office

Downing Street

Privy Council Office

C Wren, etc.'. Progress was slow but according to Sir Edward Hertslet, later Librarian of the Foreign Office, the handsome stone building that cost £40,000 to erect answered the purpose for which it was built admirably. The building was finished in 1834, but was demolished in 1862 to make way for the new Foreign Office. The archives were moved to Sir James Pennethorne's Public Record Office building in Chancery Lane, completed in 1858.

The Redevelopment of the Foreign Office (Old Public Offices)

'First, the old Foreign Office is awfully tottery,
Its bottom a quicksand, its walls all awry:
Its standing or sinking an absolute lottery –
If the fall of the roof should open that to the sky?
What piles of foul litter from basement to attic!

What dust, meant in John Bull's eyes to be thrown!
What red-taped and docketted lies diplomatic.
Which, but for that smash, never daylight had known!'

Punch, 4 August 1855

The Foreign Office did not exist before 1782. Before that there were two Departments of State, the Northern and Southern departments. Administrative reforms in 1782 resulted in the Government's Northern Department becoming the Foreign Department and its Southern Department becoming the Home Department with responsibility for the colonies. The Right Hon. Charles James Fox was the first Secretary of State for Foreign Affairs, but stayed in office for two periods of a few months only. His Under-Secretary was Richard Brinsley Sheridan, the playwright and MP for Stafford. The staff were then housed in Cleveland Row, St James's, but shortly moved to more spacious premises in the Cockpit and then to Downing Street (Lord Sheffield's House). By the late 1820s they had taken over numbers 16, 17 and 18 Downing Street as well as two houses in Fludyer Street situated south of and parallel to Downing Street.

Sir Edward Hertslet, the distinguished Foreign Office Librarian from 1857 to 1896, complained that despite an ever-increasing workload, the old Foreign Office consisted of a block of several houses in a sad state of disrepair, into which staff were literally 'crammed'. The larger houses contained some fine rooms with windows overlooking the Park, but the smaller ones with windows giving on to Downing Street or Fludyer Street were in a very tumbledown condition, so much so that when the adjoining houses at the King Street end of Downing Street and later those at that end of Fludyer Street were taken down, the block forming the east end of the Foreign Office had to be shored up, which for many years gave the Office 'a most unsightly, not to say undignified appearance'.

The foundations were unstable, there were cracks in the walls and ceilings and inexplicably, heavy printing presses were kept on the top floor and vibrated destructively throughout the old houses. The Colonial Office premises at No 14 Downing Street, occupied since 1798 were described by a Parliamentary Select Committee in 1839, with some understatement, as 'decrepit to a certain degree'.

Sir Horace Rumbold, in his *Recollections of a diplomatist* (1902), wrote of the old Foreign Office that it was 'dingy and shabby to a degree,

49 *Sir James Pennethorne (1801–71). Architect. Appointed in 1840, with Thomas Chawner, joint surveyor of houses in London in the Land Revenue Department; appointed, in 1843, sole surveyor and architect, Office of Woods. Designed Victoria and Battersea Parks, the Public Record Office in Chancery Lane, Somerset House, and produced numerous designs for government offices in London.*

50 *Sir George Gilbert Scott (1811–78). Architect. Appointed architect to the dean and chapter of Westminster Abbey in 1849; architect of the Old Public Offices, including the India Office with Matthew Digby Wyatt; designed the Albert Memorial and St Pancras Station and Hotel.*

made up of dark offices and labyrinthine passages – four houses at least, tumbled into one, with floors at uneven levels and wearying corkscrew stairs that men cursed as they climbed – a thorough picture of disorder, penury and meanness'. However, the state of the old Foreign Office had not gone unnoticed. Several plans were put forward for rebuilding it and other public offices, by Decimus Burton, Sir John Soane and later by Henry Seward, Surveyor of Works and Buildings. But thoughts of immediate Foreign Office improvements were overshadowed by the fire which devastated the Houses of Parliament in October 1834.

Decimus Burton's series of proposals for rebuilding the public offices were prepared between 1836 and 1839, and were approved in 1839. But despite the Foreign Office and Colonial Office buildings being condemned as both unfit and unsafe by the House of Commons Select Committee on Public Offices in 1839, nothing more was done until 1853 when Sir James Pennethorne, architect to the Office of Works, was asked to draw up new plans. By then the outside fabric was in even worse condition. In 1852 a ceiling had fallen down, narrowly missing Lord Malmesbury, then Foreign Secretary. Subsidence in the old buildings necessitated new foundations and rebuilding of the front wall.

The Public Offices Extension Act 1855 allowed for compulsory purchase of all privately-owned property on the site between Crown Street and Fludyer Street, but there was much opposition to what George Bankes called an 'extensive scheme to enable Cabinet Ministers to entertain foreign visitors and their friends'. In the end only a proportion of the money needed for compulsory purchases was allowed and Pennethorne's scheme was shelved. In 1856 a government competition for plans for a new Foreign Office and a new War Office on the Downing Street site was announced. There were, in fact, to be three competitions: one for the War Office, one for the Foreign Office and a third to show how the whole area of Whitehall could best be laid out so that the two new buildings could be part of a comprehensive scheme.

Drawings were submitted in a wide variety of styles and were exhibited in Westminster Hall for the public to see. There were 9,000 visitors on the first day, and 7,000 on the second. Coe and Hofland's winning scheme for the Foreign Office was in French Second Empire style as were those of Garling for the War Department, and Charles Barry, son of Sir Charles, for the Foreign Office. Several others were in Gothic mode, and two were classical in concept. Not everybody approved of them, Sir John Trelawney MP remarked that 'Bricks and mortar too often lead to bread and water . . . I would rather see great men in little offices than little men in great offices.' The Government refused to agree to anything involving heavy expenditure at that time, and once again the plans were shelved.

In 1858 yet *another* committee on redevelopment was set up. The committee recommended that the buildings be laid out according to a block plan, and that the Government buy up the remaining privately-owned houses together with the block of buildings lying between King Street and Parliament Street.

Lord Palmerston's government fell in 1858 and a new Tory administration chose Sir George Gilbert Scott as architect of the Foreign Office and Home and Colonial Offices in November 1858 (though he had only come third in the Foreign Office competition). He was also appointed joint designer of the India Office with Matthew Digby Wyatt, who was architect to the East India Company. However, Lord Palmerston became Prime Minister again in the summer of 1859 and a 'battle of the styles' dominated the rebuilding for thirty months from January 1859 onwards. Palmerston favoured the classical Italianate style, while Scott's first design had been Gothic. But everyone agreed that something must be done:

> 'The Foreign Office is tumbling down, . . . the Colonial Office is following its example, . . . we want a new India Office, . . . the State Paper Office is crammed full and has not space for two years' more papers . . . '
>
> Lord Palmerston speaking in debate
> 8 July 1861, *Hansard*, 3rd series, clxiv, cols 507–550

51   *Lord Palmerston (1784–1865). Henry John Temple, 3rd Viscount. Statesman. Served in the Admiralty and War Office and became Foreign Secretary in 1830 in Lord Grey's administration, which post he kept for eleven years. In opposition 1841–6. In 1846 he became Foreign Secretary again, and was Home Secretary from 1852 to 1855. Served as Prime Minister 1855–8 and 1859 until his death in 1865.*

Scott then put forward a design for a Byzantine edifice which Palmerston dismissed as 'neither one thing nor t'other – a regular mongrel affair'. Palmerston, being Prime Minister, had the whip hand and eventually got his wish for a classical building. Scott later recalled how he 'bought some costly books on Italian architecture and set vigorously to work to rub up what though I had once understood pretty intimately, I had allowed to grow rusty by 20 years' neglect'. Finally he produced the classical design which was approved by Palmerston and, after lively debate, by Parliament. Palmerston declared at the time:

> 'The battle of the books, the battle of the Big and Little Endeans, or

of the Green Ribbands and the Blue Ribbands at Constantinople
were all as nothing compared with this battle of the Gothic and
Palladian styles. I must say that if I were called on to give an
impartial opinion as to the issue of the conflict, I should say that the
Gothic has been entirely defeated.'

Work on the block began in 1861–2, and the staff moved out to
Pembroke and Malmesbury Houses in July 1861. The foundations were
finished in 1863. The walls of the Foreign Office were up to first floor
level by June 1864, but both the Foreign and India Office buildings fell
behind schedule. The Foreign Office was finally completed at the end of
March 1868, the staff returned from their temporary home in June, and
the new Foreign Office opened for business in July. Palmerston had died
in 1865 while still in office and so never saw the finished building. His
successor, Gladstone, commented acerbically: ' . . . desiring a classical
Foreign Office, the British Government employed the best known
Gothic architect of the day to erect it'.

After the Indian Mutiny in 1857, the India Office was established
to govern the sub-continent, and at first occupied the premises of the old
East India Company in the City. However, this building was too small
and isolated for efficiency and a new office was erected on the site
contiguous with the Foreign Office. The exterior of the India Office was
designed by Scott and the interior by Wyatt. The internal court, renamed
Durbar Court in 1902, was thought by Wyatt to be his finest
achievement. It was originally intended as an open courtyard, but was
glazed over in 1868 and transformed into a magnificent ceremonial salon.
The façade facing St James's Park contained statues of Governor-
Generals of India. The new India Office opened with an official breakfast
at the end of November 1867.

Scott's plans for the Home and Colonial Offices were approved
in 1870 and extended the block to Whitehall. They were much less
elaborate and contained no state reception rooms, being 'internally of a
plain and utilitarian character', remarked *The Building News* for 10 April
1874. *The Builder* in June of that year stated that the 'general design
scarcely excites enthusiasm', but added that 'the detailed ornament goes
far to redeem this, and is good in every way . . .'. Much later, Sir William
Harcourt (Home Secretary 1880–5) is said to have likened his office to a
railway waiting room. The whole scheme was completed in 1875.

The Home Office moved into the centre of the block between
the Local Government Office on the King Charles Street side and the

Colonial Office on the Downing Street side. The front of the building has a façade decorated with carved ornaments and sculpture by Henry Hugh Armstead and John Birnie Philip, sculptors who had previously worked with Scott on the Albert Memorial.

Although from the exterior the Old Public Offices looked like one building, they housed five separate ministries (see map on p. 71), each being self-contained. It was not until the 1980s that it was possible to walk internally from one to another.

Scott again faced carping criticism from the Select Committee on Public Offices and Buildings in 1877 over the lack of ventilation, dark corridors, damp and smells. The building of the Victoria Embankment may well have contributed to the dampness, but Scott's architectural design and planning was blamed. He died not long after, in 1878, and his achievement was recognised by burial in Westminster Abbey.

Downing Street

By the 1820s Downing Street was largely occupied by government offices. A Treasury minister resided in No 10, the Chancellor of the Exchequer in No 11 from 1828 onwards. The Judge-Advocate-General dwelt at No 13; No 14 was the Department of War and the Colonies; and No 15 became part of the Foreign Office at No 16 in 1825. The next two houses on the south west return of the street, with two more fronting on to Fludyer Street, were also absorbed by the Foreign Office by 1825 and houses further west contained the West India Department, and Tithe Commission. In 1876, No 14 was demolished and the south front of No 13 rebuilt.

In 1824 all crown leases of premises east of No 10 Downing Street were terminated and the houses pulled down in the following year to allow for the building of Soane's new Privy Council and Board of Trade offices. No 12, however, was a private residence until 1863 when it was sold to the East India Company but not occupied by them. In 1862 the house was used by the Marine and Railway departments of the Board of Trade, but a fire in 1879 gutted it, leaving only the basement and ground floor. The upper part of the house had to be demolished, and the ground floor was converted into rooms suitable for dinners and receptions. No 13 was later renumbered No 12.

The frontage to No 10 Downing Street is surprisingly modest. Behind that ordinary façade hides a building older than it looks, having been grafted on to George Downing's original speculative houses of the previous century. Many of the principal rooms are on the first floor and include Soane's state dining room dating from about 1825 and below it a large vaulted kitchen by Kent. Two Soane rooms are on the first floor of No 11.

Several prime ministers chose not to live at No 10. Lord

Melbourne, Sir Robert Peel, Lord Russell, the Earls of Derby and Aberdeen and Lord Palmerston all preferred to stay in their own houses. So No 10 was used for official purposes but not as a house until Disraeli revived the custom of living in the official residence, and moved there in 1877.

No 9 Downing Street housed the Judicial Committee of the Privy Council, founded in 1833 under the Judicial Committee Act of that year. Its heart was the Privy Council Chamber in the Soane/Barry Offices fronting onto Downing Street. The façade of No 9 was as plain as No 10, but behind it lay a room 'splashed with a splendid sickness of Sienna marble, murals, red carpeting and elaborate plaster-work'. When Sir Charles Barry carried out his reconstruction of the Treasury Offices he removed the ceiling and the Ionic columns framing the doorways and erected a flat roof. He also obliterated the murals but left the lower part of the oak panelling on the walls.

Privy Council Office, Board of Trade and New Treasury Offices

Rather confusingly the old Treasury Building is not the home of the modern Treasury, which occupies the Government Offices in Great George Street. The old Treasury was actually composed of two separate

53 *The Eastern Question: a Cabinet Council in January 1877, when Benjamin Disraeli (Lord Beaconsfield) was Prime Minister. 'Many in the crowd that assembled in Downing Street . . . to watch the Ministers as they arrived must have been struck with the meanness of the exterior of the Prime Minister's residence, compared with the palatial edifices of the adjacent Foreign Office and Treasury.' Members of the Cabinet were discussing the problems caused by the collapse of the Ottoman Empire and the battle for control of its former territories. On the right is the Earl of Beaconsfield, to his left is the Earl of Derby (Secretary for Foreign Affairs), on his right Lord Cairns (Lord Chancellor), and the Duke of Richmond (President of the Council). In the chair nearest the reader is the Earl of Carnarvon (Colonial Secretary).*

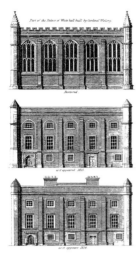

54 *Restoration of the old Tudor Tennis Court. Three views engraved by J. Basire from drawings by J. Carter, The Gentleman's Magazine, December 1816. Henry VIII's Tennis Court was used as Government offices in the 19th century, but in 1815 the façade was found to be dangerous, with large stones falling on the pavement, and repairs were carried out. The views show: 1. Restoration of the battlements and spires to the turrets; 2. As the building appeared in 1815; 3. As it appeared in 1816 with all the remaining mouldings cut away, five splays to the buttresses in lieu of two, the entire face of turrets, parapet and grounds to upper storeys masked over in brickwork. The façade was demolished in 1846 for Barry's extension to Soane's Treasury.*

buildings linked by Cockpit Passage. At the rear was Kent's Treasury, with the garden of No 10 Downing Street on its north and Horse Guards Parade on the east. Fronting onto Whitehall is Soane's Treasury Building, later rebuilt by Charles Barry. At the beginning of the century Cockpit Passage extended through a multifarious group of buildings, some being part of the old Whitehall Palace, others converted offices adapted from Palace outbuildings. Charles II's tennis court was demolished in 1809 but nothing was done to develop this site until Soane's work began in the 1820s.

The section known as Dorset House to the north included the site of what was known as the Great Close Tennis Court or Old Tennis Court. The lease of Dorset House reverted to the Crown in 1808 and from that date it was occupied by the Home Department and the Indian Board of Control, its adaptation into offices having been carried out by James Wyatt, Surveyor to the Office of Works. The front of the Old Tennis Court was in a dangerous state by 1815 and there were reports of large stones falling from it on to the pavement, but the façade endured until 1846 when it was demolished for Sir Charles Barry's extension to Soane's Board of Trade and Privy Council office.

The India Board moved into new quarters in 1810 and its old rooms were taken over by the Privy Council which had previously inhabited 'chilly and decayed' buildings between the Tennis Court and Kent's Treasury. In earlier times these rooms had been used as lodgings by the Duke of Monmouth, natural son of King Charles II.

The Board of Trade, which had been abolished in 1782 and then reconstituted in 1786, had moved into the whole of the lodging fronting onto Whitehall, once used by the Duke of Montagu, Master of the Great Wardrobe after the fire which destroyed Whitehall Palace in 1698. The Board had formerly occupied the northern part only. Its work grew and new departments proliferated until by 1820 officers were complaining about 'the great dilapidation of the building, its great insecurity and its entire inadequacy from want of accommodation for the ordinary business of the Office'.

Sir John Soane was asked to draw up plans for a new building and put in an estimate of £14,222 for a brick building with stone ornaments and a frontage on to Whitehall of 82 feet. His first designs contained a triumphal arch across Downing Street, adorned with sculptures and complemented by a similar arch opening into St James's Park from the far end of Downing Street. These two arches were intended to stand across a

55 *Offices of the Board of Trade, 1814. Lithograph by Luke Berrington (1850) shows the Whitehall frontage before Soane's new building was erected. After the abolition of the Board of Trade in 1782 and its subsequent reconstitution in 1786, it had been allotted the Montagu premises on the park side of Whitehall.*

processional road to the houses of Parliament, but this part of his plan was not carried out.

The Treasury ministers wanted the front rooms to be made larger and preferred a stone frontage (thus increasing the estimate to £17,200) and instructions to proceed were given in October 1823. The old Privy Council adjoining the Board of Trade to the south was also to be rebuilt on the site of crown property in Downing Street and on the west side of Rochester or Clarendon House, partly occupying the one-time site of Captain Thomas Cooke's (Master of the tennis courts) lodgings. In December 1823, Soane designed a façade from the corner of Downing Street extending to Treasury Passage, which would give a frontage along Whitehall of 150–160 feet. The Downing Street frontage was set back and arranged at a different angle to King Street.

There were several planning meetings between Soane and ministers before the Corinthian version of a continuous columnar façade was approved in June 1824. The work was to be done in stages. However, yet more changes were demanded and eventually it was decided that the columns were to reach only in front of the ground and first floor storeys. By November 1824 the new Board of Trade was ready for its roof.

Work began on the Privy Council Offices in December 1825

56   *Sir John Soane (1753–1837). Architect and founder of the Soane Museum. Worked with Henry Holland till 1776; architect to the Bank of England 1788; Clerk of Works at St James's Palace and the Houses of Parliament, 1791; architect to the Department of Woods and Forests 1795; 1815 appointed one of three architects attached to the Office of Works. Designed the Privy Council and Board of Trade Offices, 1824–7, and the State Paper Office in 1829.*

57   *Whitehall, 1825, lithograph by H. Monnier. Shows as background the new Soane building for the Privy Council and the Board of Trade, at its junction with Downing Street. The building is unfinished and the columns only reach half way along the Whitehall frontage. In the foreground is a stage coach and, to the right, a hearse.*

and by September the following year the building was nearly finished. Meanwhile the estimates continued to soar. Soane confessed in a private memo in 1826: 'I am in a fever about the estimates. So many alterations and additions have been made at different times, and so many estimates dovetailed into each other that I am mortified at the result of such mixed calculations.' By November 1826 the estimated costs had climbed to just under £76,200. In December 1826 it was decided not to include Treasury Passage in the frontage.

Soane's work was cut short in 1827 with the result that his building was left unfinished and asymmetrical with a façade reaching from Downing Street to the Old Tudor Tennis Court, which was allowed to stand for another 19 years. The northern wing, which had been intended to house the Home Department, was not built at all. Soane's finished building attracted much criticism, one MP unkindly referring to 'that extraordinary range of buildings which had been commenced at the Treasury . . . with its one tier of buildings so strangely heaped upon the top of the other, it resembled a double stand on a race course'.

By the 1840s the work of the Railway and Statistical departments of the Board of Trade had increased so much that the staff were overflowing their offices, and in 1844 the architect Sir Charles Barry was asked to draw up new plans for extending the accommodation. A writer in *The Builder* remarked: 'It is also in contemplation to pull down the old building at present occupied by the department of the Home Secretary of State [the Old Tennis Court] which has long disfigured that portion of

Whitehall, and to erect a more sightly structure in conformity with the new front of the Board of Trade.'

Barry's design raised the elevation and continued it as far as Dover House, to mask the old premises then used by the Home Office between Dover House and Treasury Passage. He provided for another storey, for twenty-five new rooms in the Board of Trade, five in the Privy Council and sixteen for the Home Department. His optimistic estimate for this scheme was just under £11,000 but grew to over £26,000 as work proceeded. His biographer, Alfred Barry, remarked that the altered building was practically new in design and spirit, and showed the growing taste for richness and vigour of effect visible in Barry's later Italian style, in contrast with the classicism of the original.

The Old Tudor Tennis Court was demolished to provide the site for the north wing of the Offices. It was not greatly missed. A writer in *The Builder* (12 September 1846) commented that 'an eyesore in one of our noblest thoroughfares will at last be removed', although traces of it still remain today. The Home Department was entirely rebuilt at an estimate of £11,745, producing an additional twenty-two rooms.

The only part of Soane's work to be left reasonably intact was the judicial wing of the Privy Council in Downing Street on the Dorset House site. Soane's façade was dismantled and rebuilt, using his masonry

58 *Board of Trade, Soane façade, 1828. (By T. H. Shepherd and engraved by M. Fox. Published in* Elmes's *Metropolitan Improvements: London in the 19th Century, 1827–30.) In December 1823, the architect Sir John Soane, designed a façade with a frontage from Downing Street to the Treasury Passage. The Board of Trade was to occupy the northern part. The building was completed in 1827 and had a classic stone façade with columns to the ground and first floors and a high balustraded parapet screening the top storey.*

and columns, but the columns were set deeper into the façade. Another storey was added to the top and a new roof constructed. The building thereby gained additional height, was made more symmetrical and the colonnade of the south pavilion was removed so that the whole façade now stood on a single line.

59   *This 1886 engraving shows a reception at Dover House, now home of the Scottish Office. The house, designed by James Paine, was completed in 1758. In 1787 it was assigned to the Duke of York and Albany. During the Duke's occupancy, in 1788 a portico facing the street, a circular hall and dome, together with a grand staircase, were built to the designs of Henry Holland. A swap was made in 1793 with Lord Melbourne and 'Melbourne House' flourished until 1830 when it was bought by Lord Dover and became known by its present name. The house was taken over by the Crown in 1885.*

The total cost of Barry's work came to £44,976 18s 9d, including his commission. However, the Treasury, in the person of Sir Charles Trevelyan, objected violently to the excess over estimate for which Barry had failed to obtain official permission. The Commissioners decided that Barry's commission would be calculated, not on the actual cost of the work, but on the approved estimate only.

Melbourne, later Dover House

Melbourne House had been the home of Viscount Melbourne since 1792 and thereafter that of his son, who was Prime Minister to the young Queen Victoria. In the early 19th century the house was a hub of political, aristocratic and cultural society, and was also notorious for the antics of its young chatelaine, Lady Caroline Lamb and her affair with Lord Byron. Byron was also a close friend of the older Lady Melbourne, Caroline's mother-in-law. In a letter to her, dated 6 November 1812, he wrote: 'I presume that I may now have access to the lower regions of Melbourne House, from which my *ascent* [to Lady Caroline] had long excluded me.'

The name was changed from Melbourne to Dover House in 1832, the lease having passed to the first Baron Dover whose son and son's widow lived there until 1885. The house is said to have been offered at one time to the then Prime Minister, Mr Gladstone, as his official residence in 1884, but he turned it down as being so large that he would be obliged to 'receive' there, and he preferred to be private! Dover House was instead allocated to the first Secretary for Scotland, the Duke of Richmond and Gordon, and later became the Scottish Office. The portico of the house is opposite the site of the old Holbein Gate belonging to Whitehall Palace.

Horse Guards and Paymaster General's Office

Between 1803 and 1805 the original single-storey blocks connecting the wings with the centre of the Horse Guards building had two more floors added to give extra space for staff. This work was carried out by the Horse Guards' then surveyor, Thomas Rice. The care of the

60 *Sir Charles Barry (1795–1860). Architect. Designed the new Houses of Parliament in collaboration with Augustus Pugin after the fire of 1834 and extended and remodelled the Board of Trade and Privy Council Offices 1844–6. Other projects included the Royal Institute of Fine Arts in Manchester, the Reform Club, Halifax Town Hall and Bridgewater House.*

THE HORSE GUARDS PARADE.

61 *The Horse Guards, a cartoon view in 1890 of a throng, including various dignitaries, in front of the Horse Guards; there are vignettes of the French Gun on Horse Guards Parade, and a mounted sentry on duty.*

Horse Guards building was made the responsibility of the Office of Works in 1817. Before that it had been a separate department with its own surveyor. Additional space was needed in the mid-19th century and the architect Sir Charles Barry was commissioned to design an extension to the buildings by raising the height. He produced an elaborate scheme which was never acted upon.

In 1860 the War Office Department was moved from Horse Guards to larger premises in Pall Mall, and later the Commander-in-Chief and his staff were also moved out, not without protest, to Pall Mall. By the turn of the century the Foot Guards too had gone, leaving only a few senior officers behind.

Two striking guns now stand on Horse Guards Parade, adding a fine ceremonial air, and underlining a British tradition of action abroad. The Turkish cannon is a bronze 52-pounder by Murad, captured from the French at the battle of Alexandria in 1801. The other is a French gun,

62 *The Horse Guards. Peace illuminations to celebrate the end of the Crimean War, 1856.*

a 12-inch bronze mortar made to celebrate the raising of the siege of Cadiz after the battle of Salamanca in July 1822. It was presented to the Prince Regent and originally placed in St James's Park in 1816 before finding its present home.

The Paymaster General's Office came into being in 1836, consolidating the duties of the Paymaster General of the Forces, Treasurer of the Navy, and of the Ordnance and Treasurer of Chelsea Hospital. Its headquarters was the former Army Pay Office building in Whitehall adjoining the Horse Guards. This had been enlarged by the building of a four-storey extension to the north, a single yellow brick bay, added in 1806. Shortly before the consolidation, the rooms used as the Paymaster General's official residence were converted into offices. Twenty years later, Sir Charles Trevelyan reported to a Select Committee on Government Buildings that the Whitehall building was unsuitable for its purpose.

Seemingly nothing was done, because in 1860 the Paymaster General of the day vividly described conditions in a petition to the Treasury, saying that 'claimants of all classes, such as General and other Officers, Widows of Officers, Bankers' Clerks, public servants . . . and others of a more doubtful character . . . are all mixed together in a mass so dense that, on some days it is difficult to make one's way through them, and great delay arises from this cause in obtaining payment . . . '.

Extra accommodation was found, but the volume of business and staff had also increased and in 1882 the clerks added their complaints:

'The present room is almost uninhabitable . . . the room is on a level with the street and the absence of a basement floor or even cellarage renders it exceptionally damp and cold. The windows looking towards Whitehall are small and low. They at no time admit sufficient light and the dust and noise they do admit preclude the possibility of their being used for the purpose of ventilation.'

But still nothing was done, on the excuse that the building might be demolished and the site used for expansion of the War Office and Admiralty. The staff had to wait for improvements until the next century.

The Admiralty

In a report dated 31 August 1855 concerning Ripley's Admiralty, Sir James Pennethorne said that it rested upon a timber platform laid over a bed of river deposit six or seven feet thick, which was soft and full of water and therefore the building had settled more or less in every part. In the 1990s the Admiralty is still sinking, and many of the floors and corridors are uneven.

Before the 1830s the Admiralty had two functions: the Admiralty proper, concerned with the operational side, and the Navy

63 *Nelson's funeral cortège, 1806. The body lay in the Admiralty overnight and was then conveyed from Whitehall to St Paul's Cathedral on the 9th January for the funeral, on a magnificent open hearse decorated with a carved representation of the head and stern of* The Victory, *under an elevated canopy in the form of the upper part of an ancient sarcophagus, with six sable plumes and a viscount's coronet in the centre, supported by four columns representing palm trees . . . the whole upon a four-wheeled carriage drawn by six horses.* [Gentleman's Magazine.]

Board which dealt with dockyards, the supply side and servicing the Fleet. On entering the hall, visitors are faced with E. H. Baily's original model for the statue at the top of Nelson's Column in Trafalgar Square. Facing the door are two hooded hall porter chairs (about 300 years old), which stood in the original Admiralty Building.

The old Captain's waiting room where naval officers used to assemble to await calls to the Board Room is now known as Nelson's Room and is full of Nelson memorabilia, with contemporary prints tracing the progress of the cortège from Greenwich by river and road. Nelson's body was brought from Whitehall Stairs to the Admiralty and placed in the Captain's Room, which was hung with black cloth and lighted with wax tapers. Here it lay during the night of 8 January 1806 before burial in St Paul's Cathedral. Tradition has it that after Trafalgar, Nelson's body was preserved in a barrel of rum for the long journey home. On arrival at Greenwich the barrel was opened up, the body laid to rest in a more fitting manner, and the rum drunk by the assembled multitude. To drink a tot of this liquor was thought to be a great honour!

Another memorial to Nelson is to be found in the Board Room where there is a white spot on the wall by the fireplace, known as the Nelson spot because it is at his height (5' 4"). This represented the minimum height for a commission in the Royal Marines under the 1847 regulations.

Under the Public Offices Site Act of 1882, houses in the little enclave of Spring Gardens, once a pleasure garden, were bought for the improvement, enlargement, and rebuilding of the Admiralty and War Office at a total cost of £458,000. The author of a monograph on the Admiralty Board Room reminisced:

64 *LCC Offices, Spring Gardens, by Howard Penton, 1900. Spring Gardens was once a royal, then a public pleasure garden. The offices were erected by the Metropolitan Board of Works in 1860 and taken over by the London County Council in 1889.*

65 *The survey of Spring Gardens was made in 1804 by Thomas Chawner, an architect attached to the Land Revenue Office.*

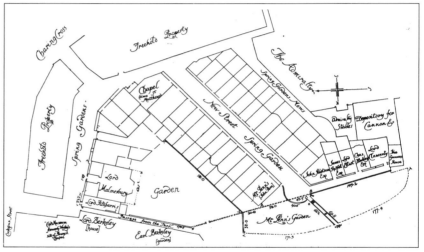

'The generation is fast disappearing that remembers the old Spring Gardens with its tottering houses (where the Mall now runs proudly under the Admiralty Arch) and the melancholy cow near the Admiralty from which the venturesome could obtain a mug of "fresh" milk.'

An architectural competition to design the new Admiralty and War Office was then held, and won by the Halifax firm of John and Joseph Leeming in 1884. The winners were to be paid £600 for the drawings and £24,400 for the completed building. The Leemings' designs involved demolition of the Admiralty and all other offices and houses on the site. They proposed to erect a lofty stone structure, capable

of containing under one roof all the staff of both departments, at a cost of about £700,000. The building was to be in two blocks, the first ready in four years, and the whole in ten. Work began on clearing the site but in 1886 all was in the melting pot once more and another Select Committee began to deliberate on the whole question of rebuilding.

A bizarre – possibly terrorist – outrage took place at the Admiralty in April 1885, when the 'Great Admiralty Explosion' occurred in a ground floor room. The room was wrecked and the 'able but autocratic' Assistant Under-Secretary Swainson was seriously injured. Lord Northbrook, sitting in the room above, was lifted from his seat and thrown on to the hearthrug. The authorities concluded that this was a criminal act (several dynamite explosions had occurred in the previous year or two), though the cause remained a mystery despite extensive investigation. It was rumoured, however, that Swainson himself was responsible.

In 1887, Shaw Lefevre, First Commissioner of Works, gave evidence to the Select Committee on the Admiralty and War Office concerning the long and tangled history of committee reports and recommendations, proposals to purchase, and alternative schemes for siting and building of new Admiralty and War Office buildings, either near the Houses of Parliament, or in Great George Street, on Spring Gardens or the Fife House site. He recalled that property valued at £241,000 in Great George Street, Parliament Street and King Street had

66 *Design for a new Admiralty by the competition winners in 1864, John and Joseph Leeming. The design involved demolition of the Admiralty and all other buildings on the site, and erection of a building capable of containing all the staff of the Admiralty and War Office. The plan was abandoned due to cost and time factors, although extensions to the Admiralty were finally undertaken by Leeming & Leeming in 1895.*

67　*Terrorist outrages were not unknown in London in the 1880s and 90s. The illustration, annotated by its former owner 'the building in front [i.e. facing] is near the Red Lion Tavern in Parliament Street', shows the scene after such an explosion. The building on the left is presumably the Home Office (now the Foreign and Commonwealth Office) before GOGGS and the arch across King Charles Street were built. The 'Dynamitards' caused several explosions in London, unsuccessful attempts including one at the foot of Nelson's Column. In the four years between January 1881 and January 1885 alone, twenty-five dynamite explosions were carried out or attempted by Irish or Irish-American conspirators.*

been bought in the 1870s in anticipation of building work. But nothing had happened. Two banks on the Spring Gardens site (Drummonds and Biddulph's) had actually been pulled down in the late 1870s and the Drummonds' site was offered to the Government, which took no action, so both banks were rebuilt and the Spring Gardens site therefore considerably reduced in size.

The Select Committee concluded that the Leemings' scheme for the Admiralty and War Office should be abandoned, not because they disapproved of the designs, but because they felt that by making additions to the Admiralty all that department's requirements could be provided for in a shorter time and at less cost. They did, however, recommend that the staff of both departments should be housed close together.

At last extensions to the Admiralty were carried out at the end of the 19th century as a result of the 1887 Committee's report. The additional buildings were designed by Leeming & Leeming. The old Admiralty building remained and the first part of the extension along the side of Horse Guards was ready for occupation in 1895 and is today known by civil servants as Old Admiralty Building. When the contractor began work on the foundations he found the gravel subsoil above the clay was heavily waterlogged, and had to line the cavity with concrete walls and a floor. Sir James Pennethorne's report about the Admiralty building's foundations appeared to be as relevant at the end of the century as it had been in 1855. A further extension by Aston Webb (including Admiralty Arch) was finally ready in 1911.

War Office

Many plans were drawn up for a new War Office during the course of the 19th century. Nearly all of them were rejected or in abeyance until the 1880s. By the middle of the 19th century the War Office was still housed in a number of buildings in Pall Mall, to the great inconvenience of all concerned. A Select Committee reported in 1856 that it was unsatisfactory that the War Department had to carry on its business in no less than ten different places.

After the conclusion by a Select Committee in 1887 that the most recent scheme to combine the Admiralty and War Office should be abandoned, matters were at a standstill for the next five years. Then an Office of Works minute of 14 December 1892 set the ball rolling again. The writer, Shaw Lefevre, First Commissioner, said that although five years had elapsed since the report, nothing had been done about a new War Office and vacant land in Whitehall owned by the Office of Woods had long been lying idle. He suggested that the only possible site for a new War Office would be in Whitehall opposite the Admiralty. The land would cost £390,000 and it would take about two years to acquire it all and eight years to build. However, the Treasury did not agree to his suggestion, saying that 'present engagements in respect of public buildings are already sufficiently large'.

But the site of the new War Office where Carrington House formerly stood was eventually acquired under the authority of the Public Offices Whitehall Site Act 1897 and the foundations were begun in 1899. This time there was no competition for the 'best' plans, but the architect was chosen by the Office of Works from a panel of names submitted by the Royal Institute of British Architects. The plans were prepared by the architect William Young, designer of the Glasgow City Chambers, who died at an early stage of the work in 1900. His chief wish had been to produce a classical building which would harmonise with the adjacent Banqueting House. The work was carried on under the supervision of his son and partner, Clyde Young, and Sir John Taylor, retired chief architect of the Office of Works.

The London correspondent of the *Birmingham Daily Post* wrote, on 12 March 1900, about an 'interesting archaeological discovery' made during the

'course of the extensive excavations now being conducted on the

68 & 69 *In the mid-19th century the staff of the old War Office were inconveniently housed in several offices in Pall Mall. Many plans were put forward for a new War Office, and a combined War Office and Admiralty in a spacious new building was proposed for the Admiralty site. Eventually foundations were laid for a new War Office on the site of Carrington House on the river side of Whitehall and the building, designed by William Young, was completed in 1906.*

70 *Carrington House: 'On the left is part of the thoroughfare known as Whitehall Place, the building at the corner of which was lately standing though all houses between it and the Banqueting House have been pulled down and the narrow thoroughfare known as Whitehall Yard has been widened into Horse Guards Avenue.' On the right and near the Banqueting House is Carrington House. Houses between it and Whitehall Place were latterly occupied as offices. Since the drawing was made in 1886, considerable changes have taken place.* J. P. Emslie: Illustrated Topographical Record of London: changes and demolitions.

site of Carrington House in Whitehall where the new office is to be erected. About five or six feet below the surface the remains of several clearly-defined and well-made roads have been laid bare, the direction of which throws an interesting light upon the topography of this part of Whitehall two or three centuries ago. It is scarcely to be wondered at also that in a spot so crowded with historic associations, situated as it is within a few yards only of the Banqueting House of Whitehall, where Charles I was executed, some human remains also should have been discovered'.

Victoria Embankment

The building of the Victoria Embankment marked a significant stage in the development of Whitehall as we know it today. As the Thames is a tidal river, the problem of flooding has always been an ever-present threat, one not resolved on the southern bank until after the Second World War. The overall risk was not finally alleviated until the opening of the Thames Flood Barrier in 1984.

John Stow's *Survey of London* paints a vivid picture of the year

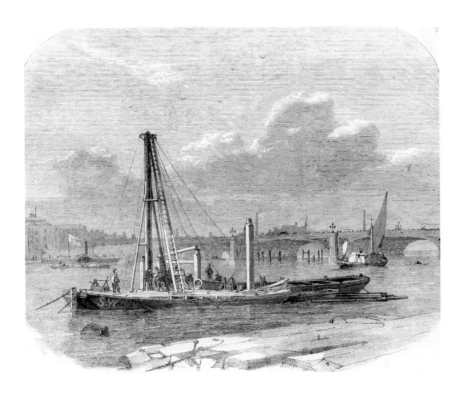

71 *The Thames Embankment, begun in 1864 and completed in 1870. The engraving shows the driving of the first pile in front of the Duke of Buccleuch's mansion. The foundation stone was laid near Whitehall Stairs by Mr John Thwaites, chairman of the Metropolitan Board of Works. The first section, from Westminster to Waterloo Bridge, was contracted to George Furness for £520,000. At Westminster Bridge the roadway was set back about 30 feet from the face of the Embankment wall and the intervening space was reserved for a promenade and steamboat pier. The riverside path between Westminster Bridge and the Temple was opened to the public in 1868.*

1236 when the river Thames overflowed the banks and 'in the great palace of Westminster men did row with wheryes in the middest of the Hall, being forced to ryde to theyr chambers'. Pepys noted in his *Diary* for 20 March 1660: 'At Westminster, by reason of rain and an easterly wind, the water was so high that there was boats rowed in King Street and all our yards was drowned . . . ', an experience often repeated in the intervening years.

Before the embanking of the Thames and reclamation of the foreshore, a causeway ran from Whitehall Yard to the river, once used by those arriving or departing by wherry, where a man employed by the Office of Works was stationed to sweep off the mud left by the ebbing tide. The Thames Embankment Act 1862 described the 'improvements and works' authorised as including the making and maintaining of an embankment and viaduct on the left bank of the river, running from the Middlesex end of Westminster Bridge. It would terminate near Blackfriars Bridge, with an approach road and new streets, including one near Whitehall Stairs, passing through Whitehall Yard and finishing in Whitehall, opposite the Horse Guards. The Act was intended to provide 'with the greatest efficiency and economy for the relief of the most crowded streets by the establishment of a new and spacious thoroughfare for the improvement of the navigation of the river'.

The construction of the Victoria Embankment was started in 1864, (the first stone being laid on the north side in July that year, not far from Whitehall Stairs), and completed in 1870. The embankment extended from Blackfriars to Westminster Bridge and to achieve a gentle curve, the river wall on the north bank was brought forward by up to 300 feet, unfortunately demolishing historic Whitehall Stairs in the process, together with piers, wharves and docks.

The last time Whitehall Stairs had been used for a ceremonial procession by water was when Prince Albert opened the New Coal Exchange in the City. With the Prince of Wales and the Princess Royal (Queen Victoria was unwell), he proceeded to the opening in the state barge, starting and ending the journey at Whitehall Stairs, and accompanied by the City and Admiralty barges, including the barge that had carried Nelson's body from Greenwich to Westminster. 'At Whitehall Stairs there was a gay gathering of boats and crafts of various periods and styles of decoration . . . the bridges were crowded with spectators' reported *The Illustrated London News* on 3 November 1849.

During the 19th century there was constant journalistic

72   *Reception of Princess Alexandra (Princess of Wales) into London in 1863, with the royal procession passing Trafalgar Square. Northumberland House is in the background and Big Ben can be seen in the distance.* The Illustrated London News *commented that 'The vast area was crowded in every part from an early hour in the morning by loyal subjects of her Majesty who were anxious to do honour to the affianced bride of the future King of England.'*

discussion about London improvements and a writer in *The Builder* was quick with suggestions for making the new Embankment more attractive: 'Now that the noble quay walls and landing piers are finished, what cause most concern are the dingy and desolate aspect of the reclaimed foreshore and the dread that the long intervals now exhibiting old ruinous stables, store-houses, and wharfs may not be occupied by buildings and façades suitable to the fineness of the site . . . ' The writer envisaged that Whitehall Place could be opened out and extended, with shady trees and seats for the public.

The Victoria Embankment was a wide and convenient thoroughfare but marred by the lack of a good approach from Charing Cross. The only two routes were via Villiers Street and Whitehall Place, and to reach it directly, the Metropolitan Board of Works could only

73 *Northumberland House; drawn by H. West and published in* Partington's National History and Views of London, *1834–5.*

74 *Contemporary postcard showing the corner of Parliament Street opposite the Houses of Parliament, decorated to celebrate the Diamond Jubilee of Queen Victoria in June 1897.*

think of one solution – straight through Northumberland House which was, as they pointed out, the last relic of the great palaces of the nobility which formerly skirted the banks of the river. Although their sentiments may be difficult to understand today, the Board felt that there was little to justify keeping Northumberland House, beyond the associations which surrounded it, and they reported that while its demolition must be regretted 'there was little to recommend its preservation'.

So the last of the riverside mansions, that of the Percys, Howards and Seymours, was sacrificed, and in 1874, unwillingly sold by the Duke of Northumberland to the Metropolitan Board of Works for half a million pounds. The Duke had long resisted pressure to sell to the Board but was eventually forced to give way, despite a strong public conservation campaign. Many people felt this destruction to be a needless act of vandalism. Thus the final establishment of the modern routing of the roads adjacent to Whitehall was accomplished.

75. *The lease of the Metropole Hotel in Northumberland Avenue, built 1882–3, was acquired in 1936 to house staff in the Ministries of Labour and of Transport.*

The Charing Cross and Victoria Embankment Approach Act 1873 empowered the Board to make a new street to the Embankment and Mowlem & Co constructed Northumberland Avenue, 1,000 feet long and 90 feet wide, which was opened on 18 March 1876. It was the only road, remarked *The Builder*, to be laid out by the Board of Works at a profit, due mainly to the absence of trade interests and to eager speculation in the sites. It cost £711,491 to build, but the Board recouped £831,310 by disposal of the vacant land for hotels and other buildings. Radiating from it were Whitehall Avenue and Horse Guards Avenue, opened by the Prince of Wales on 6 June 1893.

A railway running between Waterloo and Whitehall was proposed in the Waterloo and Whitehall Railway Act of 1865. This would have begun in Great Scotland Yard and terminated near the arches of Waterloo Station and, had it been built, would have transformed the whole area, but, as so often, the plan never came to fruition.

Whitehall Court

Whitehall Court was built by the firm of Archer and Green, working closely with Alfred Waterhouse, architect of the National Liberal Club at the north end of the site. He was also the designer of the Natural History Museum, the Prudential building in Holborn, and Manchester Assize Courts. Whitehall Court – 'a palace of flats' – consisted of luxury apartments and self-contained suites varying in size from seven to twenty rooms with rents at £300–£800 per annum. Built in French Renaissance style, its towers and cupolas can be seen to dramatic effect on the Whitehall skyline when viewed from St James's Park. (Sir Hugh Casson referred to it in the 1950s as the 'fairy-tale castle' effect.) The block was built between 1885 and 1887 and boasted many famous residents, including George Bernard Shaw, H. G. Wells and Banister Fletcher. Several clubs were also housed there.

The National Liberal Club and Whitehall Court were both lit by electricity from the start. The National Liberal Club was opened in 1887 and, like its neighbour, was built of Portland stone with a roof of green slates. It was on an awkward irregular site, but managed to accommodate six large public rooms on four different levels linked by a striking spiral staircase.

Banqueting House, Chapel Royal and the Royal United Service Institution

In 1808 it was decided that the Chapel Royal (ie the Banqueting House) should be used as a military chapel for the Horse Guards. An annexe was added, the old galleries taken down and two double-decker balconies put up to allow for a larger congregation. The work was supervised by the architect James Wyatt. Further alterations were carried out in 1814 when charity concerts were held at the Chapel Royal in aid of Germans who had suffered during the Napoleonic wars.

But the building began to deteriorate. In 1829 the Horse Guards stopped using the chapel, and it was closed for extensive repairs to the exterior which were carried out by Sir John Soane. A new roof was built and the exterior stonework renewed entirely in Portland stone. Inigo Jones had originally used Oxford stone for the basement, Northamptonshire stone above, and Portland stone for the external columns, pilasters and balustrades, so giving a subtle gradation of colour to the façade that had now been lost. Sir Robert Smirke was commissioned to restore the interior in 1834, and the work was finished in 1838. He removed Wyatt's gallery and reconstructed that designed by Inigo Jones. He also added an organ loft, had the organ repaired and oak floors and pews installed. The entablatures of the pillars were gilded and an altar-piece added.

76   *Queen's Treasury 1820. (Engraved by Thomas Dale from drawings by R. B. Schnebbelie.) Shows two views of the East and West fronts. The house was first used as the Queen's Treasury during the time of Queen Caroline, wife of George II in about 1727 and remained standing until 1884. The top view shows the East front from the river. The Treasury is on the right and has an arched entrance; the adjoining house on the left was first used as the Almonry Office in 1819. The lower view of the West front has soldiers changing guard at the Almonry Office. To the left is a small picture of the passage to the Privy Stairs and on the right is an old window in Henry VIII's Whitehall Palace.*

Towards the end of the century, use of the building as a place of worship was discontinued and in 1890 Queen Victoria agreed to a proposal by the Chapel Royal Commissioners that the building should be lent to the Royal United Service Institution as a museum. In June 1892 the RUSI accepted a Treasury offer of an 80-year lease of the ground, and most of the interior fittings, including the organ, were transferred to other buildings or sold. Sir Aston Webb and Ingress Bell built the new three-and-a-half bay four-storey RUSI premises immediately south of the Banqueting House. The two buildings were linked on the ground floor by a large doorway; a further gallery was also added. The new museum was opened by the Prince of Wales on 20 February 1895 and the RUSI's occupation continued until 1964.

A contemporary newspaper cutting relates that on 27 June 1891

78   *Office of the Education Department, Whitehall, in the Treasury Building (in the late 20th century to be the Cabinet Office building), seen from down Whitehall Gardens and across Whitehall. (Sketch by Herbert Railton c.1880.)*

the Banqueting House was used for a reception given by the Secretary of State for War to the Prince of Wales,

'when some part of its ancient magnificence was revived, but it is many years since anything has occurred there to equal in beauty and extravagance the wonderful pageants which Whitehall witnessed under the Tudors and the Stuarts, when the Court, if not a school of morals, was a school of manners . . . Now that the Chapel Royal seats have been cleared away it is easier to appreciate the beautiful proportions of the famous chamber designed by Inigo Jones . . . when the Banqueting House was turned into a chapel, which, by the way, is said never to have been consecrated, it was said of this rather inappropriate ceiling:

Aloft we view the Bacchanalian King;
Below the sacred anthems daily sing.

This splendid ceiling, which was touched from time to time by first-rate artists, including Cipriani, is in excellent preservation, and we believe it is a fact that the authorities have been offered many thousands of pounds for it.'

Horse Guards Avenue and Whitehall Gardens

A contemporary account written in 1905 vividly recalls the desolation of the east side of Whitehall as it had been 20 years before, an area that had since been covered by Whitehall Court and Horse Guards Avenue:

'Scattered about the waste and uneven ground, and overgrown with grass and weeds, lay the ruins of Fife House; its gardens were dug up, though some of the elm trees remained, the stables were dismantled, and the gateways in Whitehall and Middle Scotland yards thrown down; the Palace Beer Buttery was being "wrecked". Extending from the end of Whitehall-yard lay the stones of the causeway sloping between two side walls to the public river-stairs . . . the exposed stones of the south wall abutting on no 6

77 *Distribution of the Royal Maundy at the Chapel Royal (the Banqueting House) in 1842. It was the custom for the same number of poor men and women as the Sovereign's age to attend divine service in the Chapel on Maundy Thursday. Bread, meat and fish were served to them and each received red and white leather bags containing the Maundy money, and linen and shoes. The full ceremony, including the washing and kissing of the feet of the poor, was last carried out at Whitehall by King James II.*

79 *Chartist procession taking the Great National Petition to the House of Commons in 1842. Demonstrators carried banners inscribed 'Liberty', 'Universal Suffrage', 'Vote by ballot', 'Reform'. The engraving shows the column passing the Banqueting House and Gwydyr House and stretching up to the junction at Downing Street where the road divides into Parliament Street and King Street.*

Whitehall-yard and of the north wall, still bore green marks of water'.

Lord Fife died in 1809 and his executors sold the lease to Lord Liverpool. The property reverted to the Crown in 1868 and in the following year Fife House and the adjacent Little Fife House were pulled down. The next house to the south west, on the north side of Whitehall Yard, was Vanbrugh House, butt of many jokes. The interest in this house was sold in 1845 to the Naval & Military Library and Museum which was incorporated in 1860 as the Royal United Service Institution. The staff moved in 1895, taking many of the fittings with them, to their new home in the Chapel Royal (formerly the Banqueting House) in Whitehall. Vanbrugh House was demolished soon after in order to clear the site for the projected new War Office.

Whitehall Gardens, which lay behind the Banqueting House, consisted of a block of houses with gardens running down to the river (until the Victoria Embankment was built) on the site of the former Whitehall Palace apartments of the Earl of Bath, the Maids of Honour, Mr Chiffinch, keeper of the granary, the Countess of Suffolk, and part of the Queen's Wardrobe. The houses were erected early in the 19th century, from 1806 onwards, on the east side of what had been the Privy Garden.

80   *Whitehall Yard, 1893. Drawing shows the rear of the Chapel Royal/ Banqueting House, soon to become the home of the Royal United Service Museum. The statue of King James II by Grinling Gibbons stands in the right forefront.*

In the first half of the 19th century, this district enjoyed a brief importance as the focus of government. No 1 was occupied by the 14th Earl of Cassilis from 1806 to 1846 and Disraeli lived in No 2 from 1874 to 1878 while Prime Minister. It is said that Cabinet meetings were held in his house as he disliked crossing Whitehall and was not at the time well enough to do so. When his lease was coming to an end, he moved into No 10 Downing Street because he could not manage his 'terrible steep Whitehall stairs'. His house was later used by the Committee of Imperial Defence and, during the First World War, by the War Cabinet.

Viscount Cardwell lived in No 3 from 1846 to 1855. No 4 was built by Sir Robert Smirke in about 1824 for Sir Robert Peel, who died there in 1850 in dreadful agony after being thrown from his horse; No 6 was on a site between the Stone Gallery and Queen Mary's 'terras walk'. In 1851 Pembroke House (No 7) was annexed by the Government for use by the Copyhold, Enclosure and Tithe Commission, and afterwards by the War Office and the Ministry of Transport. The Foreign Office occupied Pembroke House and Malmesbury House, from 1861 to 1868 while their new offices were being built. In 1865–6, the Board of Trade moved in from Treasury Buildings. No 8 (Malmesbury House) was lived in by the Earl of Malmesbury until 1861 and was then taken over by the Passport Office.

The first Montagu House was pulled down in 1859 and the

81 *Sir Robert Peel's House (No 4 Whitehall Gardens), designed by Sir Robert Smirke, and completed in 1824 when Peel was Home Secretary. He was Prime Minister in the 1830s and again in the 1840s. In 1850 he was thrown from his horse near Hyde Park Corner, was taken to his house and died there three days later.*

second built almost immediately afterwards, between 1859 and 1862, to a design by William Burn using much of the old materials. Burn built it out of Portland stone on a concrete raft, in French Renaissance style with steep roofs, corner turrets and tall chimneys. The house cost a staggering £100,000, and was generally admired, *The Illustrated London News* describing it as of 'stately and imposing aspect'. The house was taken over by the Ministry of Labour in 1917; the site is now part of the Ministry of Defence main building.

Gwydyr House became the first home of the Reform Club in 1838 and was rented by the Crown in 1842. It was afterwards occupied by a variety of official bodies, including the Poor Law Board, the Local Government Board, the Charity Commissioners and the Ministry of Land and Natural Resources. It was later used by the Air Ministry and in the 1940s by the War Cabinet. From 1965 to 1969 it was the home of the Redcliffe–Maud Royal Commission on Local Government. The Welsh Office first occupied the building in 1971.

Gwydyr House has remained more or less unchanged since it was built in 1772, and still retains the look of a private house. An extension was built on the south side in 1898 which projected into the Privy Garden. A correspondent in *The Times* wrote that 'the new rooms will be placed at the back of the garden and will not extend along its full length. The statement which has been made that the beauty of the garden, as seen from Whitehall, will be destroyed is therefore erroneous.' At the same time it was proposed to move the statue of King James II

82 *Gwydyr House as it is today, having had the exterior brickwork cleaned. The house was built in 1772 by John Marquand and has been preserved outwardly almost unchanged.*

which was hidden away in the court behind the Banqueting House to the front of this garden facing Whitehall.

More Government offices moved into Whitehall Place during the 19th century. At one time No 5 housed successively the Commissioners for auditing public accounts, the Auditor of the Civil List, and in 1823 the Colonial Audit Office. In 1833 it was used by the Commissioners for French and Danish claims and the Excise, and in 1840 part-occupied by the Ecclesiastical Commissioners. The Poor Law Commissioners established under the 1834 Act only stayed briefly in 1834, near the old State Paper Office.

Other Departments were in Whitehall Yard. Pelham House (No 1) was inhabited by the Comptroller of Army Accounts from 1812 to 1835, and then became the home of the Secretary to the Chief Commissioner of Woods until 1855. The Exchequer Seal Office was in Cadogan House (No 2), on the site of the gallery which had divided Pebble Court from the Great Court in Whitehall Palace. No 3 (Cromwell House) was the office of the Auditor of the Civil List in 1826. Beneath was 'part of an old cellar' which was, in fact, the Tudor wine cellar, a remnant of York Place which had not been entirely destroyed in the fire that devastated Whitehall Palace.

Scotland Yard

When Peel's Metropolitan Police force was established in 1829, its headquarters was set up in Great Scotland Yard and No 4 Whitehall Place was taken over for police offices, later expanding to include No 5. The police stayed there until 1890 when they moved to New Scotland Yard, between Cannon Row and the Embankment, almost opposite the Home Office (now FCO). A blue plaque on the wall of Nos 3–8 Whitehall Place commemorates the site of the original headquarters.

Cannon Row is of historic interest because of its connection with the last days of King Charles I. According to his faithful companion, Sir Thomas Herbert, two days before his execution, the King took an emerald and diamond ring from his finger and told Herbert to carry it to a lady living in Cannon Row. Having delivered it, Herbert was given by the lady a small cabinet closed with three seals, on two of which were the King's arms, and told to return it to the King. The next morning, after prayers, the King is said to have broken the seals and revealed within the box diamonds and other jewels, mostly broken Georges and garters. 'You see', he said, 'all the wealth now in my power to give to my children.'

The new police building was on a site that had in 1875 been set aside for a National Opera House. Completion of this project had been hoped for by 1877 but it was abandoned for lack of funds. The Opera House, designed by Francis Fowler, was the pipe-dream of the well-known impresario Colonel J. Mapleson. It had been planned to be larger than the theatre in Covent Garden and as magnificent as La Scala, Milan. The foundation stone had been laid in December 1875, and the Opera House was intended to back on to Cannon Row and to be adjacent to

83 *New Scotland Yard. This sketch by Howard Penton shows the new police building designed by Norman Shaw and completed in 1890, a building some compared unfavourably with Crosse & Blackwell's jam and pickle factory which it faced across the river.*

the District Railway covered way. But the expense was prohibitive. *The Musical Times* reported that the cost of the concrete foundations alone had risen from £2,500 to £33,000 and took much longer to lay than expected because of flooding into the excavations. When over £103,000 had been spent, and there was no money left for the roof, the project was abandoned and the whole sold for a mere £29,000 – and later resold for £500! The site was first offered to the Metropolitan Police in 1883 and was acquired for them in 1886.

Some of the foundations and footings of the Opera House were used for the new police building. Norman Shaw was appointed architect for it in 1887 (a personal nomination by the then Home Secretary, the Right Hon. Henry Matthews MP); there was no competition for the appointment. The police had chosen facing materials of Dartmoor granite and Portland stone because they could be quarried by convict labour, and would therefore be cheaper. Shaw agreed to granite for the lower floors but introduced red brick between bands of Portland stone for the upper storeys. He wrote in a letter to A. R. Pennefather, Receiver of Police, in January 1887: 'it is a serious question whether a building with a grey granite base, a white stone upper part and a slate roof might

84 *The aborted National Opera House of the well-known impresario, James Henry Mapleson (1830–1901), known internationally as The Colonel, so long a thorn in the side of the Metropolitan Board of Works, but never completed. The Builder commented in 1876 that 'The treatment is thoroughly French and the festive and operatic element is not lost sight of in the decorative adjuncts.'*

85 *Plan showing the proposed site of the Colonial Museum on the plot of the ill-fated National Opera House. The location was, however, eventually used for the new police building which utilised some of the original foundations and footings.*

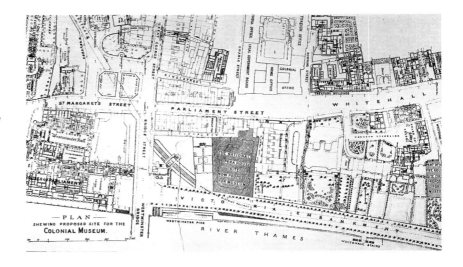

not look very cold, and whether it would not materially gain by the introduction of a warm material like red brick'.

The design of the building was controversial. The Press and public approved of it on the whole; but Sir William Harcourt, ex-Home Secretary, disliked it, alleging that it was rather inferior in architectural beauty to the premises (a jam and pickle factory) belonging to Messrs Crosse & Blackwell on the other side of the river. Norman Shaw responded to Sir William's criticism by saying that his creation was 'a genuine building in which we have no sham or shew fronts, all is of the same quality and in the court it is the same. In order to secure this . . . I have reduced the ornamental features to a minimum, relying on the bulk and outline to give the desired character.'

The building was a quadrangular block with a central courtyard and large open space on the west side between it and the rear of the Parliament Street houses. It had a brick-vaulted crypt, ground, mezzanine and three upper floors. Shaw added gables to increase the accommodation. The building was completed in 1890. The aim, said Norman Shaw, 'had been to have less of what I should call "style" and more of what I should call "character"'.

In 1896 he was appointed as consulting architect to the Metropolitan Police architect Dixon Butler 'on all questions relating to the treatment and design of the building to be erected at the Embankment end'. By the following year the police needed more space and acquired the Cannon Row site to the south, which was used to build Cannon Row Police Station and the extension to the police headquarters on the site of the old Civil Service Commission (completed in 1912 and again designed with Richard Norman Shaw). It was matched to the earlier north block, to which it was joined by an archway and a bridge. Cannon Row Police Station was linked with it on the west side.

The Board of Control/Civil Service Commission building had stood on the east side of Cannon Row. When Westminster District Railway Station was built in the 1860s, the Civil Service Commission insisted on elaborate girdering to preserve their garden. Under the Thames Embankment Act 1862, the Metropolitan Board of Works had, at their own expense, to fill up, level and wall or fence the bed or foreshore by Somerset House and the Board of Control.

Richmond Terrace

Richmond Terrace occupies part of the site of the orchard of Whitehall Palace and runs at right angles to Whitehall. The site became a Bowling Green after the Restoration, and later the Privy Garden. Two important houses were built there in the 17th century for the Earl of Loudoun and the Duke of Richmond, and Richmond House was rebuilt early in the 18th century. But in 1791 Richmond House had accidentally burnt down and was not rebuilt. The Terrace was designed between 1819 and 1822 by Thomas Chawner or Henry Harrison (there is some doubt as to which), and in 1822 the lease was bought by the Crown and granted to George Harrison, a local builder, who erected eight houses in the following three years. No 8 was used first by a firm of land agents and later by the Board of Health. The Board of Trade's Railway Department occupied Richmond Terrace in the late 19th century. The other houses were in private hands until the original leases expired in 1921 and were then gradually converted to public offices.

Among the Terrace's famous occupants were William Huskisson (1826–7 and 1829–30) one-time President of the Board of Trade and later Colonial Secretary and Leader of the House of Commons, who was knocked down and killed at the opening of the Manchester–Liverpool Railway in 1830. Others were the first Viscount Halifax (1832–6), Joint Secretary to the Treasury, Secretary to the Admiralty, Chancellor of the Exchequer, and Secretary of State for India; and the Earl of Onslow (1880–1912) who held a variety of posts, at the Board of Trade, as

Governor of New Zealand, at the Colonial Office and as President of the Board of Agriculture.

Parliament Street houses

The existence of Parliament Street and King Street created the effect of an island of buildings, and these survived almost to the 20th century. The little buildings standing between Parliament Street and King Street were pulled down in two stages: the northern block in the 1870s and the south block between King Charles Street and Great George Street at the close of the century, to prepare for the erection of the Government Offices, Great George Street. Immediately before this demolition the area was still very much a living entity with shops on to the street.

Archibald Milman, writing in the journal *Lords and Commons* in March 1899, laments King Street's passing:

'King Street is doomed! . . . to those who know what it represents (and to know is to care), the obliteration of this ancient way comes as a shock. What memories will follow it to the limbo of forgotten things? From the dawn of our history, King and statesman, warrior and priest, merchant and beggar, the people of England and the stranger guest, have come and gone by this way, and no other, to Westminster.'

At the same time, the old Red Lion pub in Parliament Street faced rebuilding. This inn had been described by Charles Dickens as the hostelry where, as a young boy, he went in and 'said to the landlord behind the bar, "What is your very best – the VERY *best* – ale, a glass?" . . . "two-pence" says he. Then, says I, just draw me a glass of that, if you please, with a good head to it.' He later recalled the scene in *David Copperfield*.

Two huge government building projects were commissioned in 1898: the Government Offices on the Great George Street site, and, further up Whitehall, opposite the Horse Guards, the War Office. They would be years in construction but were to underline the future character of the street at either end.

Among the buildings on the side of Parliament Street nearest the river is No 44, a building of white stucco with three storeys and a balustraded parapet. The ground floor was occupied by a Post Office from about 1900 until it was closed in the mid-1980s, while the upper parts were by then disused. Nos 45 and 46 Parliament Street are mid-19th century blocks of chambers, built in Portland stone, with three bays to each and on five floors.

The ornate No 47 was the former Whitehall Club, designed in what was described at the time as 'florid Italian', by C. Parnell and built between 1864 and 1866. It was occupied first by the Club until 1905, and then by the firm of S. Pearson & Son Ltd, until the building was compulsorily purchased by the Government in 1963. It has been described as 'one of the best examples of mid-Victorial classical architecture of its kind'. No 53 is an ornate four-storey façade banded in red brick and white terracotta, built in French Gothic cum-renaissance style by Huntley Gordon in 1896.

The façade of the southern block of buildings was renovated in 1990–1 as part of the establishment of the Parliament Street Building for the use of the House of Commons, and as Bernard Weatherill, Mr Speaker, observed in October 1991, this 'has preserved a fine townscape and some magnificent interiors'. One can only underline his remark that 'one simply cannot understand the thinking that endorsed, only twenty years ago, the destruction of such fine work, and its wholesale replacement by concrete and glass'; happily a plan, like that for the Foreign Office, that was never realised though soon after, instituted for Bridge Street.

169.C. THE CENOTAPH. WHITEHALL. BEAGLES POSTCARDS.
H.M. KING GEORGE UNVEILED THE PERMANENT MEMORIAL,
11TH. NOVEMBER, 1920., THE ANNIVERSARY OF ARMISTICE DAY.

88 *The Cenotaph – 'an empty tomb uplifted on a high pedestal' –
was originally intended as a temporary structure. But a permanent
Cenotaph (see postcards left and below), designed by Sir Edwin
Lutyens, was unveiled by King George V on Armistice Day 1920.
Street decorations for coronations had been put up for hundreds of
years, and conceived by such distinguished designers as
Christopher Wren and Inigo Jones. Elaborate arches were erected
by Commonwealth countries for the coronations of Edward VII and
George V, and the streets festively decorated.*

5
PEACE AND WAR:
THE TWENTIETH CENTURY

'Whitehall is growing quietly into a fine thoroughfare, and if the whole of each side can be
filled by Government buildings, which offer far more opportunity for architectural effect than
business premises can ever hope to offer, London will possess at least one street
worthy of its importance.'

Architectural Review, vol. 28, 1910

THE beginning of the 20th century saw the completion of the changes in Whitehall
that had been launched in the previous century. The War Office building was completed in 1906,
and the Government Offices, Great George Street rose in two stages – the first finished in 1908, the
second in 1917. Immediately after the war a temporary Cenotaph was put up in Whitehall
for the 1919 peace celebrations, and replaced a year later by public demand, with a
permanent monument. The Whitehall Gardens site – bounded by the Victoria Embankment,
Whitehall Gardens, Horse Guards Avenue and the grounds of Montagu House – was chosen for
new government buildings. Excavation in 1925 revealed the original brickwork floor of Wolsey's
Tudor wine cellar, and the steps to Queen Mary's Terrace. Work on the new building began
in 1939 but the war put a stop to it. During the war several bombs fell on Whitehall
and many buildings were extensively damaged.

Classic designs

Over the 18th and 19th centuries Whitehall underwent massive alterations, from a rambling palace with numerous tiny buildings to a street faced with elegant Georgian and more elaborate Victorian structures. The idea of concentrating public offices in one place had been outlined by Inigo Jones in the 17th century, and was taken up again in the 19th century by Sir Charles Barry and other contemporary architects in their designs for a new Whitehall. The 19th-century plans extended well into the next century before they were set in bricks and mortar, and the Victorian ethos survived until the First World War. The new century was to see yet more sweeping changes – bigger buildings, reflecting the growth and complexity of government and administration, and the depradations of war upon the structures themselves.

The classic designs of the first decade of the 20th century, as elsewhere in London, inform the character of the street we know today, linking the various surviving earlier styles into an acceptable unity of variety, grand in effect, yet maintaining a fundamentally human scale.

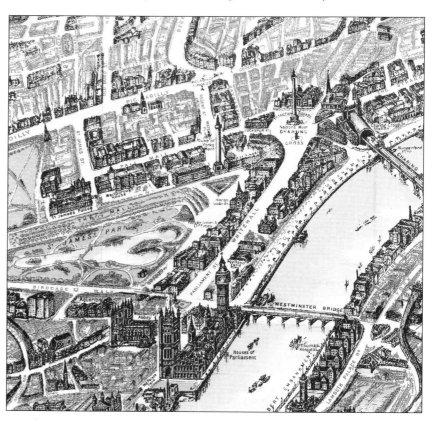

89 *London on the threshold of the 20th century. Detail of the* ABC Guide to London, *with enlarged pictorial plan of Central London, 20th century edition, 1901.*

Even while the nation endured the Second World War and London was being bombed nightly, ideas for its future development were being prepared for the London County Council. Professor Patrick Abercrombie and J. H. Forshaw proposed a pedestrian precinct round the Houses of Parliament and the Abbey, with a dual carriageway leading from Westminster Bridge along Great George Street and into Birdcage Walk and Broadway. They also suggested building a new and compact government centre that would stretch from Marsham Street as far as Northumberland Avenue at Trafalgar Square.

Government Offices, Great George Street

The architect John Brydon, whose previous work included two London hospitals and Chelsea Town Hall, was commissioned in 1898 to prepare designs for the New Public Offices, a building on a massive site stretching from Parliament Street to St James's Park. The project was intended to provide space for several expanding ministries, but as not all the money for it would be available at once, the section under consideration was only to be part of a larger whole. The plans show a building containing a large circular central court, inspired by Inigo Jones' 17th-century designs for a new Whitehall Palace, of 160 feet in diameter,

90 *Government Offices, Great George Street. The building was designed by John Brydon, who died soon after work started, and was completed in 1908 by Sir Henry Tanner of the Office of Works. At the time of its construction it was described as the most important building to be erected since Barry's Palace of Westminster. Much later it was said not to be 'so romantically interesting as Sir Gilbert Scott's Foreign Office, nor so gentlemanly reticent and delicately finished as the Treasury block, but it has a range of expression which the War Office has not' (Prof. C. H. Reilly,* Country Life, *9 February 1924).*

flanked by a square court on either side, each with four subsidiary courts or light-wells.

The building was to be connected with the Home Office and Treasury blocks by a triple arched bridge that crossed the end of King Charles Street, and with a similar bridge across the narrower opening of Downing Street. Popularly known as GOGGS from its initials, it was built of Portland stone in ornate baroque revival style with large columns above rusticated lower storeys and ornamented with towers. It had entrances on all frontages for the different departments occupying it.

By tragic coincidence, Brydon, like William Young, architect of the War Office, died soon after work on his building started. The task was taken over by Sir Henry Tanner, chief architect to the Office of Works, who made several, not always happy, alterations to the design. It was completed in the summer of 1908 and occupied by the Local Government Board and the Board of Education. *The Times* judged it a 'sober and businesslike' building, 'more consistent than Sir George Gilbert Scott's India Office close by, but perhaps a little less distinguished than the new War Office'. *The Builder* found the exterior architecture 'rather tame', while the *Architectural Review* thought that 'on the whole the building is not a successful achievement'. At this stage the building, formerly known as the New Public Offices, consisted of the frontages to Parliament Street and King Charles Street, part of the front to Great George Street and more than half of the circular courtyard.

Many MPs felt that GOGGS was unnecessarily extravagant and that staff would increase proportionately to the space available. Nevertheless, in 1910 all the buildings on the north side of Great George Street were pulled down to make room for the second part of the building. The extension to St James's Park involved the disappearance of Delahay Street, once known as Duke Street and one-time home of the infamous Judge Jeffreys. *The Graphic* for 9 December 1909 mourned the loss of: 'this quiet interesting way, with its respectable and picturesque old houses' that was to be merged into the government's huge scheme. Also facing demolition was the remainder of the northern portion of Great George Street up to Storey's Gate.

The New Public Offices were completed in 1917 and the Board of Trade moved in. The building occupied a five-acre site bounded by Parliament Street to the east, Great George Street to the south, King Charles Street on the north and St James's Park to the west. The principal entrance was in Parliament Street and had a decorated pediment by

91 *Stone head over doorway of Government Offices, Great George Street, facing the park. A similar head appears on various other entrances to the building, and also on the archways of the bridge between GOGGS and the Old Public Offices.*

Bertram Mackennal with a seated figure representing Government, and on each side Law and Order. Groups on the figure's left represented Trade and the spirit of Shipbuilding, those on the right symbolised Education and Art. Other sculpture was by W. S. Frith and Paul Montford. The central panel on the bridge, by Montford, contains allegorical representations of the work of the Boards of Local Government and Education, of the Home Department, and of trade and industry.

The connecting bridge was built between 1910 and 1911. Towards Great George Street the end towers rose to turrets. The north and south façades were of four storeys each, with an attic storey in the centre. A contemporary writer in the *Architectural Review* concluded that the edifice 'may on the whole be pronounced a success. It is by no means a brilliant work, but it possesses a considerable dignity'. Perhaps of more significance to a later generation was the basement of the St James's Park frontage, which contains the bunker later used as the Cabinet War Room, Map Room and Churchill's bedroom during the Second World War.

Between the wars alterations were made to provide yet more

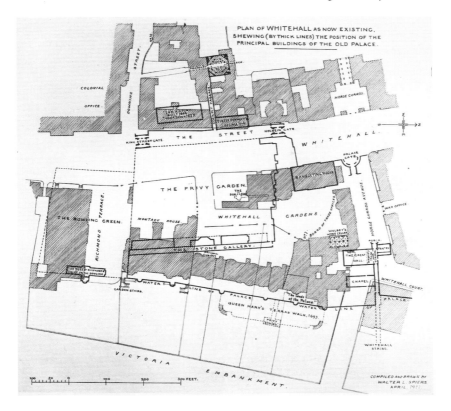

92 *Walter Spiers' plan showing the positions of the former buildings of Whitehall Palace standing on the site, in relation to the buildings there in 1911.*

staff accommodation. Large existing offices were subdivided and basement offices created beneath the courtyards. During the Second World war, the Air Ministry moved in, together with many Treasury staff, following the bomb damage to the Treasury Building in October 1940.

Foreign Office

Increases in staff to deal with matters arising from the First World War led to a severe lack of space in the Foreign Office building. George Gilbert Scott, the original architect, had regarded the Foreign Office as 'a kind of national palace, or drawing room for the nation', and one centred on its fine rooms. His splendid suite of three rooms – conference, dining and grand reception room – was used for receptions, dinners and conferences until the First World War, when accommodation pressures led to its being annexed as offices for the Contraband Department.

The Suite acquired its future name and moment of glory in 1925 when the Locarno Treaty, which guaranteed Germany's borders with France and Belgium and aimed to promote stability and harmony, was signed there by Britain, Germany, Belgium, France and Italy. The inhabitants of the offices were moved out and portraits hung on the walls to disguise their shabbiness. It was refurbished later that year in parchment, black and gold. Once again the Suite was brought into less glamorous service for the Second World War and occupied by cypher clerks. General de Gaulle had his sitting room in the Grand Reception Room during the war. Afterwards, plasterboard partitions subdivided the

93 *Contemporary postcard of Sir Henry Campbell-Bannerman, Prime Minister 1905 to 1908.*

94 *Sir Edward Grey, Foreign Secretary from December 1905 to December 1916. From his office he made his now celebrated remark: 'the lamps are going out all over Europe. We shall not see them lit again in our lifetime.'*

rooms into small offices once again, and false ceilings were erected. Only many years later, between 1990 and 1992 would these rooms' full splendour be recaptured.

No 10 *Downing Street*

No 10 Downing Street was not always the most welcoming of homes to its inhabitants. Sir Henry Campbell Bannerman regarded it as a 'rotten old barrack of a house', and his wife thought it a house of doom. Margot Asquith, wife of the next Prime Minister, described it as 'liver-coloured and squalid', its exterior giving 'little idea to the man in the street of what it is really like'.

It must have been expensive to live in, too, in the early days, because until 1878 the cost of fitting out the whole house had had to be borne by its tenant, but in that year it was agreed that the Treasury should furnish and carpet all those rooms that were used for official purposes. By the end of the 19th century, nearly all the furniture was supplied from official sources, and only supplemented by the incoming Prime Minister. Despite this, Ramsay MacDonald, first Labour Prime Minister, found he had to supply linen, china and silver at no little expense.

When Neville Chamberlain became Prime Minister in 1937, substantial alterations were carried out to No 10. The living quarters were moved up one floor, and a new staircase built to reach them. Large windows were put in and the former bedrooms on the same floor as the state rooms were turned into offices. The basement kitchen was modernised and the drawing rooms redecorated. These alterations cost £25,000.

After the war, part of the second floor was converted into a self-contained flat for the Prime Minister, but Churchill took this over for himself and his secretarial staff during his second term of office. He and his wife moved down again to the first floor.

Coronations

The Office of Works, among its many duties, was responsible for organising state ceremonies such as Coronations, Remembrance Day, Trooping the Colour, and the State Opening of Parliament. Its staff advised on the decoration of Government buildings for special occasions,

Coronation of King George V,
Canadian Columns, Parliament Street, Westminster.

95 *Postcards showing
decorations and arches put
up in honour of the
Coronations of Edward VII in
1902, and George V in
1911.*

Whitehall with Coronation Decorations.

and supervised their floodlighting, and the erection of stands for the public.

Queen Victoria who had reigned for so long had seldom appeared on ceremonial occasions. From 1877, when she was invested as Empress of India, to her Diamond Jubilee in 1897, royal ceremonial acquired a new confidence. In retrospect they were rehearsals for the Coronation of Edward VII in 1902 and George V in 1911. These became particularly musical festivities with works specially commissioned for the 1902 and 1911 Coronations by Elgar, Parry, Stanford and Sir Walter Parratt. Edward VII also revived the processional State Opening of Parliament, for which the newly integrated Whitehall provided a fitting backdrop.

For the 1902 Coronation of Edward VII, the Treasury authorised expenditure of £600 for illumination of the principal Government buildings on the line of the Coronation route. The Scottish Office had 'a suitable device over the portico at the entrance of Dover House, illuminated by gas'. In front of the Banqueting House was a crystal illumination, also lit by gas.

Nine years later, during the preparations for the Coronation of George V, the President of the Royal Institute of British Architects wrote to *The Times* in March 1911, recalling street decoration for past Coronations when Inigo Jones or Christopher Wren were in charge: 'The triumphal arches designed in the seventeenth century were artistic

96 *Contemporary postcard of King Edward VII at the corner of Parliament Street as he passes into Parliament Square to open Parliament in February 1906 on a foggy day characteristic of winter London before the passing of the clean air legislation.*

achievements far in advance of anything that is seen now-a-days'. Westminster City Council adopted a design for Whitehall without arches, but consented to the erection of an arch by the New Zealand government in the centre of the roadway north of the two refuges and opposite Whitehall Gardens. This was the precedent for other arches to be built for the celebrations, notably by the Canadian provinces.

'Illuminated devices' were displayed at night on buildings under the jurisdiction of the Ministry of Works, but the Ministry objected to 'any decoration of the Banqueting House, which is one of the most beautiful buildings in the kingdom and which in our judgement would not be decorated in any sense by the scheme suggested' [by its occupants, the United Service Institution].

97   *Victory march of the Allied troops in Whitehall, passing the temporary Cenotaph, designed by Sir Edwin Lutyens, 19 July 1919.*

98   *'Passing the Cenotaph at which His Late Majesty had so often paid Armistice Day tribute to those who fell in the Great War: the funeral procession of King George [V] in Whitehall during the journey to Westminster Hall on 23rd January.' Illustrated London News, 1 February 1936. As the procession reached the Cenotaph, the mounted police, the Artillery drivers and the walking bearer party of the Grenadier Guards turned their heads towards it, as then did King Edward, his brothers and other mourners.*

The Cenotaph

The Cenotaph was at first intended to be merely a temporary structure. When a Cabinet Committee was considering the arrangements for peace celebrations in July 1919, they felt that a saluting base in Whitehall was needed for the march past of allied troops through London and Sir Edwin Lutyens's name was put forward as the most suitable architect. He designed a temporary edifice, constructed in lath and plaster and painted to look like stone. It was to be erected for a few days only, and was adorned with flags and wreaths. But 'owing to the hold which it immediately took on the public imagination', it was impossible to remove it for some time.

99 *David Lloyd George, Prime Minister 1916 to 1922. In 1919 he had visited France and was much affected by the ceremony in Paris in remembrance of the war. He decided that Britain too should have its own memorial and was the first to suggest a catafalque that soldiers could salute; from this suggestion grew the idea of a Cenotaph.*

100   *Earl Haig. Commander-in-Chief of the British Armies in France 1915–18. Equestrian bronze by Alfred Hardiman, signed by the sculptor in 1936. Erected by Parliament in 1937 in Whitehall, looking towards Westminster.*

As the days went by, more and more wreaths were placed round its base, and the public demanded its replacement with a permanent memorial of the same kind. A leader in *The Times* declared:

'Simple, grave and beautiful in design, it has been universally recognised as a just and fitting memorial of those who have made the greatest sacrifice. It ought undoubtedly to be erected in a more permanent form among the monuments of London, though not on its present site.'

On 13 August 1919, in a reply to a Parliamentary Question, the Government agreed to 'reproduce the existing temporary Cenotaph in all respects in permanent form . . .'. For suggesting the memorial in the first place, Sir Edwin Lutyens gave credit to the Prime Minister, Lloyd George. Sir Edwin's daughter, Mary, mentions in her biography of her father, that Lloyd George had sent for him in June/July 1919 and said that the Government wanted a 'catafalque' erected in Whitehall as a saluting point. Lutyens himself recalled:

'My original drawing, now in the Imperial War Museum, shows what the Cenotaph was like when it first shaped itself on paper before me. I called it a Cenotaph, conveying the simple meaning of an empty tomb uplifted on a high pedestal.'

The people wanted an identical design for the permanent structure, and the words: 'The glorious dead' also survived unaltered. The site of the Cenotaph, too, was unchanged. No cross was engraved on it, but Lutyens stated that it contained at least 22 crosses, either on or associated with the flags forming part of the monument. The permanent Cenotaph was unveiled by the King on Armistice Day 1920, and was a column of Portland stone, surmounted by a laurel wreath, with three flagstaffs on each side. There were no vertical lines and the horizontal planes were spherical to a common centre. Lutyens had wanted flags to be sculpted in coloured marble, but was overruled by the Cabinet.

James Bone paints a striking picture in his book, *London Echoing*, of the unveiling of the Cenotaph, when the women relatives of the dead were gathered on the south side of Whitehall. After the official ceremony was over, three mounted policemen rode down the road calling for people with flowers to come through:

'I was looking down on the crowd in black, packed close and orderly like slates on a roof. "Hold up your flowers!" the constables on horseback cried . . . And so, suddenly, there in the twinkling of an eye, the black mass was transfigured into whiteness like hedgerows in May. We on the roof saw nothing beneath us but white flowers where a black crowd had been.'

The Paymaster General's Office

No 36 Whitehall, the Paymaster General's Office, is a hybrid building, originally built in 1732–3 by John Lane, with a single yellow brick bay added to the north end in 1806. The frontage to Horse Guards Parade was much more elegant. It was of Portland stone, and had once been the Park front of No 37 Great George Street which was demolished in 1910 to make way for the new Government Offices. The frontage was removed and re-erected in its present position by the Office of Works, seemingly without any prior consultation with the Paymaster General's Office, while other improvements were being carried out to the interior. The west front of the Office, overlooking Horse Guards Parade, had to be completely rebuilt to accommodate the new façade. Further alterations were carried out in 1919–20 when the Office was extended by taking in the ground floor fodder store (formerly the Horse Guards stables).

The increase in work caused by the First World War and the consequent rise in the number of payments expended on weapons, fuel, wages and rations, plus pensions, meant that the Office was acutely short of staff. Many men joined up and a large number of temporaries were recruited. By 1919 the number of staff was over three times what it had been. The overflow moved into temporary huts erected on Horse Guards Parade, but after the war they were rehoused in bungalows in the gardens of Montagu House on the other side of Whitehall.

All too soon, rumblings of war re-echoed across Europe and twenty years later preparations by the Office included the erection of an air-raid shelter on Horse Guards Parade. The then Assistant Paymaster General decided against evacuating his staff, despite Government plans to move the whole office to Lytham St Anne's, and they stayed where they were – but at some cost in casualties.

Admiralty House

In 1904 it was proposed that a new house for the First Lord should be built at the back of Drummonds' Bank at Charing Cross because the existing one was not large enough for its purpose, though some people did not agree with this suggestion. In 1908 Lord Selborne wrote that 'experts had advised . . . that the present First Lord's house would perish of senile decay before 30 years'. Three years later, Churchill, then First Lord, was only too happy to live elsewhere, assisted by a lodging allowance of not less than £700. In January 1912 it was settled that the First Lord should relinquish his official residence at the Admiralty, keeping only the ground floor for dinners and receptions – but in the event the First Lord resumed occupation in 1913!

Before the First World War, and possibly afterwards, some senior officers in Government departments who had individual rooms were provided with chamber pots, and messengers were detailed to empty them. In the Admiralty, and doubtless elsewhere, chamber pots were graded according to rank; officers made do with plain pots, crested ones were provided for more senior echelons, while Rear-Admirals and above had crested *and* fluted pots . . .

An unassuming room along a long corridor was the home of the Director of Naval Intelligence during the First World War. Among his team was an officer who later became Admiral Sir William James and who, when a child, had been the model for his uncle, the artist Millais' famous painting 'Bubbles'. There the naval codebreakers decoded the Zimmermann telegram of 16 January 1917 to the German Minister in Mexico, which announced unrestricted submarine warfare. It went on to say that should the United States not remain neutral, Germany proposed an alliance with Mexico plus financial support for Mexico to reconquer lost territory in Texas, Arizona and New Mexico. The contents of the message were made public in March 1917 and aroused much protest, which helped persuade Congress to accept the idea of joining the war. The USA declared war on Germany on 6 April 1917.

But life at the Admiralty was not entirely composed of affairs of state. Among the ranks of buff files was one entitled: 'Care of Office Cat: request for increased allowance'. (Provision for the cat's maintenance was included each year in the Navy Estimates.) In April 1921 the Admiralty binder asked for a rise of 1/6d a week to provide milk for the office cat as: '13/- a quarter does not go very far now'.

His request was referred up through the Office Keeper to the Accountant General and via the Financial Secretary to the First Lord. The First Lord hesitated

'to commit the Treasury to this increased charge without being assured of the support of those of my colleagues on the Board who are better qualified than I to judge of feline necessities . . . All that I insist on is that, whatever decision is come to, it must not involve a Supplementary Estimate, or any discussion in Parliament. In these times, when it is incumbent on all good citizens to practise frugality and to share any necessary privations, it would be detrimental to the Admiralty and repugnant to its feelings to confer a bonus on its own cat — unless some special and temporary circumstance, such as an increase in her family, can be adduced in support of the present claim.'

Other senior and distinguished officers had their say, but the rise was approved in June 1921 by the Financial Secretary and supported by the First Lord 'as considerations of humanity preclude any further delay in coming to a decision in this matter'. Cats were on the pay roll of a number of Government departments, and the allowance was drawn until 1940 when the office cat (presumably not the same one) died as a result of injuries sustained in an enemy air raid.

Admiralty Arch

Sir Aston Webb, the distinguished architect who had built the Royal United Services Institution building next to the Banqueting House in the late 19th century, had won first prize in a competition held in 1901 to upgrade the Mall into a grand processional route, with his proposal to construct an elaborate colonnade at Buckingham Palace and a triumphal arch at the Charing Cross end of the Mall. Before then there was no direct means of reaching Trafalgar Square from the Mall and Buckingham Palace. Webb designed the Admiralty Arch as part of the Queen Victoria memorial, comprising the Arch, the Mall, the Victoria Monument and the re-facing of Buckingham Palace. The Arch was also designed as an extension to the Admiralty offices, and the requirements for office space and houses for the First Lord and First Sea Lord were

101 *Postcard of the Coronation procession of King George V via the newly-built Admiralty Arch, designed by Aston Webb. The wrought iron and bronze gates were only just finished in time.*

incorporated in the planning brief provided by Henry Tanner, architect to the Office of Works.

The initial plans were published in 1904 and attracted much attention. *The Architectural Review* commented in November 1909 that 'only in our own land would a Government be found to demand the combination of a triumphal arch, an office building and an official residence in a block that shall be both convincing and expressive. The new building is neither. No archway can soar to grandiloquence when crushed under a row of offices.'

The building was finally completed in 1911. The three pairs of wrought iron and bronze gates to the archways were the largest of their kind in the country when built. They were also finished in 1911, just in time for King George V's Coronation procession. The south block of the Arch acted as an extension to the Admiralty main building, with its entrance placed opposite the Admiralty in a side street. The north block was planned as two separate semi-detached houses for the First Lord and the First Sea Lord, both of which offices had enjoyed official residences for over 250 years.

When the First Lord was asked to give up his house in the Admiralty for offices, he objected on the grounds that it had been the historic home of the First Lord since the Admiralty was built. The Cabinet agreed with him and the First Sea Lord was then given the larger of the two houses. But this was too grand for his status, so part of the upper floor was annexed for office accommodation even before the building was completed. (The gradual encroachment of office space into residential areas continued until recent times.) The first occupant, Admiral of the Fleet Sir Arthur Wilson, took up residence in 1911.

From the start, maintenance costs were a problem, as a proportion was paid by the occupant and those without a private income found it hard to manage. Official salaries were severely cut in the late 1920s, and in 1931 the then First Sea Lord offered to give up his house in return for an allowance. The Treasury agreed to a rent allowance of £500 a year, subject to a 10 per cent cut, but the proposal was not pursued and the compromise of reducing the accommodation to a flat was reached.

The Citadel

The Citadel, called by some 'Lenin's Tomb', a mysterious and monolithic structure, was designed by W. A. Forsyth and erected in 1940. It is a fort composed of concrete blocks, now covered with ivy, and is an extension to the Old Admiralty Building. The foundations are 30

feet below the surface. The Citadel consists of a maze of rooms containing a secret wartime communications system. It was designed to withstand a 1,000 lb bomb; it has no windows and narrow corridors. The third and final extension to the Admiralty stands half hidden behind this building.

Kirkland House

In 1926 Glyn Mills Bank applied to the Government for renewal of its lease at Whitehall Place from October 1928, but it also put forward an alternative suggestion – it offered to erect a five-storey building at what was then called 37–41 Charing Cross, and occupy the ground floor, letting the upper floors to the Office of Works. This plan was approved in principle, and Glyn Mills were permitted to build on the site plus part of Buckingham Court and the north-east portion of the Old Admiralty Building. The Bank was granted a 99-year lease, and sublet floors one to six to the Office of Works.

The new building was named Kirkland House, but the address became Whitehall. In 1930 the London County Council approved the renaming as 'Whitehall' of that part of Charing Cross which lay between Whitehall Place and Northumberland Avenue on the east side, and the corner of Charing Cross and the continuation of the Mall on the west side. At that time the roadway was only about half as wide as in Whitehall itself and there was, as now, a great deal of traffic congestion. The

103 *Whitehall in the snow. On the right is the Whitehall Theatre 'so clean and simple in its line that it makes the new Government offices, banks and public houses of that great thoroughfare look as if they need a shave' (Professor C. H. Reilly,* Architect's Journal, *14 January 1931). Note the stepped curb to the right of the picture, as the pavement on that side is higher than that opposite.*

Admiralty moved into the upper part of Kirkland House in September 1930, paying a rent to Glyn Mills which exactly matched the rent the Bank was paying to the Office of Works for their lease.

The Whitehall Theatre

The Whitehall Theatre – a white hall itself – opened on 29 September 1930. It stood on the site of Ye Old Ship Tavern, established in 1650. The site stretched back to Spring Gardens and the theatre, called by a contemporary writer 'a dream in black and silver', was designed by Edward Stone. On its opening day, with a performance of Walter Hackett's play *The Way to Treat a Woman, The Times* stated '. . . there can be no doubt from the first glance at its tower-like façade with tall windows, the Whitehall Theatre prepares you for something brisk and up to date. What it suggests is the atmosphere of combined comfort and alertness, not without a certain heartlessness, which becomes the modern comedy.'

The policy of comedy was superseded by light entertainment during the Second World War. This striking Art Deco theatre also gave its name to the genre of 'Whitehall' farce. Brian Rix began to stage a series of topical farces in 1950 and these continued throughout the 1960s. Under new management, *Pyjama Tops* opened in 1969, much to the dismay, it is said, of some MPs, who felt that it was not a suitable piece for the venue. The theatre became a war museum in 1983 and in 1985 was sold, refurbished and restored. It reopened in Spring 1986.

Great Scotland Yard Recruiting Office

In 1904 the Board of Works was asked if it wished to accept the tenancy of the Clock House belonging to the Office of Woods and at the time occupied by the Inspector of Reformatories. It was not the most desirable of offices, a government official describing it thus:

'The present offices are objectionable in many ways and it may be doubted if any Government office is so meanly or more depressingly housed . . . Quite recently, on entering the office I had to step over the body of a dead rat.'

In 1907 a scheme was drafted by the Commissioners of Woods for rebuilding their offices and eventually, when leases expired, rebuilding the whole block facing Whitehall Place eastwards. They also

104   *The Clarence Pub sign, Whitehall, opposite the Whitehall Theatre.*

105   *Front door of the Ministry of Agriculture, Fisheries and Food in Whitehall Place. Shows the doorway ornamented with figures riding a fish and a bull.*

intended to form a 40-foot wide street for the remainder of the length between Northumberland Avenue and Whitehall; this would involve removing an archway leading into old Scotland Yard. Formal authority was given for the move of the War Department's Recruiting Office to the proposed Scotland Yard site, just behind the Clarence Public House, by the Treasury Commissioners in April 1908. The premises were ready for occupation in March 1911.

Close to the Recruiting Office stood the old London County Council Fire Station. The building was set back to allow for the horses to be attached to the steam fire pumps, and had an observation tower for the watch-keeper to take bearings of fires. During the Second World War it was used as a club for war correspondents from neutral and friendly countries. It is now the premises of the Civil Service Club.

Board and Ministry of Agriculture

No 55 Whitehall housed the Office of Woods and Forests, a building built between 1906 and 1909 by John Murray, who had been appointed Crown Architect and Surveyor in 1904. It was erected on land occupied formerly by old buildings that stood on part of the Whitehall Palace garden and was a five-storey structure of Portland stone, a rectangular box with two-column Ionic colonnade, and a more restrained continuation of Brydon and Young's Government Offices baroque. 'Some attempt has been made to establish a relation with the adjoining War Office', stated *The Builder*. A rear extension in classical style was added in 1951–2 by C. E. Mee, a Ministry of Works architect. The central entrance bears a coat of arms flanked by allegorical figures representing Agriculture and the Sea and Fisheries, sculpted by James Woodford (see illustration on facing page).

In 1906 the Board of Agriculture & Fisheries occupied Nos 4, 5, and 8 Whitehall Place and various other homes in St James's Square and Delahay Street. They were anxious that their scattered staff should be brought together under one roof and were 'suffering from excessive congestion'. The site comprising Nos 9, 10 and 11 Whitehall Place was available on lease from the Commissioners of Woods, and in 1909 the Office of Works took a lease for 99 years with the intention of building, at an estimated cost of £72,000.

Completion of the building was expected to be in 1915. It was then pointed out that it would not be big enough to house the whole staff so the Fisheries Department remained in their premises at No 43 Parliament Street. However, the then Prime Minister Lloyd George stepped in and decided that the new building should be occupied by the Ministry of Munitions and that it was imperative that they should be settled in 'regardless of cost' by June 1915. It was then named Armament Buildings.

The Ministry of Agriculture & Fisheries moved into Whitehall Place East in 1920. The architect of that building was H. N. Hawks, who died in 1911 and had been architect to the Office of Works. The style was described in *The Builder* as that of the English Renaissance 'freely treated'.

Old War Office

The Old War Office is a baroque revival building, faced in Portland stone, begun in 1899 and completed in December 1906. The final cost was over £1.2 million. The site was originally that part of Whitehall Palace which included the kitchen quarters, the offices of the Jewel House and the King's Herb House. Later, Carrington House stood there, but was demolished to clear the way for the building of the War Office.

The site was an irregular one – a trapezium with all four frontages of unequal length. It was very close to the Thames and the ground was damp and not solid enough to support so large a building without reinforcement. The architects therefore set it in a huge concrete tank that extended out under the pavement, 30 feet below ground level, its base 6-feet thick and sides between 3 and 7 feet. The War Office occupied a whole block of Whitehall between Whitehall Place, Whitehall Court and Horse Guards Avenue. There was no official opening ceremony for the new building.

The Builder thought the original drawings were 'of very graceful design and rather in the spirit of Wren . . .'. The designs showed the west front of the Office to be set back a little from the former building line, thus bringing the building in line with the front of the Banqueting House. Clyde Young, son of the architect, who completed the building, said that 'the dimensions of the order, the level of the cornice, and the height of the building (80 feet) were accordingly made to line with the Banqueting House as nearly as the internal arrangements would permit'.

It was originally proposed that the new building should one day be architecturally connected with the Banqueting House by a decorative screen across the end of the street facing Horse Guards Parade.

The two lower floors were rusticated with large columns above them and at each corner of the building was a baroque turret crowned with a cupola surmounting a circular half-pavilion. These turrets hid the fact that there were no right-angles on the corners. A reporter for the *Building News* approved of the towers, saying that: 'the best features externally are the great angle towers which mask the fact that the site is irregular and form admirable terminations to the façades.' As each front was of a different length, each contained different detail and contemporary opinions differed as to which was the best.

Inside, the general plan, according to Clyde Young, was of a single annular corridor, with rooms on the outer sides looking on to the four streets, and having corridors running north and south, allowing for easy communication between the staff. The grand staircase was built of Painswick stone, with alabaster balusters and two Brescia marble columns at the foot of the stair, with chequered marble paving on staircase and entrance hall. The staircase started with a central flight, divided into two and then returned to one landing immediately above. Five more ordinary staircases were provided for general use.

Thirteen chimney pieces from the old War Office were restored, cleaned and placed in the principal rooms on the main floor. These principal rooms were approached either from the main entrance on Whitehall or by the grand staircase. They included the Secretary of State's room, that of the Permanent Under-Secretary, the Chief of the General Staff's office and three interconnecting War Council chambers, all panelled in oak and lit by elegant electroliers.

Those visitors who were sufficiently eminent arrived by carriage and entered the quadrangle via a handsome loggia on Horse Guards Avenue while lesser mortals had their own entrance at the back of the building. Elaborate iron gates fronted on to Horse Guards Avenue. The sculptures at the corners of the top of the building were designed and executed by Alfred Drury and represented Peace, War, Truth and Justice, Fame and Victory.

The War Office was none too roomy even when it opened, but with the advent of the First World War more space was definitely needed. On 9 October 1914 the Office of Works told the Treasury that the War Office's requirements could best be met by adding another storey in four sections to the top of the building. War concentrated the minds of Treasury staff wonderfully and authorisation arrived on the following day. Work started on the first two sections at once, but increases in staff far exceeded previous estimates and temporary staff accommodation already had to be supplemented by 'the hiring of a room at the Savoy at the rate of two guineas per day'. Again Treasury authority for an extension was forthcoming and a fifth storey of temporary wooden huts spread over the War Office roof. This conglomeration was unofficially called Zeppelin Terrace. The National Liberal Club was requisitioned in September 1916 and dubbed the War Office Annexe.

Banqueting House

A schoolboy recalled how, in Easter 1944, the Officers' Training Corps from his school went to the Banqueting House to see an exhibition on the Battle of Waterloo. Upstairs, Field-Marshal Montgomery was holding his final pre D-Day conferences. Several members of the ATS (Auxiliary Territorial Service) and Military Police thronged the building. The boys went upstairs for their lunch, passing the hat-rack with Monty's beret hanging on it.

Across Horse Guards Avenue the Banqueting House continued to be occupied by the museum of the Royal United Services Institution until 1964. In the early 20th century the ceiling-paintings by Rubens were restored and mounted on laminated board. During the Second World War they were removed for safe-keeping and after the war taken to the Kensington Orangery where Ministry of Works restorers removed the old varnish and retouching. They were then put back in their traditional order in the Banqueting House.

Some years later the Banqueting House was to be used for a ceremonial occasion that never was. In the lobby hangs an outline contingency seating plan, dated 7 November 1936, for the proposed wedding and Coronation of King Edward VIII and Mrs Simpson. The drawing shows the exterior decoration of the Banqueting House with festoons, garlands and flags.

Whitehall / Victoria Embankment: private roadway

In 1935 came the first proposal to build a private road 80 feet wide leading across the front of Richmond Terrace to the Embankment. The width was to allow planned Government buildings to have good light and car parking space. The Commissioners of Works and Westminster City Council agreed terms on drainage, maintenance, pipe-laying and so on in June 1936, but the scheme then lapsed until 1949. In 1936, Nos 2, 3, 6, 7 and 8 Richmond Terrace were adapted for use by Cabinet Secretariat staff.

The rebuilding of the Whitehall Gardens site

The Public Offices (Sites) Act 1912 made provision for a site to be acquired for new buildings for the Board of Trade and other departments. The Act also laid down a building line as agreed between the Government and the House of Commons. This was fixed on the line of Whitehall Court and the National Liberal Club, but it did not relate to land south of Whitehall Gardens.

A Committee formed in 1912 decided to hold an open competition to select designs for the new offices in Whitehall Gardens. The site of the projected building was bounded by the Victoria Embankment, Whitehall Gardens, Horse Guards Avenue and the grounds of Montagu House. It consisted of several 18th and early 19th century residences including Cadogan, Cromwell, Malmesbury and Pembroke houses.

But there was an older building under Cadogan and Cromwell House – variously called the crypt, the undercroft, or the Tudor wine cellar. A unique historic brick-vaulted room, originally built by Cardinal Wolsey for York Place, and recorded and drawn by the architect Smirke in 1810, it had a fine ribbed and vaulted ceiling in cut brickwork, which spanned from the side walls onto a central row of columns. Excavation carried out after 1925 revealed more of the crypt, including the floor with the original brick stillages on which the casks used to rest. The room was used as a luncheon club room by the Board of Trade before the buildings above and beside it were demolished in the late 1930s. At that time the whole of the brickwork was covered in plaster. A condition of the competition was that this building should be preserved intact and incorporated in the new offices.

At the time no provision was made for preservation of any other work on the site: 'This is the more to be regretted as in Pembroke House and Malmesbury House a great deal of fine plasterwork and panelling and a number of chimney-pieces and other features exist, which are eminent-ly worthy of preservation, being indeed far finer examples of eighteenth century work than the Wolsey room is of the sixteenth.' Mr C. Peers, from the Office of Works, made an impassioned plea to preserve these rooms untouched and in their same position. He particularly noted as outstanding the principal staircase, conference room, President's room and alcove room in Pembroke House. And, indeed, when the com-

petition rules finally came out they mentioned the preservation of certain rooms and other parts of architectural and historic interest, either in situ or by re-erection. Several architects complained that to preserve the rooms in situ could mean producing entirely new designs and that idea was finally abandoned, except for Wolsey's wine cellar.

Other requests had to be considered. These included one from the Board of Trade that a miniature rifle range be included in the new building! A letter to an assessor from Sir Lionel Earle, Permanent Secretary to the Office of Works, states the need for a terrace, because the then Permanent Secretary to the Board of Trade, Sir Hubert Llewellyn Smith, attached great importance to a terrace in times of acute trade difficulties.

'. . . on many occasions where apparently no agreement was possible, they [opposing trade factions summoned to the Board of Trade] have gone to cool their heads either on the terrace or in the garden: and after an hour or two in the fresh air, influenced perhaps by the surroundings of nature, they have come in in a very reasonable frame of mind, and a settlement has been effected.'

107 *Pembroke House. The second Pembroke House, built in the 18th century to designs by Sir William Chambers, was used by Foreign Office staff while Scott was building their new premises, and was demolished in 1938 for redevelopment.*

Plans for the site were judged by three assessors who chose ten finalists. Three hundred pounds was paid to the successful competitor, although the assessors received £400 each! The winner, chosen in January 1915, was E. Vincent Harris, later architect of several civic halls and Exeter University buildings, among others. His design placed the historic rooms by themselves in a courtyard on the ground floor. Although a winner had been selected, 'owing to the need of husbanding the national resources during the war, the Board of Works intend to postpone erection of the building'.

However, the Board began to buy up property on the site, in particular Montagu House and its grounds. Montagu House had been occupied by the Dukes of Buccleuch from 1862 to 1917 and then taken over by the Ministry of Labour and the Ministry of Munitions, and some temporary buildings had been erected on the garden and forecourt by the Office of Works. The house was at that time held on a lease expiring in January 1954 at a ground rent of £906 5s and land tax of £119 3s 4d.

The sale of Montagu House to the Office of Works is a story of haggling that is the equal of any house purchase battle fought out today.

108 *Montagu House. The second Montagu House was built in 1859–62 for the second Duke, from the designs of William Burn in the French Renaissance style, and occupied by the Dukes of Buccleuch. Hospitality was lavish and it is said that by custom anyone who knew the family could call in for lunch. Owing to its position near Whitehall, there were daily contingents from the Foreign Office, Admiralty, War Office and even a Minister or the Prime Minister himself.*

In November 1917 Lionel Earle, Permanent Secretary to the Office of Works, asked the Duke to give him first refusal for the house and by return, the Duke wrote that he had had an offer for it. An internal Office of Works memo stated that the Duke's leasehold interest, for Government office purposes, was about £60,000, and 'if it be considered really desirable . . . for the Government to obtain the premises over the head of the prospective purchaser . . . the only way open to us is to obtain from the Duke the lowest figure (not exceeding £70,000) he would be prepared to accept and submit it to the Treasury'.

A valuation of the house in December 1917 says 'the property occupies an important position in Whitehall between Whitehall Gardens and Richmond Terrace. The mansion is erected in stone and stands well back from Whitehall to which it has a frontage of about 167 feet. There is a courtyard in front with entrance gates from Whitehall Gardens. From an entertaining point of view the mansion is an ideal one, the reception rooms are of regal proportions, several of them open on to the terrace with steps down to the ornamental grounds'. Messrs Hamptons valued the house for use as a private dwelling at £40,800 and the Office was of the opinion that it was worth £60,000 plus an extra £5,000 for the advantage of acquiring the Duke's interest immediately. The Comptroller of Supplies was instructed to negotiate and get the lowest price he could manage – up to £70,000. But the Chancellor of the Exchequer saw the valuations and refused to go higher than a valuation of £45,000 made earlier by the Office of Works.

The Duke wrote again to Lionel Earle in December saying that he would much prefer to sell to the Government than to anyone else, adding that the house cost about £120,000 to build and immense sums had been spent on the foundations. He authorised his solicitor to sell to the Government at £50,000 and Lionel Earle writes on the file that: 'I told him, in order to bargain a bit, that I did not think I was authorised to offer more than £48,000'. This was later raised to £49,000, which the Duke accepted. Subsequently, Earle wrote to the Treasury that the Royal Colonial Institute had now offered the Duke £60,000 and had begged him to use his influence to leave Montagu House as a future home for the RCI. 'This of course is interesting from the point of view of showing that we have in fact made a wonderfully good purchase, particularly as the cost of the temporary buildings amounts to over £14,000, and that we are actually paying the Duke an inclusive rent for the house and land at the rate of £5,000 a year.' A bargain indeed.

In 1934 the architect Vincent Harris was recommissioned to provide a building not only to accommodate the Board of Trade, but also for staff from the Ministries of Air, Transport and Labour. The proposed building was discussed by the First Commissioner of Works and the London County Council in July 1934. The open space on the west frontage was to be preserved and the south frontage to Richmond Terrace would have an 80-foot wide roadway. The statutory building line of 1912 as extended southwards would be complied with. In December 1935 the Cabinet approved a proposal from the First Commissioner of Works to erect a building on both the Whitehall Gardens and Montagu House sites.

It was decided that the new building would go up in two stages. The first, on the Whitehall Gardens site, would include, as well as Nos 7–10 Whitehall Gardens, premises in Horse Guards Avenue, part of the open way of Whitehall Gardens and forecourt on the Horse Guards Avenue frontage. The second section would be on the Montagu House site with its forecourt and temporary building in the front and the rear with its two temporary buildings. The more recent additions to Gwydyr House would be demolished at the same time, leaving the house in its original condition. The new building would, however, be designed as a whole, and the architect would ensure that Wolsey's wine cellar was not disturbed.

There was concern as to the importance of protection against air attacks on the new building. The architect gave assurances that the building 'embodies all possible modern developments which are consistent with a reasonable but not parsimonious economy'. 'The proposed Whitehall building will resist the effects of bombing better than any other building in Whitehall. It will provide more protection against air raids than the War Office, the New Public Offices, or, to a greater degree still, the Home Office.'

It appeared that the building would also have to be capable of infinite expansion because accommodation was urgently needed for the Ministry of Labour, the Ministry of Transport and 'if it should prove possible, one of the four departments now housed in the New Public Offices'. And so in 1938 several handsome 18th-century town houses were demolished to clear the site. Among them were Cromwell House, Malmesbury House, Pelham House and Pembroke House. Work on the new building began in 1939, but was discontinued at the outbreak of war.

Also on the site, and revealed by excavations for the new

109 *Queen Mary's Steps, built in 1691. Fragments were unearthed when excavation was carried out for the Whitehall Gardens building. Part of the northern flight of stairs has been repaired, and a section of the terrace and river wall reconstructed.*

government building, were Queen Mary's Steps. In 1691 Christopher Wren had designed for the Queen a terrace overlooking the Thames in front of the old river wall of Whitehall Palace. This terrace projected about 70 feet into the bed of the river and was approximately 285 feet long with a curved flight of steps at each end. The upper portion of the northern flight of steps has now been repaired. This, and a reconstructed section of the terrace, can be seen today, with a rebuilt part of the river wall behind and above the terrace.

43–44 *Parliament Street*

Numbers 43 and 44 Parliament Street, built in the 18th century, had originally been privately occupied, but by the 19th century they were being used as offices. The Clerk of the House of Commons and the Journal Office had rooms there and the Liberal Party occupied No 43 later on as did the Ordnance Survey Office. No 44 was used by the Transport Board and during the early 20th century the premises were temporarily occupied by the Board of Trade's Labour Department and then the Fisheries Department of the Board of Agriculture. The ground and basement floors were let for a branch Post Office from 1900 onwards. This replaced the Post Office in King Street (demolished in 1899) which, as the main Westminster receiving office, had existed for a century.

The Fisheries staff were removed from No 43 in May 1940 as it was not practicable to provide a proper air raid shelter for them. Later War Office staff moved in and after the war the house was occupied by the German section of the Foreign Office.

Redevelopment plans for this area were first mooted in the 1920s. A scheme was suggested in 1929 which considered using the Montagu House site for rebuilding, with Richmond Terrace being retained for Government staff. In 1931 the Government proposed to acquire the leasehold interest in some of the houses, for use by the Prime Minister or the Cabinet Office or Ministry of Labour, but as the cost of adapting the houses was felt to be iniquitously high, the proposal was not taken further.

Another plan was prepared in 1935 by the architect William Curtis Green, for development of the block bounded by Richmond Terrace, Parliament Street, Bridge Street and Victoria Embankment as public offices. This was approved by the planning authority and the Royal Fine Art Commission in 1936, and involved the demolition of Richmond Terrace. The development was to be on classical lines in order to harmonise with the surrounding buildings by Inigo Jones, Kent, Soane, Scott and Brydon. The eastern end was completed in 1940, but the war put a stop to further work, and the building was taken over by the Metropolitan Police as an extension to New Scotland Yard. In 1949 it was agreed that an open scheme behind the Terrace façade, and ending at the Whitehall entrance to Richmond Mews as a complete building, be chosen.

Scotland Yard

The 20th century has been characterised by the proliferation of bureaucracy, and in this the police were no exception. By 1931 they had begun to need more space than was available in their present premises and were well aware of the projected future development of the Whitehall site. They pressed the advantages of building a police extension north over the garden of No 1 Richmond Terrace. Two bungalows had been erected on the site and the garden during the First World War and demolished in 1923–4. A temporary brick building was erected in 1925–6 and occupied by Ministry of Labour staff.

William Curtis Green, possibly best known for designing the

Dorchester Hotel, was appointed consulting architect in 1935 (at a consultant's fee of £3,000) for the scheme to provide additional headquarters accommodation for New Scotland Yard and for redevelopment of the Richmond Terrace property. The new building was planned to be on that part of Richmond Terrace lying immediately to the north of New Scotland Yard, but would hardly touch the houses in Richmond Terrace, and would extend over No 1's garden including the site of the temporary Ministry of Labour building. Work began in December 1936. The extension was opened in 1940 and was known as the Curtis Green Building.

The impact of war on the buildings of Whitehall

There were limited bombing raids on London during the First World War, from 1915 onwards. At first they were made by Zeppelins; later, bombs were dropped from long-range aircraft and fell in many parts of the capital. Whitehall survived comparatively unscathed, although at least one shell penetrated No 41 Parliament Street.

The effect of the Second World War on the Government buildings of Whitehall was felt principally over two periods of time, set well apart. There were heavy air raids from Autumn 1940 to Spring 1941, and raids from January to March 1944. On Wednesday 11 September 1940 the first bomb to hit Whitehall fell on the south side of Horse Guards Avenue, but there were only minimal casualties. On that same night a bomb fell at the front of the Horse Guards and another near the Cenotaph. There was also some damage to the Colonial Office.

A delayed action bomb on the pavement outside the Scottish Office (Dover House) could have caused serious damage both to the Scottish Office, and to the Banqueting House opposite, had it exploded immediately. However, a sandbag wall was hastily built round it and was just high enough to temper the blast when the bomb went off. Three large bombs fell in the quadrangle of the War Office. It sustained a number of direct hits although damage, apart from shattered windows, was confined to the upper levels and the stonework.

The Paymaster General's Office was bombed in early October 1940. The southern part of the Whitehall frontage was reduced to a pile of rubble, with rooms and basement in ruins:

110 & 111 *Bomb damage to Whitehall in the Second World War. Three bombs fell in the quadrangle of the War Office, but damage, apart from broken windows, was confined mainly to the stonework and the upper part of the building. The Paymaster General's Office was much more severely damaged. It was hit in October 1940 and the Whitehall frontage adjoining the Horse Guards was almost entirely destroyed. 'Nearly all the government buildings and the shelters beneath them are either wholly unsafe or incapable of resisting a direct hit' (Winston Churchill,* Their Finest Hour, *1949).*

'The air was filled with dust and pension vouchers, and all around was confusion, heightened by the simultaneous bombing of three other buildings in close proximity.'

In that raid four were killed and three injured, including an Admiralty clerk. No 36 Whitehall was declared unsafe, and the staff moved to other buildings in central London.

Early on 17 April 1941, fires were reported near the Citadel, the concrete fort in St James's Park which was an extension to the Old Admiralty Building. The eastern part of the Admiralty south block was hit by a high explosive bomb. Another fell in the quadrangle. The structure stood firm, but within all was ruin – ceilings and walls down, doors and windows blown out. The Board Room's ceiling was shattered by blast, its panelling and carving splintered and the two sea pictures facing the windows lacerated. Afterwards the carvings and panelling were stored safely in a disused Underground tunnel, the pictures taken away for restoration and the table and chairs recovered. The Admiralty Board continued to meet in their stripped Board Room until major reconstruction work began in earnest in November 1946. The Board Room ceiling was restored as an exact replica of the original design of diminishing octagons, no two of which were exactly the same shape or size.

Barry's Whitehall block and Kent's Treasury were both used by Treasury staff until damaged by bombing in 1940. On 14 October 1940 a high explosive bomb fell in Treasury Green at the rear of Soane's Judicial Wing and severely damaged the Downing Street block. Sir John Martin, former Parliamentary Private Secretary to Churchill, describes in his memoirs how 'the mess in the house was indescribable – windows smashed in all directions, everything covered with grime, doors off hinges, and curtains and furniture tossed about in a confused mass'.

Churchill was dining with friends in the garden room under the Cabinet Room that evening. In *Their Finest Hour*, published in 1949, he wrote:

'Several loud explosions occurred around us at no great distance, and presently a bomb fell, perhaps a hundred yards away, on the Horse Guards Parade, making a great deal of noise . . . having got up to order the servants to leave the kitchen and go into the shelter, I had been seated again at table only about three minutes when a really very loud crash, close at hand, and a violent shock showed that the house had been struck . . . the kitchen, the pantry, and the offices on the Treasury side were shattered . . . The devastation was complete.'

The underground Treasury shelter across the court had been blown to pieces by a direct hit and the three civil servants on Home

Guard night duty were killed. As Churchill said, Downing Street consisted of houses 250 years old, shaky and lightly built by the profiteering speculator whose name they bore. At the time of Munich, shelters had been built for the occupants of No 10 and No 11 and the rooms on the garden level had their ceilings propped up with a wooden under-ceiling and timbers, but neither these rooms nor the shelters were effective against a direct hit.

Three days later a similar type of bomb fell on the Treasury Building near Treasury Passage and penetrated into an air-raid shelter, exploding at ceiling level. The surrounding sections had to be demolished for safety, or had already collapsed. Several stone columns on the Whitehall façade were displaced, staircases made unsafe and roof timbers shattered. Many of the finest rooms were destroyed. The Downing Street block also suffered further superficial damage. At the time, the Whitehall block was considered beyond repair and complete demolition and rebuilding were recommended. Kent's Treasury and Dorset House fortunately suffered only light damage.

The Whitehall block was vacated and some temporary repairs carried out at a cost of about £5,000, were completed in March 1941. But the building remained vacant until 1943 when, because of the growing shortage of office accommodation in Whitehall, the north end was reconditioned at a cost of £11,000. It was ready in October and work began on the south end. A third explosion on 22 February 1944 in Whitehall outside the Treasury Building and near the Parliamentary Counsel's entrance, did considerable damage to the stonework of the Whitehall frontage and to the roof, partitions, ceilings and windows. Rooms occupied in the reconditioned north end were vacated once more, and so much damage was done to the south end that reinstatement work was abandoned. The building was just made safe and weatherproof.

The Ministry of Works and Buildings was set up in 1940 as an administrative department to take charge of the wartime building programme, but it also absorbed and continued the building, accommodation and supply functions of the old Office of Works. It co-ordinated planning for post-war reconstruction and dealt with wartime decentralisation of government accommodation to provide for new post-war departments. It also acted as guardian and preserver of historic buildings and ancient monuments. With the advent of war the Ministry played a vital role in co-ordinating the use of buildings and land by

Government departments, and adapting a variety of premises for the services and civil service staff.

Air raid precautions for Whitehall divided the area into seven sectors, with a post in each continuously manned. The Ministry of Works and Buildings was in charge of patrolling the streets both day and night, a duty which was carried out by the various departments. The sectors with Government wardens included: 151: Admiralty – Government offices, banks and the Whitehall Theatre; 152: Ministry of Agriculture & Fisheries – Northumberland Avenue, part of Whitehall Place and Whitehall; 153: War Office – Whitehall Court, part of Whitehall Place and Horse Guards Avenue; 154: Home Office – Horse Guards arch to Whitehall, King Charles Street, Guards memorial; 155: Ministry of Labour – part of Horse Guards Avenue, Embankment, boundary between Montagu House and Richmond Terrace; 156: Ministry of Works – Old and New Public Offices, King Charles Street, Whitehall, Great George Street.

Ministers were expected to stay at their posts in London at the height of the war. The Prime Minister, in answer to a Parliamentary Question on 18 July 1940, replied: 'I have asked Ministers whose duties are intimately connected with the conduct of the war to arrange as soon as possible to sleep in their offices at the centre of Government.'

In May 1940 a sandbag pillbox was erected at the corner of Great George Street and Horse Guards Road for the Home Guard. A machine-gun post guarded the entrance to the Cabinet War Rooms and the Prime Minister's apartment.

112 *Field-Marshal Viscount Slim. Sculpture by Ivor Roberts-Jones, unveiled in April 1990 on the green in front of the Ministry of Defence building. Put up by the Burma Star Association.*

London underground

At the beginning of the Second World War a tunnel was built 100 feet below Whitehall which connected with all the main Government departments via smaller tunnels and shafts. It was used for telephone and telegraph lines, transmission of mail and heating, and for physical access between buildings.

Second World War government citadels in the Whitehall area were at Montagu House, the Admiralty, the War Office and the Cabinet War Rooms, and at Marsham Street. By the end of 1941 the combined citadels could hold a few thousand staff. After the war, the fear of nuclear

113   *War-time roof spotters overlooking Whitehall, with the tower of Big Ben in the background. Mr Bowler and Miss Simpson, two of the many members of the staff of the Dominions and Colonial Offices, taking their turn at this duty.*

114   *The gates under the archway leading from the Dominions and Colonial Offices to No 10 Downing Street. The policeman's tin hat reminds us that it is war-time.*

attack led to the construction of yet more tunnels, which could take thousands of essential staff if necessary.

The best known of all the underground tunnels were the Cabinet War Rooms underneath the western side of the Government Offices, Great George Street. As early as March 1938 Major-General Sir Hastings Ismay, the deputy secretary (military) to the Cabinet, asked the Office of Works to draw up plans to provide a safe emergency war room for the Cabinet and Chiefs of Staff that would be protected against enemy attack. This war room had to have facilities for meetings, a 24-hour a day Map Room, secure communications, and eating and sleeping facilities for staff. The Government Offices were chosen because the steel-framed structure of the building was exceedingly strong, and it was close to all the main ministries as well as to Downing Street. The rooms were protected with steel supporting beams and blast walling.

The War Rooms were ready by late August 1938, but the aftermath of Munich led to temporary closure of the basement. Work, however, continued on improving facilities and the War Cabinet was set up in September 1939. On 30 September 1940 a bomb fell at the north-western corner of the Government Offices and this, plus the other raids on Whitehall, hardened Churchill's resolve to improve the security of the Cabinet War Rooms.

On 22 October 1940 Churchill authorised the construction of more overhead cover above the War Room, and also priority for completion of a Whitehall deep tunnel to allow secure communications and access between bomb-proof citadels in and around Whitehall. The sub-ground floor above the basement was filled by a reinforced concrete slab, three feet thick, and a concrete wall was built along the external wall of the Government Offices at ground level – part of which may still be seen in place. In December 1940 the Prime Minister and Mrs Churchill moved into new quarters, known as the 'No 10 Downing Street annexe', above ground in the Government Offices, and lived there until the end of the war. The concrete slab was extended towards the centre of the building in December 1940 and extended further in spring and autumn 1941. Each time accommodation and office space were expanded, existing offices subdivided and corridors utilised.

At the end of the war, the original rooms such as the Map Room and its annexe, the Cabinet War Room, Churchill's office and bedroom and the transatlantic telephone room were left just as they had been during the closing days. In 1948 they were preserved as a museum under the supervision of the Cabinet Office, with visitors allowed in by special arrangement. Responsibility for the museum was transferred to the Department of the Environment in 1975, and in 1981 the then Prime Minister, Mrs Thatcher, decided that the rooms should be opened to the public. The Imperial War Museum now looks after the Cabinet War Rooms for the Department, and they were restored and re-opened to the public in 1984. They were renovated again in 1993.

115 *The interior of the India Office (now Foreign and Commonwealth Office) was designed by Matthew Digby Wyatt. The Court, styled 'Durbar Court' in 1902, was built as an open courtyard but almost immediately a glazed roof was added (in 1868) transforming it into a magnificent ceremonial reception hall. The sides consist of three storeys of columns and piers supporting arches; the floor is made of Greek, Sicilian and Belgian marble. It was first used in 1867 for a reception in honour of the Sultan of Turkey. Restoration of the former India Office was carried out between 1984 and 1987.*

6
POST-WAR TO
PRESENT-DAY

'What is particularly frustrating for architects is that while ambitious schemes were commissioned and abandoned, anonymous piecemeal additions, often of miserable quality, were going on all the time, giving Whitehall a reputation for undistinguished clutter that amazes foreign visitors used to more sophisticated centres of government.'

Stephen Games, 'Whitehall farce', *RIBA Journal*, April 1980

AFTER the war several government buildings had to be shored up and rebuilt, while Downing Street and the Treasury Buildings both needed major repair. Fragments of Tudor building were discovered during work, and excavation of the Treasury site revealed Roman and Saxon remains, and substantial portions of the Whitehall Palace tennis courts and precinct walls.

The Whitehall Gardens building, that had been stopped and started since 1913, was finally finished in the 1950s and since 1964 has housed the Ministry of Defence. A new Richmond House was built and property between Cannon Row and Parliament Street adapted to provide accommodation for MPs as phase 1 of an ambitious rebuilding scheme, completed in 1991. Phase 2 is currently under construction. Restoration of the Old War Office and the Horse Guards has recently been completed. The Old Public Offices, housing the Foreign and Commonwealth Office are now being carefully restored and refurbished. Many other buildings are currently under repair.

Whitehall's restoration and redevelopment

The strictures at the head of this chapter could have applied equally well to Whitehall Palace in the 16th and 17th centuries, and to the burgeoning growth of government buildings in Victorian London. The history of the street known as Whitehall is not one of the implementation of long-term considered development and planned layout. Nevertheless some civil servants were aware of the historical sites on which their modern buildings stood, and in two instances particularly, this shows: in the careful preservation of the Tudor wine cellar beneath the present-day Ministry of Defence, and in the archaeological excavations carried out during restoration of the old Treasury and Downing Street.

Since 1945 the historic character and personality of Whitehall has finally been revealed but not without several determined efforts by vested and blinkered interests to destroy it, 'and not without haphazard redevelopment that indicates that there is no comprehensive plan for Government office building in general and none for Whitehall in particular', according to a writer in *The Architect & Building News* (December 1969).

Planning for London's redevelopment started well before the end of the Second World War. In 1943 the London County Council

116 *Detail of portico on Government Offices, Great George Street, now the Treasury.*

published the County of London plan, by J. H. Forshaw and Patrick Abercrombie. The following year, Professor Abercrombie's *Greater London Plan* proposed five ring roads round London to divert traffic from the centre, a traffic-free precinct around Westminster Abbey and the Houses of Parliament, and defined a large area of Westminster stretching from Trafalgar Square to the Tate Gallery as the Government centre.

In the context of the redevelopment of Whitehall, a Ministry of Works memorandum pointed out in 1967 that over the last fifty years only one major headquarters building, Whitehall Gardens, had been erected and that 74,000 civil servants were scattered in leased premises. (In the early 1980s, the Department of Trade and Industry, for example, was located in forty buildings in central London.) Redevelopment was required to concentrate departments and accommodate staff more efficiently. This was, of course, before the policy of office dispersal was widely promulgated.

Government Offices, Great George Street

After the war, more temporary offices were carved out of the Government Offices, Great George Street, to accommodate a further increase in Treasury staff. In 1962, the Board Room, originally designed for the Board of Education, was taken over for Rab Butler, then newly appointed as Deputy Prime Minister and Secretary of State.

Since the 1970s, single development projects and piecemeal repairs and maintenance have been carried out in the building, mainly to provide more space and apparently without the sympathetic regard to its history which is evident in the restoration of the Foreign and Commonwealth Office across King Charles Street. The courtyards have been used by contractors for storage and, as elsewhere in Whitehall, there is flooding in the basement and sub-basement. Two tributaries of the ancient River Tyburn run directly under the St James's Park façade and part of the circular courtyard. There are severe structural problems, the steel framework of the building is corroded, the exterior needs cleaning, and persistent lack of funding has added to the difficulties. Newspaper publicity in 1994 has mentioned the possibility of moving all the staff elsewhere while the necessary major restoration work is carried out, and the ministerial rooms redecorated and furnished with suitable carpets,

117 *Bird's eye view of Whitehall from the new Parliament Street Building of the House of Commons.*

curtains and lighting. Any restoration or improvement work should be more sympathetic to the history of this building than hitherto.

Foreign and Commonwealth Office

After the war Sir George Gilbert Scott's ornate building lost two of its occupants. The India Office was dissolved in 1947 after India gained its independence and some of the residual work was taken over by the Colonial or Commonwealth Relations Office and moved to Church House in Great Smith Street.

The Foreign Office expanded into these premises which were mainly used by the enlarged Germany department, but shortage of space was still a problem. The Commonwealth Relations Office, also formed in 1947, stayed in Scott's building until 1966 when it merged with the Colonial Office. The Foreign and Commonwealth Office was established in 1968 by the merger of the Foreign Office and Commonwealth Office. Plans to build a new Foreign Office in Carlton House Terrace and a new Colonial Office in Broad Sanctuary did not materialise, and over the years the structure and parts of the interior deteriorated.

In 1963 Geoffrey Rippon, then Minister of Public Building and Works, announced that the present Foreign Office building had come to the end of its useful life and should be demolished. The news was greeted with horror. Christopher Hussey wrote in *Country Life* in 1964 that the Government's resolve to pull down

> 'the sumptuous Renaissance Palace containing the Foreign Office, the Commonwealth Relations Office, the Home Office and the old India Office is the most shocking to those who admire it from outside. For a century the spectacular Italianate pile, thanks to Palmerston's inspired obstinacy, has played the visual role intended by Inigo Jones to be filled by Whitehall Palace in the centre of the historic square mile . . . '

Luckily such views prevailed, and after much public debate the offices were classified as a Grade I listed building and their destruction averted.

Nevertheless, some drastic repair work was still required. George Brown, who became Foreign Secretary in August 1966, remarked that

'the building in fact is downright inconvenient, ugly and shabby inside. People literally still work in what must have been once upon a time intended to be cupboards and in corridors. Quite senior officials interview foreign diplomats in the most incredible little cubby-holes.'

In the 1970s a full redevelopment programme was proposed, retaining only the façade and the finest rooms. This was turned down and a more modest scheme of refurbishment over a long period chosen. Eventually the whole building was occupied by the Foreign and Commonwealth Office (the Home Office having moved to a new building in 1977) and restoration of what had originally been four very different and separate departments began. The four constituent parts of

118 *The Foreign Office main courtyard. One commentator later remarked that going from No 10 through the courtyards of the FCO and GOGGS to Parliament Square is 'one of the major architectural experiences of the western world'. As Colin Amery wrote in the* Financial Times *in March 1992: 'Whitehall is a street of courtyards, almost all of which are invisible to the public.'*

the building were joined for the first time, so that staff could now circulate through the whole building, which became established in everyone's mind as 'The Foreign Office'.

As we have seen, George Gilbert Scott, the original architect, viewed the Foreign Office as 'a kind of national palace, or drawing room for the nation' and his vision is reflected in the lavishness of the grand staircase, the decoration of ceilings and corridors, and the magnificent Locarno Suite of three rooms.

The Property Services Agency started work on the former India Office on the first stage of a major scheme of conservation and restoration in 1984 and this was completed in 1987. Of much greater significance for the FCO, however, was the fact that, also in 1987, Government departments were made responsible for their own major projects, and were able to appoint architects, surveyors and contractors themselves. Departments were more able to ensure that the work matched their operational requirements and to take a proprietorial interest in quality standards and value for money.

In 1987 work began on the second phase, the refurbishment of the grand staircase, three storeys high, constructed in marble, and on conservation of the Victorian interiors with their tiled floors and walls, and ceilings stencilled in red, blue and gold, by church decorators Clayton and Bell. The series of allegorical murals by Sir Sigismund Goetze has been cleaned under the supervision of English Heritage. Goetze had painted these at his own expense during the First World War and they were put up, despite some criticism of his style, as the 'Marie Corelli of painting', round the Grand Staircase. They depicted the 'origin, education, development, expansion and triumph of the British Empire, leading up to the Covenant of the League of Nations'.

The Locarno Suite, designed by Sir George Gilbert Scott, is a splendid three-room suite on the first floor, consisting of the Reception Room, a smaller Dining Room and Conference Room. With the outbreak of the Second World War, the Locarno Suite was used by the cypher branch, and after the war was partitioned to make more offices. Refurbishment began in the late 1980s and since 1990 the Conference Room has been used for its original purpose. The Reception Room and Dining Room were restored in the following two years, and the Victorian stencilled decoration in the dining room copied exactly. The Foreign and Commonwealth Office and its architects, Cecil Denny Highton, were presented with the Europa Nostra medal of honour in 1992 for the

119 *Details of the refurbished Foreign and Commonwealth Office: including the painted pilaster by the Grand Staircase; stencilled ornament; doorway through to landing at the top of the staircase (a Goetze mural can be seen through the door); balustrades at the top of the Grand Staircase.*

'magnificent and meticulous restoration to the original design of one of the finest examples of Victorian architecture in the United Kingdom'.

The penultimate phase of refurbishment of the Foreign Office is proceeding and the project is now in its sixteenth year. Since responsibility was transferred from the Property Services Agency to the Foreign and Commonwealth Office in 1988, expenditure has amounted to over £58 million, the money being found from the FCO's own budget as part of its capital programme (1993–4). The project, on completion, will have cost about £100 million, considerably less than the estimated cost of building new premises for the Foreign Office in Central Westminster.

Restoration work should be completed in 1997 and the whole programme is expected to achieve 25 per cent more usable accommodation. The current phase covers the one-time Colonial Office and parts of the Home Office sections of the building. There are no fine rooms awaiting restoration here for, by this stage of his building, Sir George Gilbert Scott had been told to cut costs. Yet the old Colonial Office Library is a notable feature, rising through two floors, and displaying a stuffed anaconda, a gift from British Guiana at the turn of the century. The final phase will include restoration of the grand entrance to the India Office and the fine rooms which have, for many years, been used as the receiving and despatching rooms for the several thousand diplomatic bags handled each year by the Mails Branch. The Branch will move to purpose-built accommodation in a formerly disused courtyard in the Old Colonial Office.

It has been said that the magnificent restoration of the historic Old Public Offices is a significant contributory factor to the high staff morale in the FCO.

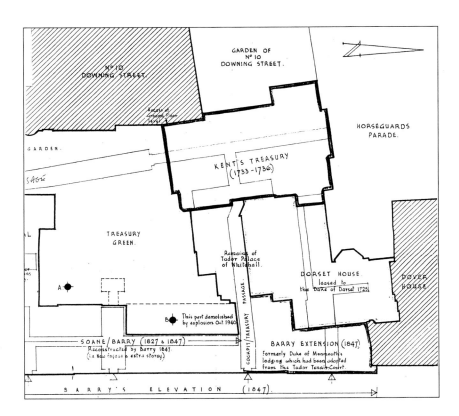

120 *Plan of Treasury Buildings, showing the remains of Whitehall Palace, the Soane/Barry façade and Kent's Treasury, and the bomb damage inflicted in October 1940.*

The Treasury and Downing Street

Reinstatement of the southern end of the Treasury began immediately after the war, in October 1945, and was finished by the following spring. Much dry rot had been found and £32,000 of eradication work was carried out. Although sufficient repairs were done to allow the buildings to be used as offices again, nothing in the nature of complete restoration had been attempted by the end of 1957. Plans for future work included the reconditioning of historic buildings such as Soane's Judicial block in Downing Street (1827), the Whitehall block built by Soane and rebuilt by Barry (1847), Dorset House and Kent's Treasury (1733–6). A Ministry of Works memo discusses these plans and mentions the restoration of the Barry façade to Whitehall, behind which a modern building could be built.

In 1954 the Ministry of Works made a survey of the structure of Downing Street and found that, though not actually in danger of imminent collapse, it would be unsafe to postpone major repairs for too long. The foundations had moved, some walls were unsupported and floors, especially in the Cabinet Room, were weak. After the Ministry made its report it was asked to draw up a detailed plan of reconstruction, although nothing was to be undertaken before mid-1958.

An independent Committee under the chairmanship of the Earl of Crawford and Balcarres considered the Ministry of Works report in July 1957 and recommended in March 1958 that Nos 10–12 Downing Street be given a major overhaul with the aim of preserving the external appearance. This would include rebuilding No 12 to its original height before the fire that had gutted the upper floors in 1879, the provision of about 50 per cent more space for staff, and preserving rooms and features of historic or artistic importance. The design for the alterations was to be approved by the Royal Fine Art Commission.

The Committee also recommended that the reconstruction of the Treasury Buildings was to be undertaken concurrently. A very tentative estimate of £400,000 for carrying out these recommendations was made, and Raymond Erith was appointed architect for the project. His report on the proposed reconstruction notes that: 'Although No 10 is old it is surprisingly well suited to its present purpose . . . I do not think the main dispositions can be altered to any advantage at all. My aim is therefore to improve the building by working within its established framework.'

121

Downing Street frontage as it was in 1959. No 12 on far left cut down to single storey building after fire in 1879. Wing of no 10 on right, which contains Soane dining room, is set back from main frontage and has single storey annex in front of it.

Downing Street frontage as proposed. No 12 rebuilt to original height. No 11 unaltered. To right of no 10 a room added on each floor in front of back stairs.

Garden front facing Horse Guards as it was in 1959.

Garden front facing Horse Guards as proposed. Main change to no 12.

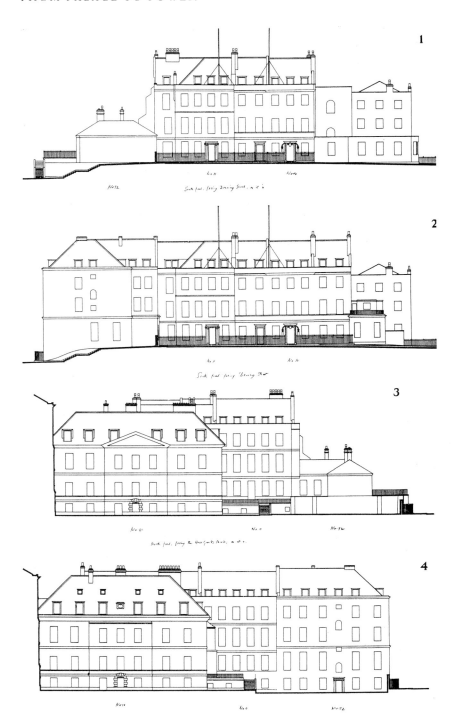

The estimate was increased by a further £100,000 in October 1959 and work planned to start in spring 1960. When a Ministry of Works Press Notice was finally issued in December 1959, it said that the combined cost of work on Downing Street and the Treasury Buildings was likely to be £1,250,000 and work would start in the summer. The Prime Minister, Harold Macmillan, wrote a personal minute about the restoration work on 7 July 1958:

'. . . the utmost care should be taken to preserve the few antiquities which still remain. In particular, the whole of the Tudor structure on the sub-ground, ground, first and second floors on the site of Cockpit Passage should be preserved intact and no new buildings added which will obscure them.'

The Crawford Committee did not consider the Downing Street houses to be architecturally outstanding, but felt that if steps were not taken soon, 'further deterioration in the structure may make it impossible to preserve some of the historic features . . . the façades of Nos 10 and 11 are survivals of a style which was common in London in the past and there is a strong case for preserving them on these grounds'. The Committee also mentioned as worthy of note the Cabinet Room, two secretaries' rooms to the east and one to the south, the first floor state rooms and staircases, and the Soane dining room in No 11.

Work began on Downing Street in the summer of 1960. Raymond Erith remarked to R. J. Minney, author of a history of No 10: 'It was not a ramshackle house as some people seem to think . . . It was substantially built, but the original foundations were not strong enough and they have shrunk.' The architect remodelled the back of Downing Street with a high stone terrace outside the windows of No 10,

122 *Tudor finds in Whitehall: Whitehall Palace, park side looking north. Parts of the building found during reconstruction work.*

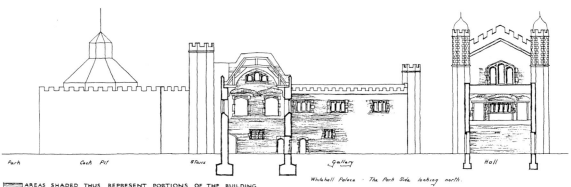

Park   Cock Pit   Stairs   Gallery   Hall

Whitehall Palace · The Park Side looking north.

AREAS SHADED THUS REPRESENT PORTIONS OF THE BUILDING FOUND EXISTING DURING RECENT RECONSTRUCTION WORK

strengthened the floor and roof beams of the Cabinet Room, under-pinning the walls with concrete to a depth of 18 feet, and added another staircase. The state rooms in No 11 were left as they were. He rebuilt No 12 from scratch as a new building in classical style to its original height.

While restoration was being carried out on No 11, several fragments of Tudor work were uncovered, including part of a garden wall. In Dorset House were found large pieces of the original flock wallpaper dating from about 1720. The blocks from which the wallpaper had been printed were still in existence and new paper was specially printed and hung in the rooms.

Restoration was undertaken on the Treasury site between 1960 and 1963 when the buildings were repaired and extended, and a modern office building was erected behind Barry's 19th-century façade to Whitehall. The old Treasury is, in fact, made up of two distinct buildings — William Kent's Treasury facing Horse Guards Parade and the Soane/Barry building with its frontage onto Whitehall. The two are connected by various corridors, the main one of which is Cockpit Passage, from where, today, visitors can view what remains of King Henry VIII's Tennis Court.

The excavations of the Treasury site under the direction of the Ministry of Works revealed Roman remains and a ninth-century Saxon settlement on the site of Treasury Green. As soon as the deep foundations had been dug, portions of Tudor buildings were found embedded in

123 *Vicky cartoon, Evening Standard, 11 May 1962.*

Dorset House above ground and remains of Whitehall Palace were discovered below ground level. These excavations were carried out with the co-operation of the contractor's staff and the help of many professional and amateur archaeologists. Parts of the Small Close Tennis Court were found, and also the contents of the garderobes and rubbish pits belonging to the Court families who had lodged on the site of Whitehall Palace. The precinct wall of the Tudor palace was traced round three sides of the site and survived to its full height under 17th-century structures in Downing Street.

One bay of the Great Close Tennis Court, which had also been used for entertainments, the major part of a corner turret and one of its windows, most of Cockpit Passage and the footings of the Small Close Tennis Court have been restored as has the two-storey gallery which also contained part of a stone fireplace. In the rebuilt offices part of the wall of the Tudor hall and a 20-foot high window have been incorporated at the end of a series of corridors and are visible through glass panels at the various floor levels. The Great Close Tennis Court had in its heyday looked like a Gothic great hall divided into bays by buttresses and topped with battlements and pillars, crowned with gilded vanes. In Dorset House the staircase was reconstructed and restoration carried out on the President's Room and two other principal rooms on the first floor. The exterior was kept intact.

Reconstruction work was expected to take two years, but a succession of strikes slowed it down and it was not finished until 1963. By March 1962 the estimated cost had shot up to £1,600,000, and in September a minute on the file states: 'We shall have spent some £20,000 on work of an ancient monuments nature on this site . . . ' In April 1962 there had been much excitement when a skull, thought to be that of the Duke of Monmouth, was dug up. It was sent for examination by the pathologist Francis Camps, but not surprisingly no definite conclusions could be drawn as to whose body it belonged.

Early in 1964 the Lord President's Office and Judicial Committee returned to their old rooms, and the Cabinet Office occupied Kent's Treasury and the central part of the old Treasury Building, now known as No 70 Whitehall.

In 1989, security gates ten-feet high were erected at the White-hall end of Downing Street, as a protective measure against terrorist attack. In February 1991 improvised mortars fired from a parked van across Whitehall fell, one in the back garden of No 10 Downing Street, and two (which did not explode) on Mountbatten Green outside the Foreign Secretary's Office. Although the blast shattered windows, the underpinning and strengthening work carried out by Raymond Erith in the 1960s prevented more serious damage.

Dover House

At the end of November 1955 the Scottish Office returned to their home in Dover House. They had occupied Dover House from the establishment of the Office in 1885 until it was narrowly missed by the bomb which hit the Treasury Building next door in October 1940. Since then, Dover House had been temporarily occupied by various tenants, including Field-Marshal Montgomery. Dover House was severely damaged in an air raid after the departure of the Scottish Office staff.

After the war Dover House was restored and overhauled. Reconstruction of floors and roofs was necessary, both because of bomb damage and because some of the 18th-century structure had become dangerous. Both the inside and outside were renovated and the 18th-century appearance restored as far as possible with redecoration in keeping with the architectural and historic character of the building. (Also in keeping is the lack of a passenger lift!) In the last few years the state rooms have been refurbished with great care, and carpets and curtains have been designed and made in appropriate style for the building. The renovation of the downstairs rooms is now complete.

The Horse Guards

Restoration of the Horse Guards started in August 1991. When the work was begun, this Grade 1 listed building was in a poor condition, largely through neglect of maintenance owing to expenditure cuts. In the 1920s, new foundations had been put in, but these had sunk at least six inches throughout the block. The building leaked and the services were in a bad state. There was damage to the stonework, which had never been cleaned and was almost black. The roof let water in, windows and stonework needed repair, and the roof required recovering.

The building is now an office block for the Army, seventy per cent occupied by Headquarters London District for the Army, and the

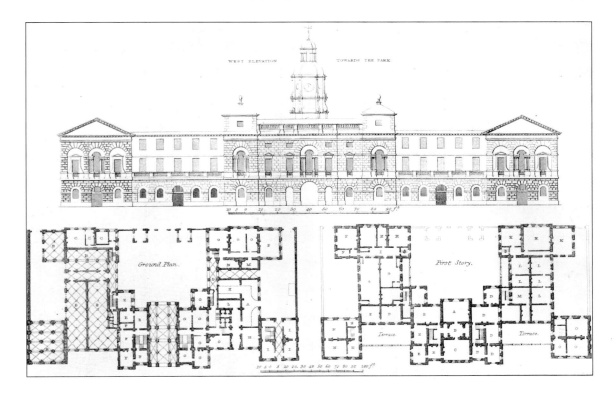

remainder by the Queen's Life Guard. At one time sixty horses had been stabled at the Horse Guards – now there are about twenty. While the re-furbishment continued, the horses were moved into temporary stables constructed on Horse Guards Parade. Foundation works for the temporary stables exposed human remains which were thought to have dated back to a time when an early rudimentary hospital occupied the site. Another theory held that the site contained a plague pit where the bodies of unfortunates were interred in mass graves as the scourge swept the capital.

The right-hand block next to the Paymaster General's Office sustained bomb damage during the Second World War and has been reconstructed. After the war an ancient and illicit cockpit was found in the basement, with a vaulted roof and timber-boarded perimeter for officers to sit and watch the fights. This still survives.

Restoration work has included stripping the roofs and finishing them in the original materials with lead, slate and asphalt. The stonework has been cleaned and balustrading repaired, and the interior has been redecorated and new services installed. Most of the changes have been to the ground floor and the operational rooms. The three bells in the tower

124 *Horse Guards. Plan taken from Pugin and Britton's* Illustrations of the Public Buildings of London, *showing the west elevation on the park side, and the ground and first floors. The ground floor was used mainly for stabling, with the upper floors used for suites of offices, and the Commander-in-Chief's room.*

were taken down for refurbishment but two were stolen from the foundry carrying out the work; their replacements may be distinguished by their much brighter sound.

Upstairs, the Duke of Wellington's bedroom when he was Commander-in-Chief has been restored to its former shape and decorated as it was in his time. The Commander-in-Chief's room was dark green before restoration, and earlier had been wood-panelled like the Board Room in the Admiralty, extending to the ceiling some 24 feet high. On the recommendation of English Heritage it has been repainted in subtle shades of stone, ivory and grey that appear to change in the sunlight, and a new carpet has been specially designed. The other main room on the first floor is now known as the Conference Room. Its chandelier has been refurbished and an original door buried in a wall has been revealed. The central octagonal hall beneath the clock tower has been repainted.

Originally the upper part of the building consisted of several suites of self-contained rooms. There are many flights of mundane stairs, but no main grand staircase. Partitions were inserted by the Victorians to form corridors and the architects wished to get back to the original elegance, but this idea was vetoed by the fire adviser. All the skirting boards, architraves and cornices have been retained as far as possible, and new radiators put in, but to traditional patterns. In June 1994, the central block was almost finished, and the main vertical services in place, with cables, ventilation, computer and electric cables all discreetly hidden behind the walls and in the basement. Target date for completion was July 1994.

125   *Gates closed in front of the Horse Guards, 1994. 'The projections of the white stone seem to take on the broken light and shadow effects of a line of chalk cliffs partly fallen away and further eroded at the base. It is lovely in any light . . .' (David Gentleman,* David Gentleman's London, *1985).*

In summer 1994, the National Heritage Department had hoped to implement a recommendation by the Royal Parks review group to ban parking on Horse Guards Parade as well as traffic on Horse Guards Road. This would have allowed tourists and pedestrians to see the parade ground without clutter and almost as it was centuries ago, as depicted in numerous paintings, notably by Canaletto, and engravings. But objections were raised on grounds of operational necessity by Cabinet Ministers and senior civil servants.

A proposal has been put to the Government for an underground car park beneath Horse Guards Parade to accommodate official vehicles, leaving the surface free for pedestrians. The private sector proposers believe that this can be done in such a way as not to intrude unduly on the character of the area and at no cost to the taxpayer. The Government has yet to respond

The Paymaster General's Office – No 36 Whitehall

No 36 Whitehall was left in a state of disrepair for many years after the bomb damage inflicted on it in October 1940. A meeting held on 5 October 1954 to discuss the programme of outstanding major war repairs postponed any work on the Office for the time being, as it was not urgent, nor easily visible from Whitehall or Horse Guards Parade. This

126 *No 36 Whitehall, old Paymaster General's Office. Its unassuming and dignified frontage to Whitehall, is considered by some to be of no architectural merit. The Portland stone elevation to Horse Guards Parade is of much more interest. It was removed from No 37 Great George Street and replaced the original brickwork façade of No 36. The interior has been almost entirely restored since a third of it was damaged in the Second World War.*

was the last major war-damaged building remaining in Whitehall. Two-thirds of the Office still stood, but the rest was so dilapidated that complete rebuilding was advised.

The Prime Minister, Harold Macmillan, occupied Admiralty House in August 1960 in preparation for the reconstruction of Downing Street. His staff and the Chief Whip's Office went to No 36 Whitehall, and the Treasury finally sanctioned repair work in November 1961. Tenders were received by December 1963, but costs rose by about one-third and once again the repairs were postponed. However, this decision was reversed in March 1964 and at last work went ahead. The interior of the existing building was gutted, except for a fine ground floor panelled room which was dismantled and then put back. The existing façade to Whitehall and the elevations to Horse Guards Parade and the Admiralty were retained.

During the early 1960s it was thought that No 36 Whitehall would be a suitable home for the Office of the Minister for Science, but his staff expanded and the building was not ready for occupation until the mid-1960s. Eventually, in September 1967, the Parliamentary Counsel and his staff moved in to the upper floors. The ground floor and basement were used by the Ministry of Defence.

Admiralty House and Old War Office

Admiralty House had been in almost constant use as an official residence for the First Lord until the Second World War. During the war the First Lord used only the upper floors, and the lower ones were taken over for departmental purposes. Once peace came, the building was restored to residential use, but at the end of 1946 it was divided into two flats, the upper one being used by the Minister for Defence, who paid rent. This arrangement lasted until the Conservatives returned to Government in 1951.

In preparation for the reconstruction and restoration work that was to be carried out on Downing Street, the Ministry of Works converted Admiralty House, No 36 Whitehall (Paymaster General's Office) and one wing of the Admiralty main building for use by the Prime Minister, his staff and the Whips' Office.

The Prime Minister moved into Admiralty House in 1960. Harold Macmillan wrote in his memoirs:

'By a miracle of organisation the operation was completed in a week and by 10 August we were duly installed in Admiralty House, a noble structure in the best style of the late eighteenth century, with magnificent reception rooms and dining-rooms and embellished throughout by fine cornices, doors and chimney-pieces.'

No 10 Downing Street was ready for occupation at the end of 1963, and Admiralty House then remained empty until 1966 when it was extensively modernised. Two flats were constructed, one for use by the First Lord and his successor, the Secretary of State for Defence. The other was occupied successively by the Commonwealth Secretary, the Chief Whip, the Chancellor of the Duchy of Lancaster, the Secretary for the Environment and the Home Secretary.

The Old War Office building operated throughout two world wars until 1964 when its functions were transferred to other Ministry of Defence buildings. However, it continued to house military personnel. The interior of the building did not change greatly and the principal rooms stayed much as they had been originally, with wooden panelling, brass electroliers and marble fireplaces.

An unfortunate lapse of taste led to the then Secretary of State's panelled room being painted over entirely in Wedgwood blue and white in the 1960s – completely out of keeping with the historic character of the room and the building. During the current refurbishment project the panelling of this room has been painstakingly stripped of paint and now glows in its former glory. Portland stone from the same quarry as was

127 *Old Admiralty Building on Horse Guards Parade, built as an extension to the Admiralty by Leeming & Leeming in 1894–5. It used to be possible to walk along the roofs from one building to the next, which allowed flagmen to raise and lower the flags on each roof-top. The routing was graphically shown in the BBC TV play by Michael Frayn:* A Landing on the Sun, *screened on 8 June 1994.*

originally used was employed for the restoration work, and the final repairs to the war-damaged stone have at last been carried out. The question of refurbishment of the Old War Office had first been mooted in 1977, but it then grew into a major scheme of restoration. Work began in 1987 and involved a complete design exercise.

On 10 January 1992, a terrorist bomb exploded in Whitehall Place directly opposite the Ministry of Agriculture, Fisheries and Food's East Block, shattering window frames and glass in that building and inflicting even worse damage to the Old War Office opposite. However, restoration work was subsequently quickly completed and staff are once more working in the Old War Office.

Banqueting House

The Banqueting House remained in use as the Royal United Service Institution's museum until 1964 when the Institute moved out, taking its exhibits with it. Several improvements were made thereafter. The windows were double-glazed to muffle the noise of traffic in Whitehall, the gallery erected by Aston Webb in 1890 across the south wall was removed and the south window restored. The walls were repainted in what was believed to be the original stone colour, the gold leaf ornamentation cleaned, and the floor was replaced with an oak strip

128 *Howard Penton's drawing shows the Banqueting House on the left, refuges and carriages in the road, and on the right the Horse Guards and Dover House, 1901.*

surface. A contemporary Press Notice mentions that excavation revealed under the floor of the crypt foundations of Tudor and Jacobean buildings on the site, and a range of early Tudor buildings backing onto Whitehall.

Rubens' ceiling-paintings were rearranged in 1972 in an order, described by John Charlton in his *Guide* to the building, that was thought to be the original pattern. The King on his throne looking towards the entrance would have seen first, and the right way up to him, the painting representing 'The union of England and Scotland', depicting Hercules (Strength) and Minerva (Wisdom). A visitor looking towards the throne from the entrance would see first, and the right way up to him or her, 'The apotheosis of James I', and then, above the throne the blessings of the King's reign, with figures symbolising royal bounty and wise government.

In 1988, the Banqueting House held an exhibition to commemorate the tercentenary of the 'Glorious Revolution' of 1688–9, when James II was overthrown and the Crown was offered to William and Mary, Prince and Princess of Orange, in the last great ceremony to be held in Inigo Jones's elegant building. The exhibition, said the organisers, depicted the moment when the balance of power finally shifted from the Crown to Parliament.

The Banqueting House closed early in 1989 for interior restoration following cleaning of the front and rear elevations, and has undergone a £150,000 refurbishment. It is now open to the public, with an absorbing exhibition on Whitehall's chequered history.

The Whitehall Gardens building

The history of the Whitehall Gardens building extends over nearly four decades from the moment when the competition to find a designer was held in 1913, to its occupation by the first staff in 1951. Mr E. Vincent Harris was chosen as architect for what was to be the new Board of Trade offices in 1915, but the First World War put paid to any large-scale building projects. However, the scheme was revived in 1934 and a number of 18th-century houses in Whitehall Gardens were pulled down to clear the site.

The outbreak of the Second World War led to deferment of the project again, but after the war work started in earnest. It was still under the supervision of Vincent Harris, but on a site extended to nearly twice

129 *View of the Ministry of Defence main building. At the Richmond Terrace entrance can be seen the air force crests substituted for the two sculptures 'Air' and 'Fire', originally proposed but never created, to complement 'Earth' and 'Water' at the other end.*

the original length, till it lined up with the Horse Guards to Downing Street on the opposite side of the road. The frontage to the embankment had to continue the line of Whitehall Court as laid down in the Public Offices (Sites) Act of 1912.

The first half of the building was completed in 1951 and occupied by the Board of Trade and the Air Ministry. Since February 1939 the Air Council had met in rooms in King Charles Street, Whitehall. Now they had a new home. The section of the building nearest to Richmond Terrace was completed and occupied at the beginning of 1959 by the Air Staff and the Department of the Air Member for Supply and Organisation.

Sir Nikolaus Pevsner thought that the building was 'a strangely undecided design'. But not all critics agreed with him. A writer in *Building* praised its 'masterly simplicity' and 'organic unity' and said that 'the beauty that the building exhales is the beauty of high intelligence and pure proportion'. High praise indeed! The building, a single block with three large internal courts and an additional upper storey set back ten feet, is faced with Portland stone. Preserved within it are the salon from Pembroke House, designed by Sir William Chambers, and a room said to be by William Kent, from Cadogan House, as well as the Tudor wine cellar.

However, this new building was not the ideal modern office. The Board of Trade had problems with rats during its sojourn at the Horse Guards Avenue part of the building. Matters came to a head when they ran along the pelmets during a meeting of the President of the Board of Trade and his staff and one fell off. History does not relate what the President said.

In those days, the Board of Trade door-keeper had a special livery of tailcoat and top hat, and his opposite number at the War Office had a similar outfit. Many government buildings had coal fires to heat them; these were lit by the women cleaners, and a civil service grade of coal porter was employed to distribute the daily allowance of firewood (cut and tied in bundles in HM Prisons).

Tunnels far below Whitehall carry communication services from ministry to ministry and Whitehall's central heating system is run from the Whitehall Gardens building, now the Ministry of Defence main building. The deep tunnels extend to various parts of London and there are citadels at Marsham Street, Parliament Square and the Horse Guards. Several books and articles have been written about these tunnels, the fear

130 *Tudor wine cellar. When the new Whitehall Gardens building (now part of the Ministry of Defence) was being built, the wine cellar was found to protrude at ground level from the Horse Guards Avenue façade of the new block. After much discussion on how to preserve the cellar without spoiling the look of the new building, the room was moved laterally on staging, lowered by 19 feet, and rolled back to its present position beneath its original site. This feat of engineering was completed in 1950.*

of nuclear attack after the Second World War, and other reasons for their being built and maintained in good repair.

The Tudor wine cellar

Among the historic rooms preserved within the new building was Cardinal Wolsey's wine cellar, but when Vincent Harris's new building was rising, he found that the cellar protruded at ground level from the Horse Guards Avenue façade of the new block, marring the main entrance front of the building. It projected over the building line by 27' × 32' and was 15' high, looking somewhat like a forgotten air raid shelter. The architect suggested removing it or sinking it below ground level, but the Chief Inspector of Ancient Monuments disagreed, saying that 'we consider the destruction of the cellar to be an unthinkable procedure, and use the word destruction advisedly to include transference to another site'.

There was much debate as to whether the cellar should remain where it was or be moved. It was eventually decided that it could not stay where it was as it seriously interfered with the appearance and layout of the new offices. Nevertheless, a public promise had been made that it should be preserved. In September 1947 the Treasury agreed that the cellar should be lowered at a cost of £32,000. This was a mammoth undertaking as the room's weight was estimated at nearly 1,000 tons and it measured approximately 62' × 32' × 20' high. The cellar was moved 43' 6" laterally on staging and then lowered by screwjacks through 18' 9" and rolled back 33' 10" to its present position more or less beneath its original site. The work was completed in 1950. The wine cellar now stands, perfectly preserved, a peaceful oasis within the drab surrounding offices and corridors.

In the 1960s the wine cellar was frequently used as a novel venue for official parties and receptions, and was open to the public on Saturday afternoons. But when the Ministry of Defence moved in to the building in 1964, they wanted to stop public admission on security grounds, much against the will of the Ministry of Works, in view of the amount of public money spent on preserving the monument. Eventually limited access was agreed upon and security arrangements completed early in 1965. In recent years the wine cellar has not been generally open to the public.

131 *Sculptures representing Earth and Water, by Charles Wheeler, at the Horse Guards Avenue entrance to the Ministry of Defence. 'To the left lay a modern structure of brutal simplicity, to the right a jovial pile of Victorian Gothic . . . The entrance to the new building, as if to soften the ferocity of its design, took the form of a classical portico over which sprawled an enormous stone woman' (Jeremy Fisher: Lambe's Tale, 1969).*

Sculpture in Whitehall Gardens

A competition was held in 1948 to find a sculptor to design and create two sculptured groups of Portland stone to stand on 40-foot pylons flanking the main entrance in Horse Guards Avenue to the Whitehall Gardens building. Henry Moore was among those invited to apply, but he pleaded pressure of work. In 1949 Charles Wheeler was chosen to produce groups representing Earth and Water for a fee of £12,600. The sculptures were in place and on view in August 1952 and the work was finished in spring 1953. The figures are each approximately 13' 6" high and 8' 6" wide. The question of the other two groups, Air and Fire, for the Richmond Terrace entrance was left open at the time but in April 1954, Wheeler was finally told that he was not to proceed with them. Instead RAF crests were used for the other entrance, and were placed on the top of the piers at a more modest cost of £1,250.

In late 1991 a review was carried out by consultants of the style and layout of the Raleigh Green in front of the Ministry of Defence main building. Suggestions for its improvement included the installation of a paved walkway in front of the military statues, encouraging people to walk there, or that the green should be re-landscaped, with a bronze

132 *Royal Air Force crest on the Ministry of Defence building, Richmond Terrace entrance.*

133 *Richmond House, the third to bear that name, built of yellow brick and Portland stone to designs by William Whitfield, and completed in 1987. Behind the façade of Richmond Terrace all has been gutted and restored, while the new portion of the building rises six storeys with a concourse in front of York and Purbeck stone. Called by Gavin Stamp a 'brilliant and joyful new building'.*

fence and entry gate, and plaques giving the history of each statue. The final outcome is eminently practical and has brought all the military statues, each standing on its own plinth, towards the front of the green. Sir Walter Raleigh's statue, because of its more delicate style and smaller scale, appears somewhat diffidently among them.

A statue of Field-Marshal Alanbrooke, by Ivor Roberts-Jones, who also sculpted that of Slim, was unveiled by the Queen in May 1993 and stands between those of Field-Marshals Montgomery and Slim.

Richmond House and Richmond Terrace

Remedial work on restoration of the Richmond Terrace Georgian façade started in October 1983, followed by major building work. The houses of Richmond Terrace and the buildings along Whitehall were refurbished, although Richmond Terrace had to be gutted behind the façade.

The whole development was completed in December 1987. Richmond House is a six-storey building with the front rooms of the first three floors rebuilt in similar style to the original, and an external cobbled road paved in York and Purbeck stone. The architect was William Whitfield. Gavin Stamp wrote about the new building in 1987:

'Where there was once the arched entrance to the mews of Richmond Terrace opposite the Cenotaph, a courtyard has appeared which is terminated by an extraordinary eruption of Tudor Gothic. It is as if a fragment of an ancient palace that had survived in this complex and much rebuilt part of Westminster had been suddenly exposed, except that the suave detailing and the mixture of yellow brick and Portland stone declare it to be entirely new. It is the entrance to Richmond House.'

Richmond House was at first allocated to the Overseas Development Agency, which carried out extensive room planning and announced a moving date to their staff in Eland House. However, in spite of the convenience of having the diplomatic and aid wings of the Foreign Office facing each other across Whitehall, it was not to be. The decision was subsequently reversed at a very high level, and the

Department of Health and Social Security was installed in Richmond House instead.

Whitehall redevelopment: the Bridge Street/Richmond Terrace site

There were repeated proposals to improve the routing of roads in the vicinity. For example, in 1949 the Ministry of Transport wrote to the Ministry of Works about the possibility of laying an 80-foot wide road on the line of Richmond Terrace, for use by through traffic in conjunction with a one-way traffic scheme for Bridge Street. Fortunately, the Ministry of Works did not agree.

In 1952 the need for a private road was again raised. This was to run behind the Banqueting House and it was also suggested that another road should go between Whitehall and the Embankment; although private, the road would be maintained, lit and cleansed by Westminster City Council. As with so many Whitehall proposals, bureaucratic delay has been a powerful weapon for good, and this proposal was abandoned in 1957 so the road remained the property of the Ministry of Works, with

134 *Picture taken from the Clock Tower (Big Ben) in about 1900, showing the corner of Parliament Street, now the site of the Parliament Street Building. The Old Public Offices, housing the Colonial, Foreign, Home and India Offices can also be seen, but at this date the Government Offices, Great George Street, had not yet been built.*

135 *Duke of Cambridge. Commander-in-Chief of the British Army, 1856–95. Equestrian bronze by Adrian Jones, 1907. Stands outside the War Office.*

posts and chains at either end, and parking allowed on both sides. The Embankment end was closed to traffic and sometimes to pedestrians, with an Air Ministry attendant controlling the Whitehall end of the road.

The pressure for more space for MPs' offices began in the 1950s. The Bridge Street site on the approach to Westminster Bridge, and encompassing Westminster Underground station, was designated for this purpose and those buildings on the site not already in Government ownership were gradually acquired. In 1959 the Government decided to proceed with major redevelopment of the whole site to give more accommodation for MPs and for permanent Government offices.

The importance of the site demanded a unified scheme and under the original proposals Richmond Terrace was to be demolished, as were Nos 43, 44, 47, 53 and 54 Parliament Street. Sir William Holford was asked to prepare a preliminary report in 1962 and proposed a shopping centre with offices above. In 1964 the Metropolitan Police were given permission to move their headquarters from their celebrated Scotland Yard building to new tower block premises in Victoria Street. The old Police buildings were sold to the Ministry of Public Building and Works in 1967 for £5.75 million when the move took place.

In 1964 Sir Leslie Martin was appointed overall consultant for the Whitehall redevelopment to ensure that the various proposals under consideration were related to each other. He paid attention to the general architectural character of the area, taking relative traffic considerations into account. His report, together with a paper on traffic by Colin Buchanan, was published in 1965. Charles Pannell, then Minister of Public Building and Works, accepted the main conclusions as a broad framework within which future development should take place.

The Martin report made three basic assumptions: firstly, Whitehall was by tradition and in the scope that it offered, the best area in which to house the headquarters staff that must be concentrated at the centre; secondly, buildings on Crown land should contribute as much as possible to a reduction of the amount of leased property; finally, as many headquarters departments as possible should be housed in the fewest groups of buildings, from the point of view of general efficiency in use of space, and for communications and servicing.

The Martin report recommendations for Whitehall included the rebuilding as a comprehensive layout of the Bridge Street site, the Great George Street site and the Foreign Office site for Government office purposes. This, if carried out, would have meant the demolition of the

Foreign Office and the Treasury! Martin also recommended that Government building on the sites at the Trafalgar Square end of Whitehall, including the old War Office site, should not proceed until a comprehensive study was made of the needs of the Trafalgar Square district in relation to Whitehall and other adjoining areas.

The Ministry announced in November 1965 that the architect for the Parliamentary building would be chosen via a Commonwealth architectural competition and that Ministry staff would design the Government offices. A Whitehall Redevelopment Policy Committee was set up and the Ministry also established a group of architects and designers, known as the Whitehall Development Group, to plan the new Government office building on the Bridge Street/Richmond Terrace site. The Group stated the requirements for the development of the site in a formal brief in August 1967. By January 1969 the Ministry of Public Building and Works had spent £2.7 million on acquisition of property by agreement and was negotiating for interests valued at just over a further half a million.

Among questions discussed by the various interested parties was whether to preserve or demolish the Norman Shaw (North) building. (This building, the former home of the Metropolitan Police, is commonly referred to as 'Norman Shaw' by civil servants, rather than as 'Scotland Yard'.) The Royal Fine Art Commission was in favour of retaining it, calling it a 'building of considerable architectural and historical interest'. The Commission also felt that the new river frontage between Vincent Harris's Whitehall Gardens block and Westminster Bridge should 'retain something of its existing varied and broken character'. Deserving of special mention was Norman Shaw (North)'s 'romantic silhouette'. Nevertheless, in July 1968, and reiterated that December, the Government announced its decision to demolish the building and Richmond Terrace.

The 'final' scheme was prepared by the Development Group and approved by the Royal Fine Art Commission in October 1969. The plans were exhibited in the House of Commons in December 1969 and later put on public view in the Banqueting House. The design showed a building extending 400 feet along Whitehall and 350 feet along Richmond Terrace, with a height of 75 feet, two basement floors, a ground floor and five floors of offices. The proposals met with a great deal of opposition, the majority of the letters urging the preservation of both Richmond Terrace and Norman Shaw (North). During this period, No 47

Parliament Street was in use as the Welsh Office and later for the Supplementary Benefit Appeal Tribunal.

From the vantage point of the mid-1990s, it is difficult to recapture the climate of thirty years earlier, before council and government tower blocks had been revealed as a mistake both in concept and construction. The revival of widespread appreciation of our architectural heritage was only just beginning, and the architects and planners of the 1960s made draconian proposals that, if implemented, would have significantly damaged the nation's image of government. We know from the history of the then contemporary Marsham Street Buildings for the Department of the Environment, due for demolition in the 1990s, what the fate of Whitehall property would have been. Disaster was only narrowly averted.

In 1970 the Government held a public inquiry to hear and report upon objections to the redevelopment proposals for the Richmond Terrace/New Scotland Yard site, with particular reference to the proposed demolition of Richmond Terrace and Norman Shaw (North).

The public inquiry 'is now unfolding, like a Greek tragedy in Church House, Westminster'. So stated *The Architect's Journal* in July 1970. Fourteen listed buildings were involved, including Norman Shaw North (Grade I) and Richmond Terrace and the Whitehall Club (Grade II). 'It is clear that as far as MPBW [Ministry of Public Building and Works] is concerned, the site is to be clear felled: Mr William Bryant, as architect to the Ministry said frankly that to maintain listed buildings would "ruin the site" from the point of view of what is to occupy it'. The Inspector, Harold Willis QC, presented his report to Peter Walker, then Secretary of State for the Environment later that year. He concluded that the Bridge Street/Richmond Terrace site did not necessarily have to be entirely cleared and that a satisfactory scheme could be provided that retained the Norman Shaw (North) building and the façades of Richmond Terrace, the latter being incorporated into a new building. The Martin scheme, he said, should not be accepted.

The winners of the Bridge Street site competition in 1972 were Robin Spence and Robin Webster. Their design for a rectangular, free-standing bronze-coloured block surrounding a central public piazza was approved early in 1973. The architects continued to work on their scheme, but opposition to it began to mount and it was abandoned in 1975 because of the high costs involved. Richmond Terrace developed structural faults in the 1970s and was declared unfit for occupation, but the listed façades were preserved to await restoration and rebuilding.

In 1972, the Select Committee on the House of Commons (Services) had agreed that the Commons should use the Norman Shaw (North) building. By October 1973 the Committee was making arrangements to adapt the main building to provide rooms for MPs and their secretaries. During the following two to three years the main building was thoroughly refurbished, its exterior cleaned and the interior remodelled to provide a new Vote Office, Library, TV studio and rooms for the Public Information Office, MPs and secretaries. The original features were retained wherever possible, the bridges leading to the Curtis Green Building and Norman Shaw (South) were closed, and the private entrance to Westminster Underground station was abolished.

Work began on conversion of Norman Shaw (South), part of the old police premises, in 1976 and it was ready for occupation by 1979. This was a much less elaborate refurbishment and the exterior was not cleaned, but the bridge linking the two buildings was reopened. Cannon Row Police Station remained in use by the Metropolitan Police until May 1985 when the police moved into the Curtis Green Building, which had been converted for their use. In late 1985 the Services Committee recommended that the old police station should also be adapted for Parliamentary use.

A further feasibility study was carried out by the architect William Whitfield on the possibility of retaining Richmond Terrace with new office accommodation behind the façades. Another plan was produced by Sir Hugh Casson and the Casson Conder Partnership in 1978. This was an infill scheme that could be undertaken in stages if necessary, incorporating some of the existing façades in Parliament Street.

The report by Casson Conder underlined the most significant considerations:

'Those buildings facing on to Parliament Street in particular have witnessed Cenotaph services and Coronation processions, victory parades and Jarrow marches. They have formed the background to great occasions of state pageantry and national history for many years and have therefore achieved a significance exceeding their intrinsic architectural value. It is our view that wherever possible these should be retained . . . The human scale and texture of Parliament Street must be respected and any new work must relate happily to those buildings which – temporarily or indefinitely – it is suggested should be retained'

These sentiments echo those aired in the House of Commons debate of 28 July 1978 on the Bridge Street redevelopment:

' . . . all good architecture should have the quality of good manners. When a new building is to intrude in an area such as Parliament Square, it should do so with some decency and delicacy.'

The new building was designed to work to the current street lines and to support the linear nature of Whitehall and the Embankment. All listed buildings on the site were to be retained, either wholly or in part, particularly the façades of certain houses in Parliament Street and the northern end of Cannon Row Police Station. The cost at 1979 prices was estimated at over £100 million and in December 1979 the Government decided not to authorise so ambitious a scheme.

Still more new proposals in 1982 were for redevelopment in two phases. The first was to conserve and adapt the property between Cannon Row and Parliament Street at a cost of £15m spread over four years, to provide accommodation for 100 MPs. The corner building on Parliament Street, which had been modernised in the 1930s, was to be retained and restored, its top two storeys removed and a small dome which had been a feature of the building replaced. The second phase was possible development of the area between Cannon Row and the Embankment for a mix of parliamentary and commercial uses.

The Parliament Street area had suffered from planning blight for many years, as the above history shows. The task that faced the planners, even of phase one, was daunting. The corner building facing Parliament Square needed restoration, the Whitehall Club at the other end of the block had dry rot and a leaking roof, and many of the old Parliament Street houses had been used as tourist shops. Phase one of the development, carried out by Ramsay Tugwell Associates, conserved and adapted the property between Parliament Street and Cannon Row.

Work began on the first phase in 1985. By 1991, five floors of offices and ancillary accommodation had been built. The rooms facing Parliament Street and Bridge Street were recreated, the cupola on the corner site was carefully reconstructed and the exterior of the building restored. The rear half of the building was rebuilt and a terrace overlooking Cannon Row formed. The centre section, which was once Nos 43–44 Parliament Street, a pair of fine Georgian houses, was also restored and the foundations underpinned. Plasterwork and joinery and the Chippendale style chinoiserie staircase in No 43 were reconstructed. These town houses are now used as residences by the Serjeant and Deputy Serjeant at Arms and other officers of the House.

The north section containing the old Whitehall Club (No 47 Parliament Street), later the offices of the Pearson company, together with Nos 45–46 Parliament Street, which date from 1870 and were also used as offices, has also undergone reconstruction and preservation. The smoking room of the Whitehall Club, with its tiled walls, is now the Research Library and the whole northern section given over to the House of Commons Department of the Library. 'In the process,' said David Ramsay, partner in the Casson Conder Partnership, 'some unique historical features will have been preserved for posterity which otherwise would have been lost for ever.'

Phase one of the £38 million Bridge Street redevelopment was completed early in 1991, and opened by the Prince of Wales in November 1991. Sixty-six MPs are now housed in this marble and panelled building. The design for phase two, encompassing the area between the Victoria Embankment and Cannon Row, has been undertaken by the architect Michael Hopkins (architect of the new Glyndebourne Opera House and responsible for the conversion of the former Financial Times building). Plans for this site, 'perhaps one of the most sensitive in the country', were put before the House for approval in early 1992. These involved a six-storey building of sandstone with a bronze roof, a glazed central courtyard, a colonnade with an entrance facing the river, and shops and cafes. Both English Heritage and the Royal Fine Art Commission were consulted on the design.

The architect's scheme, said the House of Commons Accommodation and Works Committee in February 1992, would lead to the establishment of a 'comprehensive Parliamentary campus' within a secure perimeter from Victoria Tower in the south to Richmond Terrace in the north, and from the river and Victoria Embankment in the east to Parliament Street in the west. The building's shape, height, massing and silhouette are determined by two major factors – its position in the setting of nearby listed buildings, and its founding on the substructure of the underground box excavated for the Jubilee Line extension.

The new building was planned to follow the existing building

136 *By Autumn 1994 piles of rubble and a pall of brick dust over Bridge Street heralded the final phase of the redevelopment of historic Whitehall. As rebuilding commences, backs of old buildings are briefly revealed to remind us of past building history.*

lines in Bridge Street and Cannon Row, and the main façade of the Norman Shaw buildings. Its height is intended to follow the cornice line of those buildings and will set back above that level. The skyline will be slightly lower and relieved by chimneys and towers.

The start of construction was deferred for nearly two years because of delays in authorising the Jubilee Line Extension, but finally began in Autumn 1993. Everything between Cannon Row and the Embankment east and west is being cleared, including the railway buildings. The Police Station building will remain as No 1 Cannon Row. In spring 1994 the remains of Palace Chambers and – the only significant flaw in the plan – the Grade II listed St Stephen's Club were demolished, to be followed by St Stephen's House. A huge concrete raft was then installed over Westminster Station, on which the new building will be founded.

The title of all buildings forming part of the Parliamentary Estate was transferred to the two Houses of Parliament by the Parliamentary Corporate Bodies Act 1992 and associated subordinate legislation.

Epilogue

The extensive restoration and cleaning work carried out in Whitehall, and with possible future work on the Government Offices, Great George Street, has generated a programme to refurbish Whitehall for the millennium and beyond. Work is well under way or completed at the Banqueting House, Dover House, Gwydyr House, the bridge over King Charles Street, and Clive Steps. Firm guidelines are now being drawn up to ensure the preservation of this unique architectural tapestry for appreciation by future generations.

Already, with the major renovation of the Foreign and Commonwealth Office, of Bridge Street, Richmond Terrace, the Horse Guards, and the old War Office, Whitehall has arrived at an interesting and satisfying mix of style and scale. 'The Street' is an architectural patchwork, reflecting the history of different ages, and the overall effect, apparently more by luck than judgement, mirrors a view of the British character that hitherto eluded earlier planners. Grand in effect, yet maintaining a fundamentally human scale, Whitehall is testimony to nearly five hundred years of history and power. All who come to walk this most historic of thoroughfares can now appreciate, mirrored in the architecture, Whitehall's influence through the ages.

Statues

An Act of 1854 [The Public Statues (Metropolis) Act, 17 & 18 Vic, c 33 1854] placed certain statues within the Metropolitan Police District (including those of King Charles I and King James II) in the charge of the Office of Works. It also allowed owners of other statues in the Metropolitan Police district to transfer them to the Office, with the agreement of the Treasury. The Office of Works was permitted to erect and enclose statues in any public place in the district, and to repair them at public expense.

137 *Field-Marshall Viscount Alanbrooke*

Field-Marshal Viscount Alanbrooke (1883–1963). Statue by Ivor Roberts-Jones, 1993, stands on the green in front of the Ministry of Defence building, between the statues of Field-Marshals Montgomery and Slim. Plinth is inscribed: 'Master of Strategy'.

Duke of Cambridge (1819–1904). Commander-in-Chief of the British Army 1856–95. Equestrian bronze by Adrian Jones, 1907. Stands outside the War Office.

Charles I (1600–1649). Equestrian bronze by Hubert Le Sueur, 1633, pedestal designed by Christopher Wren. Stands looking down Whitehall towards Westminster.

Lord Clive (1725–1774). 'Clive of India'. Bronze standing figure by John Tweed, 1912. Erected first in the garden of Gwydyr House and in 1916 placed at the top of the steps leading from King Charles Street to St James's Park.

Captain Cook (1728–1779). On the south side of The Mall, near the Old Admiralty Building. Bronze figure in naval uniform, by Sir Thomas Brock, 1914.

Spencer Compton, 8th Duke of Devonshire (1833–1908). [Lord Hartington]

138 *Lord Clive*

Standing bronze, in peer's robes by Herbert Hampton, 1910. Horse Guards Avenue.

Earl Haig (1861–1928). Commander-in-Chief of the British Armies in France 1915–1918. Equestrian bronze by Alfred Hardiman, signed by the sculptor in 1936. Erected by Parliament in 1937 in Whitehall, looking towards Westminster.

James II (1633–1701). Bronze standing figure in Roman dress by Grinling Gibbons, 1686. Outside the National Gallery.

Field-Marshal Earl Kitchener (1850–1916). Standing bronze in uniform, but bareheaded, set against a stone screen on Horse Guards Parade and backing on to 10 Downing Street, by John Tweed, 1926.

Field-Marshal Viscount Montgomery of Alamein (1887–1976). Bronze in battledress and beret by Oscar Nemon, 1980. Stands on the grass in front of the Ministry of Defence, facing Downing Street.

Earl Mountbatten (1900–1979). Bronze standing figure by Franta Belsky, 1983, outside the Foreign and Commonwealth Office on Foreign Office Green.

Sir Walter Raleigh (1552–1618). Bronze figure in Elizabethan dress, by William Macmillan, 1959. Stands on the grass in front of the Ministry of Defence.

Field-Marshal Earl Roberts (1832–1914). Equestrian bronze in battledress, by Harry Bates. Erected by Parliament on Horse Guards Parade 1924.

Field-Marshal Viscount Slim (1891–1970). Sculpture by Ivor Roberts-Jones, unveiled in April 1990 on the green in front of the Ministry of Defence building. Put up by the Burma Star Association.

Field-Marshal Viscount Wolseley (1833–1913). Equestrian bronze by Sir William Goscombe John, cast from captured guns. Unveiled 1920. Horse Guards Parade. Viscount Wolseley was the 'modern Major-General' parodied by Gilbert and Sullivan in *The Pirates of Penzance*.

139 *Sir Walter Raleigh*

140 *Field-Marshall Viscount Montgomery of Alamein*

Chronology

1223 Property north of Westminster purchased from the Abbey by Hubert de Burgh, justiciar of England.

1230 Hubert de Burgh transferred property to trustees.

1240–1 Trustees sold property to Walter de Grey, Archbishop of York.

1245 Property given to the See of York and became the official London home of the Archbishops of York, known as York Place.

1509 King Henry VIII acceded to throne.

1514 Wolsey became Archbishop of York and took up residence at York Place.

1529 Wolsey disgraced and left York Place in October. King Henry VIII immediately took possession.

1530–1 Cockpit built.

1531–2 Whitehall Gate built.

1532 Holborn and King Street Gates erected.

1547 Henry VIII died, and his son Edward VI acceded to throne.

1553 Queen Mary I acceded to throne.

1558 Queen Elizabeth I acceded to throne.

1559 Queen Elizabeth builds first Banqueting House.

1572 Second Banqueting House built.

1581–2 Third Banqueting House built.

≈

1603 Death of Queen Elizabeth and accession of James I.

1604–5 Small Close Tennis Court adapted for use by King's daughter, Princess Elizabeth.

1606 Third Banqueting House pulled down and a new one begun and completed in 1609.

1611 Inigo Jones appointed Surveyor to the Prince of Wales.

1615 Inigo Jones appointed Surveyor of the King's Works.

1619 Banqueting House burnt down and Inigo Jones asked to build a new one.

1622 Inigo Jones's Banqueting House completed. First masque staged there on Twelfth Night.

1625 Charles I acceded to throne.

1628 Commons put forward a Petition of Rights. Buckingham, the King's favourite, assassinated.

1629 Parliament adjourned and the King ruled without a Parliament.

1630s Inigo Jones and John Webb produced a series of designs for a new Whitehall Palace.

1633 Laud created Archbishop of Canterbury.

1637 Masquing house or hall built in the Preaching Place.

1639 King Charles I went north to fight against the Scots.

1640 Short Parliament called together in April and later dissolved. Long Parliament opened in November.

1641 Strafford executed and Archbishop Laud impeached. Parliament passed the Great Remonstrance.

1646 Charles I surrendered to Cromwell's army.

1649 Charles I put on trial 19 January, sentenced to death 27 January and executed 30 January. Royal art collection and palace furnishings dispersed or sold by Parliament over the next few years.

1652 Inigo Jones died.

1653 Cromwell declared Lord Protector of the Commonwealth.

1654 Cromwell and his family moved to Whitehall Palace.

1657 Assassination and arson attempt by Miles Sindercombe.

1658 Cromwell died at Whitehall Palace.

1660 Prince's Lodgings assigned to General Monck. Long Parliament sat for the last time and a newly appointed Parliament called for the monarchy to be reinstated. 20 May, King Charles II received in the Banqueting House by both houses of Parliament.

1662–3 King Charles II's Tennis Court built on the Brake and the Great Close Tennis Court converted into lodgings for the King's son, the Duke of Monmouth.

1663–4 Quarters built for the King's Horse and Foot Guards in what had been the Tilt Yard.

1666 Fire nearly burnt down the new Horse and Foot Guards' building.

1668 First Richmond House built.

1669 Christopher Wren appointed Surveyor of the King's Works.

1672 Upper storey of the Holbein Gate used as the State Paper Office.

1675 Cockpit pulled down.

1676 Lord Treasurer Danby's house built on the site of the Cockpit. Statue of King Charles I erected in its present position.

1677 House built for the Earl and Countess of Lichfield on the site of what was later No 10 Downing Street.

1682 Five large houses built by Sir George Downing in what became Downing Street.

1684 Part of Cockpit Lodgings bought for the King's niece, Princess Anne.

1685 Charles II died, to be succeeded by his brother James II. During James II's four-year reign three new blocks designed by Wren were erected in Whitehall Palace, including state apartments and a chapel.

1686 Statue of James II erected in Pebble Court.

1688 Gun platform next to the Banqueting House rebuilt. James II abdicated in December.

1689 Crown offered to the Prince and Princess of Orange in the Banqueting House in February, and accepted. King William III and Queen Mary II accede to throne.

1691 A fire burnt down all the buildings over the Stone Gallery at Whitehall Palace. A terrace garden for Queen Mary was begun and the Privy Stairs abolished.

1694 Queen Mary died in December. Purpose-built Admiralty built by John Evans.

1695 In February, Queen Mary's body lay in state at the Banqueting House, and the funeral was on 5 March.

1698 On 4 January fire destroyed nearly all Whitehall Palace except for the Banqueting House, the south side of the Volary Buildings and the south end of the remains of the Stone Gallery. The Banqueting House was fitted up as the new Chapel Royal and the first service was held on Christmas Day. The Treasury was established in a building on the site of the Cockpit.

1702 Queen Anne accedes to throne.

1710 The lease for a second Richmond House was bought.

1714 King George I accedes to throne.

1717 First Pembroke House, designed by Colen Campbell, built.

1718 Christopher Wren forced to leave his post of Surveyor of the King's Works.

1722 Lease for Cadogan House granted to Sir George Byng.

1723 King Street Gate demolished and the wall of the Privy Garden set back to the Banqueting House frontage. The gun platform next to the Banqueting House was removed and the arch of the Holbein Gate opened up. Old Admiralty building demolished.

1725–6 Admiralty building designed by Thomas Ripley built. Malmesbury House built.

1727 King George II accedes to throne.

1728 Internal restoration work was carried out at the Banqueting House by William Kent.

1733 The house and office of the Paymaster of the Forces was pulled down and rebuilt by John Lane. Plans submitted for a proposed new Treasury Building by William Kent. First Montagu House built.

1735 Sir Robert Walpole moved into No 10 Downing Street as its first occupant. William Kent was responsible for extensive repair work.

1736 Kent's Treasury completed.

1738 The building of Westminster Bridge was begun.

1750 Westminster Bridge opened. Old Horse Guards building demolished.

1752 Great Britain adopts new-style dating. The Julian calendar, with the New Year held on 25 March, was in official use until 1752 in Britain, when the Gregorian calendar, with its New Year on 1 January, became compulsory. Both calendars had been in common use in the Stuart era.

1752–3 James Mallors authorised to open a street from the west side of King Street to the west side of Delahay Street (Great George Street).

1753 Horse Guards central building and north wing completed to designs by William Kent, supervised by John Vardy.

1754 The house now known as Dover House was sold to Sir Matthew Featherstonehaugh MP.

1756 Pembroke House taken down and rebuilt to the designs of Sir William Chambers. Parliament Street laid out and King Street became a backwater. State Paper Office was moved from rooms in Holbein Gate.

1757 Great George Street first appears in the rate books.

1758 The street leading from Charing Cross to Whitehall widened. Sir Matthew Featherstonehaugh's house was rebuilt by James Paine.

1759 Holbein Gate demolished. Horse Guards completed.

1760 King George III accedes to throne. Adam's stone screen was erected in front of the Admiralty.

1764 Second Earl of Fife leased a site which became Fife House.

1765 Gower House built by Sir William Chambers. Whitehall Gate demolished.

1769 Fife House enlarged.

1772 Gwydyr House built by John Marquand.

1774 The State Paper Office moved to Montagu Lodgings.

1782 The Home Office was established and took over the Board of Trade's offices when the Board of Trade was abolished.

1786 Board of Trade reconstituted. Foreign Office moved to Cockpit site. Admiralty House was built by Samuel Pepys Cockerell.

1787 'York House' was assigned to the Duke of York and Albany, who had major alterations carried out by Henry Holland.

1788 State papers stored in a building between Middle and Little Scotland Yard.

1791 Richmond House burnt down and not rebuilt.

1792 Duke of York and Albany exchanged York House for Lord Melbourne's house. York House then known as Melbourne House.

1793 Foreign Office moved to Downing Street.

1796 Land Revenue Office built opposite the Admiralty on the site of the old Office of Works building. Semaphore apparatus installed on the Admiralty roof.

1798 Colonial Office moved to No 14 Downing Street.

～

1806 Part of south side of Great George Street demolished.

1807 Lord Carrington bought Gower House, which was then renamed Carrington House.

1808 Lease of Dorset House reverted to Crown and thereafter occupied by the Home Department and the Indian Board of Control.

1810 Indian Board of Control moved out and Privy Council moved in.

1817 Maintenance of Horse Guards handed over to Office of Works.

1819 State papers dispersed, some to a house in Great George Street, formerly the Agent-General's, others to Middle Treasury Gallery.

1820 King George IV accedes to throne. Almonry Office moved to an old house north of Liverpool (formerly Fife) House.

1821 Street gas lighting introduced into Whitehall and Charing Cross.

1824 Soane's new State Paper Office completed on the site of Lady Suffolk's house on the corner of Duke and Delahay Streets. All Crown leases in Downing Street east of No 10 terminated.

1825 Soane's plans for Board of Trade and Privy Council building approved. Some houses in Downing Street pulled down to allow for Soane's new Privy Council and Board of Trade offices.

1827 Work on Soane's building stopped when Whitehall façade reached the old Tudor Tennis Court.

1829 Metropolitan Police force established.

1830 King William IV accedes to throne. Melbourne House sold to Mr Agar-Ellis, who became Baron Dover the following year.

1832 Office of Works combined with Office of Woods, Forests and Land Revenues.

1833 Judicial Committee of Privy Council founded.

1834 Houses of Parliament destroyed by fire.

1836 Paymaster General's Office established.

1837 Queen Victoria accedes to throne.

1844 Charles Barry's scheme for redevelopment of Soane's Privy Council and Board of Trade building approved and work began. Old Tudor Tennis Court demolished except for part of west wall. Nos 11 and 12 Downing Street joined together.

1847 Barry's scheme for redevelopment of Soane's Privy Council building completed.

1849 Whitehall Stairs last used for a ceremonial procession by water.

1851 Office of Works separated from the Office of Woods, Forests and Land Revenues and the senior of the three Commissioners became First Commissioner and head of the new Department.

1855 Public Offices Extension Act allowed for compulsory purchase of privately-owned property on site between Fludyer Street and Crown Street.

1856 Competition for plans for new Foreign Office and War Office announced.

1858 George Gilbert Scott appointed architect of the Foreign Office and Home and Colonial Office, and joint architect with Matthew Digby Wyatt of the India Office.

1859 First Montagu House pulled down and rebuilt 1859–62 to a design by William Burn.

1861–2 Work on Foreign Office block began.

1862 New iron bridge to replace old Westminster Bridge opened.

1864 Construction of the Victoria Embankment began.

1867 India Office completed.

1868 Foreign Office completed.

1870 Victoria Embankment completed.

1873 Houses in Parliament Street pulled down in March and King Street side of street in Nov.–Dec. Charing Cross & Victoria Embankment Approach Act empowered the Metropolitan Board of Works to make a new street to the Embankment.

1874 Northumberland House bought and demolished to lay new street.

1875 Home and Colonial Offices finished. Building of National Opera House begun.

1876 Northumberland Avenue opened.

1878 George Gilbert Scott died.

1884 Leeming & Leeming won architectural competition for new Admiralty and War Office. Almonry Office pulled down.

1885 Explosion at the Admiralty. Whitehall Court and National Liberal Club under construction.

1886 Site of National Opera House acquired for the police.

1887 Richard Norman Shaw appointed architect for new police building.

1890 Metropolitan Police moved to New Scotland Yard, Victoria Embankment.

1892 Chapel Royal (Banqueting House) leased to the Royal United Services Institution for use as a museum.

1893 Whitehall Avenue and Horse Guards Avenue opened.

1895 Admiralty extension completed by Leeming & Leeming.

1897 Public Offices Whitehall Site Act.

1898 Government Offices Great George Street and War Office commissioned.

1899 King Street and the west side of Parliament Street demolished and Parliament Street greatly widened.

≈

1900 William Young, architect of the War Office, died.

1901 King Edward VII accedes to throne. John Brydon, architect of the Government Offices, died.

1906 War Office completed.

1906–9 No 55 Whitehall (Office of Woods and Forests) built by John Murray.

1908 Government Offices Great George Street, first section completed.

1910 King Edward VII dies.

1911 Coronation of King George V.

1911 Sir Aston Webb's Admiralty Arch and extension to the Admiralty opened.

1912 Public Offices (Sites) Act.

1915 Competition for design of Whitehall Gardens building won by E. Vincent Harris.

1914 War declared.

1915 Ministry of Munitions moved into new Board of Agriculture's Whitehall Place building.

1916 National Liberal Club requisitioned as War Office Annexe in September.

1917 Government Offices, Great George Street completed. Zimmerman telegram decoded by Admiralty team.

1918 Peace declared.

1919 Temporary Cenotaph designed by Sir Edwin Lutyens erected for march past of allied troops.

1920 Permanent Cenotaph unveiled on Armistice Day. Ministry of Agriculture and Fisheries moved into Whitehall Place East.

1921 Goetze murals put up in Foreign Office.

1925 Locarno Treaty signed in Foreign Office reception rooms, thereafter known as the Locarno Rooms.

1930 Kirkland House completed and Admiralty moved in to upper floors. Whitehall Theatre opened.

1934 Vincent Harris recommissioned to build Whitehall Gardens offices.

1935 Plan for development of Bridge Street and Richmond Terrace site prepared by William Curtis Green.

1936 King Edward VIII accedes to throne. Abdicates the same year and is succeeded by George VI.

1937 Coronation of King George VI.

1938 Eighteenth century houses, including Cromwell, Malmesbury, Pelham and Pembroke houses, demolished to clear Whitehall Gardens site.

1939 War declared. Cabinet War Rooms became operational.

1940 Citadel erected.

1940–1 Enemy air raids damaged several Whitehall buildings.

1943 LCC County of London plan, by Forshaw & Abercrombie published.

1944 Greater London plan, by Abercrombie published.

1945 War ends. Reconstruction of south end of the Treasury buildings.

1946 Admiralty House divided into two flats.

1947 India Office dissolved. Commonwealth Relations Office formed.

1948 Competition held for a sculptor to design two groups for the Whitehall Gardens building. James II statue moved to its present position in front of the National Gallery. Cabinet War Rooms preserved as museum.

1950 Move of Wolsey's wine cellar to its present position completed.

1951 First section of Whitehall Gardens building completed.

1951–2 Rear extension to Ministry of Agriculture and Fisheries built by C. E. Mee.

1952 Queen Elizabeth II accedes to throne.

1953 Sculptured groups 'Earth' and 'Water' completed.

1955 Scottish Office returned to Dover House.

1957 Crawford Committee on Downing Street reconstruction set up.

1959 Whitehall Gardens building completed.

1960 Prime Minister and staff move to Admiralty House. Work then started on Downing Street and Treasury Buildings restoration.

1962 Preliminary report on Bridge Street site prepared by Sir William Holford.

1964 Metropolitan Police given permission to move to new HQ in Victoria Street. Ministry of Defence took over Board of Trade's Whitehall Gardens building and Board of Trade moved to Victoria Street. Admiralty, Air Ministry and War Office became part of the Ministry of Defence. Royal United Services Institution moved out of Banqueting House.

1965 Sir Leslie Martin's report on the Whitehall redevelopment published. Government set up the Whitehall Redevelopment Policy Committee.

1967 Parliamentary Counsel moved in to No 36 Whitehall (formerly the Paymaster General's Office)

1968 Foreign Office and Commonwealth Office merged.

1970 Public inquiry on Bridge Street/Richmond Terrace redevelopment proposals held with Harold Willis QC as Inspector.

1972 Banqueting House. Rubens ceiling-paintings rearranged in different order.

1975 Norman Shaw (North) building refurbished and reopened as annexe to the House of Commons.

1977 Jubilee of Queen Elizabeth II. Home Office moved to new building in Queen Anne's Gate.

1978 Casson Conder scheme for Bridge Street/Parliament Street site published.

1979 Norman Shaw (North) building opened as House of Commons annexe.

1982 New proposals for Bridge Street redevelopment.

1983 Remedial work on Richmond Terrace Georgian façade, followed by major building work.

1984 Property Services Agency started work on restoring the former India Office.

1985 Work began on the first phase of the Bridge Street/Parliament Street site redevelopment.

1987 Foreign Office refurbishment of Grand Staircase and Victorian interiors started. Major scheme of restoration of the Old War Office began. Restoration of Richmond Terrace and building of Richmond House completed.

1991 House of Commons Parliament Street Building completed mid-1991 and opened by the Prince of Wales in November. Review of style and layout of the green in front of the Ministry of Defence main building. Commissioning of statue of Field-Marshal Alanbrooke to stand on Ministry of Defence green.

1992 Parliamentary Corporate Bodies Act passed, permitting the transference of the title of all outbuildings of the House of Commons, including Nos 38–47 Parliament Street and Norman Shaw (North) and (South) from the Department of the Environment to the House of Commons. Sketch plan for Bridge Street/Embankment Parliamentary Building by M. Hopkins published.

1993 Alanbrooke statue unveiled on green in front of Ministry of Defence main building. In Autumn demolition of buildings between Cannon Row and Embankment started, for New Parliamentary Building and Jubilee Line Extension work at Westminster Station. Alanbrooke statue unveiled in front of Ministry of Defence.

1993–4 Demolition of buildings between Cannon Row and the Embankment to clear site for phase two of the Bridge Street redevelopment.

1994 Spring. Listed St Stephen's Club demolished and major construction work on Westminster Underground Station begun. Refurbishment of former Colonial Office and of the Horse Guards completed.

Bibliography

Ackermann, Rudolph. *The Microcosm of London or London in Miniature*, with illustrations by Pugin and Rowlandson. 3 vols, 1904 edition.

Adair, John. *The Royal Palaces of Britain*. Thames & Hudson, 1981.

Adams, Bernard. *London Illustrated 1604–1851: a survey and index of topographical books and their plates*. Library Association, 1983.

The Admiralty Board Room 1725–1949. Unpublished typescript, n.d. [1949?].

Amery, Colin. 'Building for history' [proposed new Parliamentary building at the corner of Bridge Street and the Victoria Embankment]. *Financial Times*, 2 March 1992, p. 13.

Archer, Lucy. *Raymond Erith, Architect*. The Cygnet Press, 1985.

Barker, F. & Hyde, R. *London as it Might Have Been*. John Murray, 1982.

Barker, F. & Jackson, P. *The History of London in Maps*. Barrie & Jenkins, 1990.

Barbican Art Gallery. *Getting London in Perspective*. 1984.

Belsey, Hugh. 'Canaletto's England.' *The Art Quarterly of the National Art Collection Fund*, no. 15, Autumn 1993, pp. 34–6.

Besant, Sir Walter. *London in the Time of the Stuarts*. A & C Black, 1903.

Besant, Sir Walter. *Westminster*. Chatto & Windus, 1897.

Blackwood, John. *London's Immortals: the complete outdoor commemorative statues*. Savoy Press, 1989.

Bone, James. *London Echoing*, with pictures by Muirhead Bone. Jonathan Cape, 1948.

Brereton, Austin. *The Story of Old Whitehall, with a note on the Whitehall Rooms and the Hotel Metropole*. The Gordon Hotels, 1912.

Brown, Ivor. *London: an Illustrated History*. Studio Vista, 1965.

Burlington Fine Arts Club. *Illustrated Catalogue of Pictures and Drawings of Old London*. 1920.

The Cabinet Office. Unpublished typescript, n.d.

Cameron, Robert & Cooke, Alistair. *Above London*. Bodley Head, 1980.

Cairns, Lady Constance. *Memoirs*. Blacklock Farries, 1961.

Campbell, Sir Alan. 'The Foreign and Commonwealth Office building: an Italian palazzo in London.' *Rivista*, Jan./Feb. 1984, pp. 1–3.

Campbell, Duncan. 'Subterranean secrets.' *Good Housekeeping*, November 1987, p. 13.

Campbell, Duncan. *War Plan UK: the Truth About Civil Defence in Britain*. Burnett Books, 1982.

Cannadine, David. 'The context, performance and meaning of ritual: the British monarchy and the "Invention of Tradition" *c.* 1820–1977' in Eric Hobsbawm and Terence Ranger (eds), *The Invention of Tradition*. Cambridge University Press, 1983.

Casson Conder & Partners. *New Parliamentary Building, Bridge Street. Feasibility study*. May 1979.

Cecil Denny Highton & Partners. *The old Public Office Whitehall, London SW1: a history of the building containing the India Office, the Foreign and Colonial Office and the Home Office*. March 1983, amended reprint January 1985.

Chancellor, E. Beresford. *The Private Palaces of London Past and Present*. Kegan Paul, Trench, Tribner & Co Ltd, 1908.

Charlton, John. *The Banqueting House Whitehall*. Ministry of Public Building & Works. HMSO, 1964. 1st edn by Department of the Environment, 1983, reprint, 1989.

Clunn, Harold. *London Marches On: a record of the changes*

which have taken place in the metropolis of the British Empire between the two world wars and much that is scheduled for reconstruction. The Caen Press, 1947.

Clunn, Harold. *London Rebuilt 1897–1927.* John Murray, 1927.

Collins, Steve, Pond, Chris, and Seaton, Janet. *The Parliament Street Building.* House of Commons, 1991.

Completion of the new government buildings, Westminster.' *Architectural Review* 1917, vol. XLII, pp. 54–9.

Cornforth, John. 'The old India Office.' *Country Life*, 12 November 1987, pp. 164–9.

Cunningham, P. *Hand-book of London Past and Present.* New edition. John Murray, 1850.

Davies, J. H. V. 'Whitehall old and new.' *MAFF Bulletin*, vol. 7, nos 2 and 3, May and June 1963.

Department of the Environment. *Report of a Public Inquiry into the Objections to the Redevelopment Proposals for the Richmond Terrace–New Scotland Yard Site.* HMSO, 1972. (Inspector: Harold Willis).

Dillon, Viscount. *The Story of Whitehall Palace.* Published by authority of the Council of the Royal United Service Institution by William Clowes & Sons Ltd., 3rd edn 1905.

'The drama of Whitehall: once the Thames-side home of England's monarchs.' *The Sphere*, 11 December 1948, pp. 346–7.

Dugdale, George S. 'Old Whitehall.' *Journal of the London Society*, December 1952, vol. 316, pp. 158–68.

Dugdale, George S. *Whitehall Through the Centuries.* Phoenix House Ltd, 1950.

Edwards, Percy J. *History of London Street Improvements 1855–1897.* London County Council, 1898.

Emden, W. & Penton, H. *Picturesque Westminster, being a Collection of Sketches Illustrating Historic Landmarks and Places of Interest in the Ancient City of Westminster*, illustrations by Howard Penton. 1902.

Emmerson, Sir Harold. *The Ministry of Works.* George Allen & Unwin, 1956.

Evelyn, John. *The Diary*, with an introduction and notes by Austin Dobson. Macmillan & Co, 1908.

Finberg, Hilda. 'Canaletto in England.' *The Walpole Society*, vol. 9, 1920–1, pp. 20–76.

Foreign and Commonwealth Office. HMSO, 1991, 2nd edn, 1993.

Foreign and Commonwealth Office. Historical Branch. *The FCO: Policy, People and Places, 1782–1991.* April 1991.

Foreign and Commonwealth Office. Historical Branch. *Locarno 1925: the Treaty, the Spirit and the Suite.* October 1991.

Foreman, Susan. *Loaves and Fishes: an illustrated history of the Ministry of Agriculture, Fisheries and Food 1889–1989.* HMSO, 1989.

Foreman, Susan. *Shoes and Ships and Sealing-Wax: an illustrated history of the Board of Trade 1786–1986.* HMSO, 1986.

Frizzell Partnership Ltd. *PSA Historic Building Quadrennial Building Inspection: Government Offices, Great George Street, Westminster.* March 1991.

'The future of Whitehall.' *The Architects' Journal*, 17 and 24 December 1969.

Games, Stephen. 'Whitehall farce.' *RIBA Journal*, April 1980, pp. 49–58.

Glanville, Philippa. *London in Maps.* The Connoisseur, 1972.

Goodman, Godfrey. *The Court of King James 1st to which are added letters illustrative of the personal history of the most distinguished characters in the Court of that monarch and his predecessors . . . by John S. Brewer.* Richard Bentley, 1839.

Grand Architectural Panorama of London: Regent Street to Westminster Abbey, from original drawings made expressly for the work by R. Sandeman, Architect and executed on wood by G. C. Leighton, 1849. Reprint published by Henry Margary in association with Guildhall Library, London.

Green, H. J. M. & Thurley, S. J. 'Excavations on the west side of Whitehall 1960–2, part 1: from the building of the Tudor Palace to the construction of the modern offices of state.' *London & Middlesex Archaeological Society Transactions*, vol. 38, 1987, pp. 59–130.

Green, H. J. M. 'Secrets of Whitehall: evidence of Roman, Saxon and mediaeval Westminster revealed during the current rebuilding of the Treasury and Downing Street – part I.' *Illustrated London News*, 29 June 1963, pp. 1004–7.

Green, H. J. M. & Curnow, P. 'The Palace of Whitehall and after: Tudor and later discoveries made during the reconstruction of Downing Street and the Treasury – part II.' *Illustrated London News*, 6 July 1963, pp. 14–17.

Hall, Shirley. *Sir Edward Hertslet and his Work as Librarian and Keeper of the Papers of the Foreign Office from*

1857–1896. Thesis submitted . . . for the degree of Master of Arts, University of London, 1958.

Hanson, Michael. *2000 Years of London: an illustrated survey*. Country Life Ltd, 1967.

Harwood, B. *Horse Guards* 1982.

Hayes, John. *Catalogue of the Oil Paintings in the London Museum*. HMSO, 1970.

Hayes, John. 'Parliament Street and Canaletto's views of Whitehall.' *Burlington Magazine*, vol. 100, 1958, pp. 341–9.

Heath, Sir Thomas L. *The Treasury*. G. P. Putnam's Sons Ltd, 1927.

Hertslet, Sir Edward. *Recollections of the Old Foreign Office*. John Murray, 1901.

Hibbert, Christopher. *London: the Biography of a City*. Longman, 1977; Penguin, 1980.

History Today. Special issue on 1688 and the Glorious Revolution. Vol. 38, July 1988.

H.M. Treasury. *Whitehall Through the Centuries: a handbook to accompany the exhibition of old prints arranged by H M Treasury*. [1948]

The History of the King's Works. General editor, H. M. Colvin. HMSO, vol. IV part II 1982, vol. V 1976, vol. VI 1973.

Home Office. *Home Office 1782–1982: to commemorate the bicentenary of the Home Office*. 1981.

The Horse Guards' Parade: a suggested improvement by a citizen of London. O. Anacker, 1919.

House of Commons. Accommodation and Works Committee. *New Parliamentary Building (Phase 2). The sketch plan. Vol. I. Report, Appendices and Proceedings*. HC269–I, sess 1991–2. HMSO, 1992.

House of Commons. Public Information Office. *The Norman Shaw Buildings*. February (No 11).

Hurd, Douglas. 'My Foreign Office.' *The World of Interiors*, March 1992, pp. 82–9.

Hussey, Christopher. 'Foreign Office's threatened glory.' *Country Life*, vol. 135, 6 Feb. 1964, p 272.

Innes-Smith, Robert. *Whitehall: from Trafalgar Square to the Palace of Westminster*. English Life Publications, 1978.

James, Gethin & Coleman, David. 'The Government as Whitehall landlord.' *Chartered Surveyor/Chartered Quantity Surveyor*, June 1981.

James, Robin. 'Worth the wait.' *The House Magazine*, 4 November 1991, pp. 8–9.

Johnson, Paul. *The Aerofilms book of London from the air*. Weidenfeld, 1984.

Jones, Christopher. *No 10 Downing Street: the story of a house*. BBC, 1985.

Knight, C. (ed.). *London*. vols 1 & 2. Charles Knight & Co, 1841.

Kiek, Jonathan. *Everybody's Historic London*. Quiller Press, 1984.

Kohan, C. M. *Works and buildings*. HMSO & Longman Green, 1952 (History of the second world war).

Laurie, Peter. *Beneath the City Streets: a private inquiry into Government preparations for national emergency*. Rev. edn, Granada, 1979.

Links, J. G. *Canaletto*. Phaidon. Rev. edn, 1994.

Liversidge, Michael and Farrington, Jane. *Canaletto & England*. Merrell Holberton in association with Birmingham Museum and Art Gallery, 1993. [Exhibition catalogue]

Loftie, W. J. '10 Downing Street'. *Architectural Review*, vol. 15, no 89, April 1904, pp. 135–47; and no. 90, May 1904, pp. 196–206.

Loftie, W. J. *Whitehall: historical and architectural notes*. Seeley & Co Ltd, 1895.

London County Council. *Survey of London*, vols X, 1926; XIII part II, 1930; XIV, 1930; XVI, 1935.

Martin, Sir John. *Downing Street: the war years*. Bloomsbury, 1991.

Martin, Sir Leslie. *Whitehall: a plan for the national and government centre, accompanied by a report on traffic* by Colin Buchanan. HMSO, 1965.

Metcalf, Priscilla. *Victorian London*. Cassell, 1972.

Milman, Archibald. 'King Street, Westminster.' *Lords & Commons*, 4 March 1899, pp. 94–7; 'Whitehall and King Street – II.' *Lords & Commons*, 11 March 1899, pp. 130–2.

Minney, R. J. *No 10 Downing Street: a house in history*. Cassell, 1963.

'A new Government building'. *Architectural Review*, vol. 28, Jul.–Dec. 1910, pp. 54–61.

'New Government building in Whitehall,' *Building*, September 1951, pp. 340–6; May 1952, pp. 178–9.

'The new Government offices.' *Lords & Commons*, 1 April 1899, pp. 218–20.

New public offices, Westminster.' *Architectural Review*, vol. 24, July – Dec. 1908, pp. 69–85.

Oliver, Andrew. 'Notes on Whitehall and the Strand.' *The*

Builder, 17 January 1903, pp. 60–3.

Orrell, John. *The Theatres of Inigo Jones and John Webb.* Cambridge University Press, 1985.

'The Palace of Whitehall: interesting discovery of original Tudor buildings.' *The Builder*, March 3 1961, pp. 408–9.

Palme, Per. *Triumph of Peace: a study of the Whitehall Banqueting House.* Thames & Hudson, 1957.

Pearce, David. *London's Mansions: the palatial houses of the nobility.* Batsford, 1986.

Pepys, Samuel. *Diary.* Edited by R. C. Latham & W. Matthews. G. Bell, 1970.

Pevsner, N. *The Buildings of England. London 1: the Cities of London and Westminster.* Penguin, 1957.

Phillips, Hugh. *Mid-Georgian London: a topographical and social survey of Central and Western London about 1750.* Collins, 1964.

Physick, John & Darby, Michael. *Marble Halls: drawings and models for Victorian secular buildings.* [Exhibition catalogue, V & A Museum] HMSO, 1973.

Plumb, J. H. & Weldon, H. *Royal Heritage: the story of Britain's royal builders and collectors.* BBC, 1977.

Port, M. H. 'Pride and parsimony: influences affecting the development of the Whitehall quarter in the 1850s.' *London Journal*, vol. 2, no. 2, 1976, pp. 171–98.

Property Services Agency. *The Government Buildings of Whitehall: festival of architecture 1984.* HMSO, 1984 [leaflet].

Property Services Agency. *PSA Historic Buildings Register, vol. II: London.* PSA, 1983.

Pugin, Augustus & Britton, John. *Illustrations of the Public Buildings of London, with historical and descriptive accounts of each edifice.* 2nd enlarged edn, 2 vols, by W. H. Leeds. John Wheale, 1838.

Ramsay, David. 'The new Parliamentary Building: a case study' in *The Future of the Public Heritage. Report of a conference organised by the RSA–Cubitt Trust Panel*, held at the RSA on 15 October 1986. RSA–Cubitt Trust Panel, 1987, pp. 33–40.

Ramsay, David. 'The Palace of variety.' *The House Magazine*, 4 November 1991, p. 9.

Report of the Committee on the Preservation of Downing Street. HMSO, June 1958. Cmnd 457.

Richmond House Whitehall: a major restoration and new building project by the Property Services Agency. 1987.

Robinson, John M. *Royal Residences.* Macdonald & Co, 1982.

Rosebery, Earl of. 'Royal Palace of Whitehall.' *London Topographical Record*, vol. VI, 1909, pp. 23–35.

Rosser, Gervase & Thurley, Simon. 'Whitehall Palace and King Street, Westminster: the urban cost of princely magnificence.' *London Topographical Record*, vol. XXVI, 1990, pp. 57–77.

Saint, Andrew. *Richard Norman Shaw.* Published for the Paul Mellon Centre for Studies in British Art by Yale University Press, 1976.

Saint, Andrew and Darley, Gillian. *The Chronicles of London.* Weidenfeld & Nicolson, 1994.

Salaman, Malcolm C. (ed.), Charles Holme. *London Past and Present.* The Studio Ltd, 1916.

Sansom, William. *The Blitz: Westminster at war.* Oxford University Press, 1990.

Saunders, Ann. *The Art and Architecture of London: an illustrated guide.* Phaidon, 1984.

Scott, Lora V. *The War Office, Whitehall.* Unpublished Open University thesis for course on History of Architecture and Design 1890–1939 [n.d.]

Segall, Anne. 'Treasury set to quit office over repairs.' *Daily Telegraph*, 30 April 1994, p. 5. [Report on possible move of the Treasury from the Grade 2★ listed building known as Government Buildings, Great George Street, to allow major repair and upgrading.]

Service, Alastair. *The Architects of London and their Buildings from 1066 to the Present Day.* Architectural Press, 1979.

Service, Alastair. *London 1900.* Granada, 1979.

Shepherd, Thomas H. *London and its Environs in the Nineteenth Century, illustrated by a series of views from original drawings.* Jones & Co, 1829, new edition published by Frank Graham, 1970 (Illustrated Topography Reprints no. 5).

Sheppard, E. *The old Royal Palace of Whitehall.* Longman, Green & Co, 1902.

Simpkins, Peter. *Cabinet War Rooms.* Imperial War Museum, 1983.

Spiers, Walter L. 'Account of the view of the Palace of Whitehall from the river, 1863.' *London Topographical Record*, vol. VII, 1912, pp. 26–30.

Spiers, Walter L. 'Explanation of the plan of Whitehall.' *London Topographical Record*, vol. VII, 1912, pp. 56–66.

Spring, Martin. 'Foreign expansion.' *Building – Building Renewal Supplement*, 29 April 1994, pp. 31–4.

'Spring-Gardens, Charing Cross and Whitehall: 1801–1900.' *The Builder*, 7 January 1905, pp. 7–14.

Stamp, Gavin. *The Changing Metropolis: earliest photographs of London, 1839–1879.* Viking, 1984.

Stamp, Gavin & Amery, Colin. *Victorian Buildings of*

London 1837–1887: an illustrated guide. Architectural Press, 1980.

'The story of the Government Offices.' *The Builder,* 25 August 1877, pp. 852–6; 'An additional chapter to the story of the Government Offices.' *The Builder,* 8 July, 1882, pp. 37–9.

Streitberger, W. R. 'Records of Royal Banqeting Houses and Henry VIII's Timber Lodging, 1543–59.' *Journal of the Society of Archivists,* vol. 15, no. 2, 1994, pp. 187–202.

Sykes, Christopher S. *Private Palaces: life in the great London houses.* Chatto & Windus, 1989.

Tallis, John. *John Tallis's London Street Views 1838–1840, together with the revised and enlarged views of 1847, introduced and with a biographical essay by Peter Jackson.* Published in association with the London Topographical Society, by Natali & Maurice, 1969.

Taylor, Nicholas. 'The Downing Street story.' *The Architect & Building News,* 25 Dec. 1963, pp. 1031–36.

10 Downing Street.' *Architectural Review,* vol. 15, Jan.–June 1904, pp. 135–47.

Thornbury, G. W. *Old and New London: a narrative of its history, its people, and its places, illustrated with numerous engravings from the most authentic sources. Westminster and the western suburbs,* vol. III by Edward Walford. Cassell Petter & Galpin, 1873–8.

'The Times' London History Atlas, edited by Hugh Clout. Times Books, 1991.

Toplis, Ian. *The Foreign Office: an architectural history.* Mansell, 1987.

Trench, Richard & Hillman, Ellis. *London Under London.* John Murray, 1985.

Ulph, Colin. *150 Not Out: the story of the Paymaster General's Office 1836–1986,* 1985.

Visit to the site and remains of old Whitehall Palace.' *London Topographical Record,* vol. VII, 1912, pp. 31–55.

Walker, R. J. B. *Old Westminster Bridge: the bridge of fools.* David and Charles, 1979.

Warner, Malcolm. *The Image of London: views by travellers and emigres, 1550–1920.* Trefoil Publications, Rizzoli International Publications Inc in association with Barbican Art Gallery, 1987 [An exhibition at Barbican Art Gallery, Aug. 6 – Oct. 18 1987].

Weinreb, Ben & Hibbert, Christopher (eds), *The London Encyclopedia.* Macmillan, 1983.

Whinney, Margaret. 'John Webb's drawings for Whitehall Palace.' *The Walpole Society,* vol. XXXI, 1942–3, pp. 45–107 + plates.

'The War Office "old" and "new".' *Stand To! The Journal of the Western Front Association,* no 15, Winter 1985.

'The widening of Parliament Street.' *Lords & Commons,* 18 March 1899, pp. 160–3.

Winnifrith, A. J. D. 'The Treasury, Whitehall.' *Country Life,* 7 November 1957, pp. 978–81 and 14 November 1957, pp. 1034–7.

Young, Clyde. 'The new War Office.' *Architectural Review,* vol. 20, Jul. – Dec. 1906, pp. 301–16.

Acknowledgements

Without the assistance of experts in Whitehall, this book would have been much less complete. I am particularly grateful to Chris Pond, Head of the Public Information Office of the House of Commons Library; David Brown, Head of Home Estates Dept., Foreign and Commonwealth Office; Stewart Robertson, sometime Departmental Records Officer, DTI; Helen Glass of the FCO Library and Heather Yasamee, Head of Historical Branch FCO, for reading the text and for their valuable comments and suggestions.

Derek Arnold of Weston-Lewis, Clarke & Arnold, Architects; Marian Carter; John Denny and his team from Cecil Denny Highton, Architects; Cliff Cowell; Janet Driels; Bob Edmunds; Victoria Elliott; Alma Harris; Eric Miller; Derek Morris; Chris Pond; the Viscount Slim, and Alex Smith showed me round or provided extra information on particular buildings in Whitehall.

I thank the Public Record Office for allowing me to use Crown Copyright material from the following Work 12 files: 428 (pp. 169, 171); 595 (p. 171); 609 (p. 176); 682 (pp. 11, 46, 47, 150, 166, 168, 169); 731 (pp. 161, 187, 188). This material is reproduced with the permission of the Controller of HMSO. For the use of quotations from copyright works, I am indebted to David Gentleman (p. 174), Gavin Stamp (p. 184), the estate of Henry Archer (*Lambe's Tale*, p. 183), the editors of *Country Life* (p. 162), and *RIBA Journal* (p. 159).

I have found much information and help in the British Architectural Library of the RIBA, the British Museum's Department of Prints and Drawings, the Guildhall Library, the Greater London Record Office, HM Treasury (Lister Collection), the London Library, the Property Services Agency London Collection (now incorporated into the Department of the Environment Library), the Museum of London, the Public Record Office and Westminster City Archives, to whose staff grateful thanks are due.

Illustrations of London can be traced in a number of celebrated series and collections. In selecting appropriate engravings for reproduction, I have occasionally chosen later copies over the originals. Particularly in the 19th century, there are many versions of similar views by different artists, and in using those that give the liveliest representation of different periods, I may have omitted a few of the best known ones, a number of which may be found in my previous books: *Shoes and Ships and Sealing-Wax* (HMSO 1986), and *Loaves and Fishes* (HMSO 1989).

Susan Foreman,
December 1994.

Picture sources

All pictures are from the author's collection unless otherwise stated. 'Plate' refers to the colour section; other numbers are the b/w illustrations.

British Architectural Library, RIBA, London: 80.

British Museum: Copyright British Museum: Plate 4.

The collection of the Duke of Buccleuch and Queensberry KT: Plate 1.

Cecil Denny Highton, Consultant architects for the restoration of the Foreign & Commonwealth Office: 119; CDH/Adam Woolfitt: Plate 4.

CDH/Crispin Boyle: Plate 13.

Ministry of Defence: 106, 110, 111, Plate 6. Crown copyright, reproduced by permission of the Controller of HMSO.

Foreign & Commonwealth Office: 113, 114.

Greater London Record Office (Photograph Collection): 108.

Guildhall Library, Corporation of London: 47.

Crown copyright: reproduced by permission of the Controller of HMSO: 30, 55, 115, 130.

Lister Collection, HM Treasury: 24, 35, 46, 53, 57, 58, 62, 67, 70, 76, 79, 85, 87, 92, Plate 11.

Public Record Office: 120, 121, 122. Crown copyright, reproduced by permission of the Controller of HMSO.

Reg Roberson: 103.

Scottish Office: Plate 7

Solo Syndication: 123.

Stone Collection, Birmingham Central Library, reproduced by permission of Birmingham Library Services: 134.

Westminster City Archives: Plates 3 and 8.

To all the above, my grateful thanks.

Index